MAPPING THE FARM

Catherine Esmond O'Neill

William O'Neill

John Esmond O'Neill

The Farm —pre–World War I

John and Mame O'Neill

*Catherine Esmond O'Neill and
Kate Sinnott*

John and Mame O'Neill and children—1915

John and Mame O'Neill and children

Bill, Edward, James O'Neill   *Theresa O'Neill on Blue*

Barn-raising—1927

John O'Neill, Ed O'Neill, Brad Phillips—1934

Farm Holiday Association march in St. Paul—1933 (John O'Neill is eighth from left)

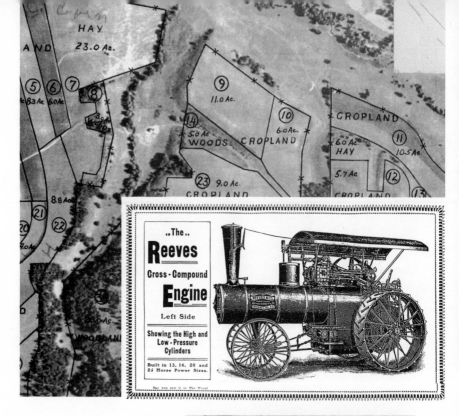

*Aerial photograph taken
by the Minnesota Soil
Conservation
Department—1941*

*The Reeves Cross-
Compound Engine*

Frances Bruski

Edward O'Neill and crew chief

Edward and Frances O'Neill

Dennis O'Neill

Bridget O'Neill

Sharon on Dobie

Mapping the Farm

The Chronicle of a Family

John Hildebrand

Alfred A. Knopf

NEW YORK 1995

This Is a Borzoi Book
Published by Alfred A. Knopf, Inc.

Grateful acknowledgment is made to the following for permission to reprint previously published material:
Henry Holt and Company, Inc.: Excerpt from "Death of the Hired Man" by Robert Frost, from *The Poetry of Robert Frost*. Reprinted courtesy of Henry Holt and Company, Inc.
Little, Brown and Company: Excerpt from "To Make a Prairie" (Poem #1755), from *The Complete Poems of Emily Dickinson*, edited by Thomas H. Johnson. Reprinted courtesy of Little, Brown and Company.

The author is grateful to the Bush Foundation for its support.

Library of Congress Cataloging-in-Publication Data

Hildebrand, John.
Mapping the farm / by John Hildebrand. — 1st ed.
p. cm.
ISBN 0-679-43009-1
1. Farm life—Minnesota—Rochester Region. 2. Family farms—Minnesota—Rochester Region. 3. O'Neill family. I. Title.
S521.5.M6H54 1995
977.6′15505—dc20   94-42902
                                                                    CIP

A song of the good green grass!
A song no more of the city streets;
A song of farms—a song of the soil of fields.

— WALT WHITMAN (1871)

The question of the survival of the family farm
and the farm family is one version of the question of who will own the country, which is,
ultimately, the question of who will own the
people.

— WENDELL BERRY (1986)

MAPPING THE FARM

ONE

It is the start of Memorial Day weekend and we are at my wife's family farm, the O'Neill farm south of Rochester, because her father is in the hospital. Black-bottomed clouds have circled all morning, but so far the day looks bright and promising. The lower pasture has greened up, goldfinches flit between the flowering crab tree and bird feeder hanging by the picture window, and thirteen new calves are grazing by the creek with their mothers. I catch a ride with my brother-in-law Steve when he drives out to check on the planting and we rumble past the barn, then head south along a fence line. Most of the corn was already in the ground when my father-in-law went into the hospital and has come up in neat drill rows no more than two inches high. The alfalfa has blossomed into a field of purple-violet flowers that will be ready for a first cutting next week, if anyone's around to cut. It sure won't be either of us.

The black pickup parked at the end of the plowed field belongs to Dennis O'Neill, my wife's cousin, who is drilling soybeans by maneuvering his tractor in figure-eight's through the dust. As he works, a cloud shadow races across the brown field, trailing rain behind it. We roll up the windows as the first big drops splatter against the windshield and wait to see if Dennis will finish planting or dash for cover. Soon the rain is coming down in torrents. Inside, the cab is snug and dry and the windshield has fogged up. Steve lights a cigarette. Then he wipes a patch clear with his hand until we can see Dennis shuttling back and forth across the muddy field as if the tractor ran on tracks.

"A true farmer," Steve says.

By the time Dennis finishes, the shower has moved into the next township and left behind a blue-washed sky. He dismounts and walks over slightly bandy-legged, as if he'd spent the morning in the saddle instead of a tractor seat. We are all in our early forties and all wear mustaches, although Dennis's has more of an overhang and would not look out of place in a Mathew Brady photograph. By way of beginning a conversation, he goes through an elaborate series of motions—taking his red feed cap off with one hand, sweeping the other over his head, pulling the hat back on, turning his head, spitting.

"Well, I'm going to quit. Field's getting too greasy anyway." Then, as an afterthought, "How's Ed?"

We'll see him tonight, I say, and offer to drive his pickup back to the yard so he won't have to make two trips. When I switch on the ignition key, the cab swells with twangy music. It smells funny too, not the sweetish, hay-smelling fermentation of cow manure but the oily, change-of-barometric-pressure that is fetor of hog. When he isn't on shift as a city fireman, Dennis and his wife raise hogs on fifty acres and farm another hundred and fifty. He is the only person I know of my generation who farms for a living, and without him these fields would go unplanted. Not that Ed and Fran haven't tried, producing seven daughters, who, between them, married an auto mechanic, a carpenter, an assistant manager at Fleet Farm, a forklift operator, a Medevac nurse, and two school-teachers—all the possibilities of small-town employment, but nobody who knows how to drill soybeans. The only son, who might have taken over the farm at one time, gave up waiting for his father to retire and moved to Wisconsin, where he works as an electrical engineer for a super-computer company.

Leaning out the window, I steer Dennis's pickup down the field road in reverse until there's room to turn around, then drive back to the yard and park by the fuel pump. On a farm the yard is not grassy lawn but the bare ground circumscribed by house and barn and other outbuildings; it is the hub of activity, the roundabout for all traffic heading in or out. Over the years, horses' hooves, iron wagon wheels, and lug tires have worn the yard down to its bedrock of bone-white limestone embedded with tiny brachiopod shells and crinoids, or "stone lilies," from an ancient sea. I've tried explaining fossils to my children, but in their boundless imaginations they cannot imagine this place as anything other than as it is right now: their grandparents' farm.

The remainder of my day is devoted to looking busy. I rototill the vegetable garden, refill the bird feeder with thistle seed so the goldfinches will hang around, and seriously consider changing my middle name to Useless.

ROCHESTER, MINNESOTA, is unique among Midwestern cities in having both the world-famous Mayo Clinic and a water tower shaped like a giant ear of corn. The town was founded on agriculture, but medicine made it rich. So many schools, parks, and public buildings are named for the Mayo brothers, Dr. Will and Dr. Charlie, that they could be Rochester's mythical twins, the town's origins intertwined with their own. Their early surgical practice centered on farm accidents, and the city's first medical museum featured dioramas of farmers having mangled limbs reattached or replaced with prostheses. Today the clinic has become the Lourdes of medical research, a place where stretch limousines whisk ailing sheikhs and celebrities in sunglasses between the airport and private suites. Even Elvis Presley slouched through here on his way to Graceland, and though the clinic is the soul of discretion, word got out ("His insides were Swiss cheese!"). The clinic is the city's largest employer. When physicians and their families settled predominantly in southwestern Rochester, outlying residents began to call the neighborhood Pill Hill, and the town's unique social stratification wasn't lost on them. At my wife's twentieth class reunion at Mayo High, the master of ceremonies was a specialist at the clinic, and the couple who received a prize for being the first to marry were also singled out because their check for the reunion dinner bounced. An alumnus from Texas who didn't attend wrote in his questionnaire: "It seemed like the rich kids vs. the poor kids. Who you were in sports was who your Doctor Dad was. I had to work if I wanted a car and spending money."

Most of Ed O'Neill's daughters work in some capacity for the clinic. When we visit St. Mary's Hospital, three of them are crowded into his bedroom. They huddle together like the Fates, discussing their father's prognosis, while he sits upright in blue pajamas and watches a game show with the sound turned off. He's been here before—heart attack, prostate cancer, back trouble—all the ailments of a body used as tool for a lifetime of hard labor. His forearm is black and blue where the IV tube disappears under a bandage. For me, there's the unnerving sensation of seeing multiple versions of my wife's face in one room.

The previous week Ed had been discing the fields in preparation for planting, and afterward complained of a sharp pain in his chest and blinding headaches. Once, in the middle of the field, he became disoriented and for one terrible moment didn't know where he was. Still, he kept putting off going to the hospital until yesterday, when the pain worsened and Fran insisted. The doctors at St. Mary's did a ventilation-profusion scan of his chest that revealed multiple blood clots in the right lung, any one of which could have broken off in the bloodstream and lodged in his heart or brain. He was admitted on the spot and given an anticoagulant intravenously to dissolve the clots. Then the doctors began troubleshooting to find the source of the clots. They administered blood tests and X rays and bone scans. They did ultrasounds and a CAT scan. They made Ed drink radium-isotope milk shakes that illuminated his internal organs as if flares had been dropped on the dark side of the moon. They mapped the interior landscape of his body, and in the end they still couldn't say why the clots had formed.

The good news, the doctors say, is that Ed will live awhile longer. The bad news is that he must forswear alcohol, which counteracts the blood-thinning effect of the anticoagulant. One reward for never having left home except to fly P-38s in the Pacific was that, at seventy-two, Ed could still have a drink at the Legion with the same buddies he'd known in high school. He'd already quit a two-pack-a-day smoking habit on doctors' advice. The same with chew. One by one, doctors had taken away the few pleasures a man had in life—but he was putting the kibosh on this latest edict.

"Jim Sheehan across the road never smoked in his life, so the doctors tell him *he's* got farmer's lung. Well, I've inhaled as much tractor dust as anyone, but because I smoked they say *I* have emphysema. Now they say I've got to quit drinking. Like hell I will."

On our way back from the hospital we stop at William T. McCoy Legion Post 92 for a drink. The oval bar is ringed with photographs of past commanders, as well as of the Post's namesake, a smiling doughboy who died in France of influenza. My wife snags a table close to the evening's entertainment, a one-man band who plays keyboard and torques his vocal cords into low gear to sing about heartaches by the dozen. The waitress who brings our brandy and water asks where Ed is tonight and Fran explains, as she will several times during the course of the night, why he's in the hospital. In the machine shed at the farm is a boxcar mounted on a truck chassis that members of the Legion's "Société des 40 Hommes and 8 Chevaux" ride in during parades behind the color guard, waving at the crowd through its open door. A silver-haired liberator swings by the table to explain that someone will be out on Sunday morning to retrieve the boxcar before the Memorial Day parade.

When the keyboard player whines that "the whiskey flows and the beer chases my blues away," it strikes me that the elegiac quality of so much country music has to do with a pervasive sense of loss, of ruined marriages and dip-shit jobs and the sweet, lost countryside itself. They are the songs of a rural diaspora. They hark back to a remembered past when land was the only true measure of wealth and one's people owned a quarter-section instead of a body shop and, by God, their name meant something in these parts. Never mind that shop work paid better or that they sold the home place to a developer and bought a split-level in town. The catch in the throat, the heartbreaking tremolo, only mask the singer's own complicity in these matters.

Last winter Ed and Fran met with an attorney, "a dapper little squirt," to consider an estate plan so the clinic wouldn't end up owning the farm if either of them went into the hospital for an extended stay. The papers were never drawn up. How is it possible that a man who owns outright 240 acres of prime farmland just outside the city, the envy of developers, should worry about passing it along to his children intact? Not that one less farm would be missed. The state of Minnesota recently decided to close its agricultural research center at Waseca and convert it into a prison because corrections has turned into the kind of growth industry farming isn't. If this farm is lost, it won't be because of crooked bankers or poor markets or even bad luck. It will be a failure from within when, after four generations on the land, the line of descent finally runs out. The end of the line is resting peacefully in his bed at St. Mary's Hospital.

But nobody at the table talks about what is going to happen to the farm. Instead, Fran tells a story about an acquaintance from the Legion, a man in his sixties who's going to be a father again, this time outside of marriage and with a woman half his age. Fran can hardly get to the punch line without laughing: "So Lucille picks up the phone and this girl asks, 'Are you his mother?' 'Mother?' says Lucille. 'I'm his wife!'"

We are back at the house in time to watch Johnny Carson's farewell monologue. The low-key exit is strangely moving, the aging-boyish face so much a fixture in that corner of the living room. As the Prince of Late Night fights back the tears, thunderstorm warnings beep across the bottom of the TV screen. The wind is picking up. Outside the picture window, the bird feeder swings like a pendulum as it's caught in the coming storm.

LAST OCTOBER, on a warm Indian summer's day, Ed crossed the road to check his mailbox and was nearly run over by a man on skis. The county had recently paved the road and now, besides the usual pickups and tankers hauling liquid manure, here was this skier propelling himself up the grade on wheel-mounted skis with blunt-tipped poles and a graceful, waltzing motion. The skier wore black Lycra tights and a swept-back plastic bicycle helmet; when Ed described him, he might have been discussing some new variety of corn borer. Paving the road had settled the dust, but the skier was a harbinger of even greater changes, an advance man for all that was coming Ed's way.

I was at the farm that day to help run calves through a squeeze chute and do painful things to them. Afterward Ed drove up in the Jeep Honcho and said, "Let's go for a ride."

I swung the stock gate open and jumped into the pickup, and then we were bouncing down the lane through the old orchard and into the lower pasture. The two-track road narrowed to a single cow path before disappearing altogether among milkweed and Canadian thistle. Ed gunned the Jeep to climb the grassy slope that marks the farm's northern border, and for a brief moment I felt airborne until we leveled off, skirting the edge of the upland where it falls away to Highway 52. It was a blue-sky day. If the radio had been on, we could have listened to a football game instead of the wash of traffic below. Ed pointed out ruts worn into the hillside, he said, by prairie schooners on the Dubuque Trail, a wagon road that ran between Iowa and St. Paul, and the route his grandparents would have taken to peruse this land. What could anyone think of this place now, whipping past at sixty-five miles an hour—hayfields, corn, something else that's green? At least that was my impression the first time I saw the farm. More of the same. The anonymity of farmland is what makes it so easily converted to other purposes.

Clearly, my father-in-law had no particular destination in mind that afternoon. We were just driving the fence lines, making a circuit of the farm to remind ourselves of how land-rich he is. In his seventies, Ed would look even more like Spencer Tracy if the late actor had spent half of his life on a tractor seat. He has the same shock of white hair and battered nose, the same gravel voice and Irish fatalism, the same short, self-deprecating laugh in place of a sigh.

Heading over east, Ed backed the truck beneath a solitary apple tree so I could lean out the window and pick. Apples thunked off the cab roof. The tree was a volunteer, a descendant of Wealthies or Duchess of Oldenburgs, antique varieties Ed's father had planted in the orchard during the Taft administration. A cow grazing on windfalls in the orchard had deposited the seed on this windblown site when she paused to shit here. The apples were small and tart, and a reminder that everything has a history.

Pitching down the other side of the hill, we rolled bumper deep through buttonweed and timothy to a willow-lined creek, a branch of Badger Run, that widens into a soggy meadow. We followed the creek up the hollow to its source, a clear spring bubbling out of a cleft in the limestone hillside. Over-hung with trees, it's the kind of grotto you want to associate with votive candles and visionary peasant girls, not a scummy green pool trampled by cow hooves. Ed's father, John O'Neill, once tried to increase the spring's flow with a bulldozer and nearly plugged it. He also told his son stories about Indians camped by the spring, watching indolently as he plowed the hollow.

Every pioneer had these stories, a kind of narrative abstract of title that linked the owner of the land to its aboriginal inhabitants. The Mdewakanton and Wahpeton bands of the Dakota lived in villages along the big rivers, the Mississippi and Minnesota, and may have hunted these upland prairies, but had vanished onto reservations by 1876, when John O'Neill jounced into Olmsted County on his mother's knee. Still, it's not hard to imagine a party of Dakotas or, more likely, uprooted Winnebagos on their way back to Wisconsin, no longer hunters but travelers like everyone else, following the creek up from the Dubuque Trail to camp out of the wind with plenty of fresh water. They might well have sat here watching a young man hitch himself behind a team of draft horses to plow the land into furrows. The Great Seal of Min-nesota depicts just such a scene—a straw-hatted ploughboy tearing up the prairie while a red man gallops off into the sunset—thus illustrating the triumph of agriculture over shift-less nomadism. The motto above the seal, *L'étoile du Nord*, is French for "The Star of the North," but most Minnesotans translate it simply as "Northern Toil." An updated Great Seal might reveal the same farmer skedaddling into the setting sun to make way for a new Wal-Mart.

Backtracking to cross the creek on a culvert, we continued east up a road overgrown with black locust planted by the Civilian Conservation Corps in the thirties to anchor the hill-

side. Branches now canopy the road, and snapped off the cab
as we drove. "They said black locusts made good fence posts,"
Ed recalled. "Well, they were wrong."

We emerged as from a tunnel into a pocket field of soybeans
called Potter's Field after the farmer who had sold it to Ed's
father, the name persisting long after all memory of its owner
had disappeared. Naming, of course, is a way of taking pos-
session of a place, of connecting yourself to it. Place names
on farms are often shorthand versions of stories for who
owned what or how it was used. To know the stories is to
understand where you are in the world, and to know that is
to understand who you are. For the most part, such names
are unrecorded and only accidentally find their way onto a
map. Twenty years ago a Department of Natural Resources
official making an inventory of watersheds asked Ed the name
of the creek that flows west of the farmhouse. "Oh, we just
call that Home Creek," he said because it was the creek nearest
home, an eponymous reference that started showing up on
topographical maps a few years later. The names tend toward
the practical, though occasionally one verges on the poetic,
like the wedge-shaped field above the orchard that hasn't held
a cow in years but is still called the Night Pasture.

From Potter's Field you can look north across Highway
52 to a mirror image of these rolling uplands that has been
zoned residential and developed into housing tracts with names
like Highland Ridge or Sylvan Acres, names unconnected to
anything like a past. Last summer's horse pasture had bloomed
almost overnight into a subdivision of view lots. The hilltop
houses are of the multilevel, many-square-feet, awesome-
garage, LOOK AT ME school of architecture, each squatting
on its own two and a half acres of view property as long as
nobody builds in front of it. Houses that solve the problem
of how to live in the country without living in the country.
Houses that would seem even more hideous if some of them

didn't belong to the sons and daughters of those who once owned the pasture.

Descending through the vault of locust trees, we followed the creek back toward the field road and, looking over the grassy bank, I spotted a piece of rusty machinery sticking out of the water. It was an old sulky-style cultivator, sunk to the hubs in duckweed. "We had that out a few years ago," said Ed, "but some kids rolled it back into the creek." The seat and wooden double-tree to which horses were harnessed were missing, but otherwise the cultivator looked complete, a machine-age fossil, a reminder of other days.

Climbing out of the hollow, we emerged from the trees onto a long, shining field. The corn had recently been picked and in the flat October light the stubble took on a metallic sheen. As the road angled across the field, it passed beneath high electric wires. And for a moment, before we crested the hill to the farmhouse below, I could see nothing ahead but the clean sweep of earth and sky, as if that were all there had ever been.

TWO

A friend of mine once spent a summer driving around eastern Nebraska trying to sell farmers aerial photographs of their farms. Stopping at the end of the driveway, he'd look for some telltale feature—a roofless silo, a wraparound porch, a shelter belt of red cedars—to distinguish this farm from all the others the company's pilot had flown over in his Cessna. Then he'd flip through a big cardboard box of photographs until he found a match, which required a practiced eye, since most farms look alike from a thousand feet above the earth. He'd slip the picture into a genuine oak frame and pull into the driveway, fervently hoping that the dog bounding toward him was friendly. He'd hold the photograph under the farmer's nose and say, "Does this place look familiar?" or "You've got a real nice place here!" The farmer, for his part, would remain stone-faced, reluctant to show too much pride until he knew what it would cost him. If my friend wasn't in the door by now, he might point out a tiny figure in the photograph. "Look, there's someone standing outside the barn!" If all else failed, he would exclaim, "Look at that corn! This picture must have been shot in late July." The farmer would break into a pie-eating grin. "Why no," he'd say. "That would have been mid-June." The trick was to get people to look closely at the photograph, to start talking about it and thereby connect themselves to what they saw before price was ever mentioned.

Too often, however, the reverse occurred, which is why my friend quit the business. He'd find himself staring at something in the photograph and asking questions he really wanted answered. He'd sit in some farmer's kitchen all morning, drinking endless cups of coffee and listening to stories about how that particular farm came to be in the shape it was. The stories might have different plots, but the overriding themes were the same. And because the land could not be explained apart from the people who farmed it, the stories covered several generations and required many hours to tell.

I am trying to form a mental map of my wife's family farm, an overview of 240 acres of the planet's surface, an inventory of this small kingdom. I have aerial photographs, quadrangle maps, soil-survey maps, plat maps, legal descriptions—no end of information, really. What I haven't got is a clue as to how all this information fits together to form the ongoing story that some people call a sense of place. Government agencies have charted this ground for their own narrow purposes, transforming the landscape into a one-dimensional set of data. What I have in mind is a series of overlays that will orient me not only to how the land lies but where we fit into it. Land itself can never be lost, only transformed; what is slipping away, day by day, is the meaning that connects us to it.

Aerial Photograph—33,000 Feet. Every ten years the Agricultural Stabilization Conservation Service charters a plane to fly over Olmsted County to photograph six square-mile sections of land from which soil maps will be drawn. The ASCS then field-checks the land against the aerial photograph, partitioning it by soil type and drainage until the resulting map resembles a paint-by-numbers chart of the Balkans. But that's not what the photographer sees as the plane flies from east to west. He has the same view of the Midwest that airline passengers have as they fly from one coast to another. The natural topography is flattened out into a great grid of section roads, all running in cardinal directions and spaced exactly a mile apart. From this elevation the land resembles nothing so much as a map of itself. The Jeffersonian grid, like the grooves left by prairie schooners, is an artifact of more expansive times, an era when democracy meant cheap land evenly divided. Thomas Jefferson, envisioning a nation of small farms rather than of cities—which he considered "sores upon the body politic"—initiated the township-range survey system as a means of distributing enough land to guarantee ordinary citizens a decent living and the republic a hedge against tyranny. The result was the landscape as a work of political imagination.

"You have noticed," the Oglala mystic Black Elk told his biographer, "that everything an Indian does is in a circle and that is because the Power of the World always works in circles, and everything tries to be round." But the first thing white men did was to square the land. Surveyors from the General Land Office did not reach southeastern Minnesota until the summer of 1853, two years after the Santee Sioux had ceded their lands west of the Mississippi in the Treaties of Traverse des Sioux and Mendota. John Ball, an eighteen-year-old surveyor from New York State, led a four-man crew laying out the exterior lines of what would become Marion Township. They pulled a length of wire links sixty-six feet long called a Gunter's chain through the tallgrass prairie and oak savannas and marked corners by pounding a charred stake into a trenched mound of dirt and planting the seeds of Osage orange or apple trees. A second surveying crew followed a week later to subdivide the township into thirty-six sections of one square mile each, crisscrossing back and forth, transforming the land into a great, empty checkerboard. Heading east on a random line between Sections 27 and 34, they crossed the hollow, wading a north-flowing creek "4 links wide," and set a temporary post to mark the quarter section. In his general description of Township 106 North, Range 13 West of the Fifth Principal meridian, the deputy surveyor wrote in a flowing pen: "In this Township the prairie and timber are about equally divided—Rolling surface + 1st rate soil. The water is clear + cold + plenty. Timber generally oak openings. All marshes are *of course* wet."

The opening of "Suland," as newspapers called the territory west of the Mississippi, brought a flood of white settlers to Minnesota. The subdivision of rolling prairie and woodlands into square sections or fractions of squares promoted not only orderly settlement but also speculation. Those who could not afford the government's price of $1.25 an acre for surveyed land could preempt land by putting up a small improvement, which gave them a year's leeway to come up with the cash; or they could purchase a military land warrant. The government had issued the warrants to veterans of wars prior to 1855, who sold them to bankers or land agents, who then sold them to settlers. Their prices were published in newspapers and fluctuated like the stock market. This process of transferring property from the public to the private sector was called—rather prophetically, I think—*land alienation*.

Plat Maps—Marion Township. Imagine a windstorm knocking flat all the tombstones in the cemetery beside St. Bridget's Church and you have a good idea of an early plat map of Marion Township: white rectangles filled with Irish surnames. Timothy Twohey, late of County Cork, preempted land west of St. Bridget's in 1854 and would later recall watching a column of five hundred Sioux pass through on their way to a reservation along the Minnesota River. The O'Neill farm was cobbled together out of four separate parcels of eighty acres each, but the property that most interests me is the northwest quarter of Section 27, the original eighty acres on which the farmhouse rests. Charles and Phoebe Hamlin of Walworth County, Wisconsin, bought the property in 1855 with a military land warrant originally issued to Jason Hogsed, a captain in the Georgia militia, who had received the eighty acres for service in the Cherokee Removal. So, while the Hamlins personally displaced no Sioux, they purchased the land, in a sense, with Indian blood. They held on to it as an investment for ten years, then sold it for $150 to Walter Brackenridge, a lawyer for the Winona and St. Peter Railroad who made his fortune speculating in real estate and put his name on quarter sections all over the county. In 1880, Brackenridge rented the land to a Pennsylvania dairy farmer and Civil War veteran named William O'Neill. Twenty years later his widow, Catherine Esmond O'Neill, made a down payment on the farm and put her own name on the plat.

Photograph. In the summer of 1915, John and Mame O'Neill and their four children pose for a photographer in front of a single-gable barn. Mame, holding the baby, wears a high-collared dress with a pleated hem, while her husband is dressed for chores in overalls, work shirt, and a straw hat. Two of the children are mounted on horses. All of them are barefoot. Catherine, the oldest girl and her grandmother's namesake, sits sidesaddle on a bay mare, her sandy hair brushed back, one leg thrown over the pommel, a strangely defiant look in her eyes. A moon-faced hired man stands gaping from the shadow of the barn door. Despite the work clothes, this is a formal photograph, meant to convey the family's prosperity and all they have made of this place. Besides the steam-powered tractor visible in the barn, a wagon and sulky cultivator (the same one I saw rusting in the creek) have been hauled into the center of the photograph. The barn, which serves as backdrop, is the family's storehouse, its bank account made visible. The photographer has ducked his head beneath the black cloth draped behind the camera but continues to motion with his hands. "Hold still!" he shouts. The words hang in the air as everyone looks straight ahead, out of their own thoughts and into the camera lens as if this were the bright future itself.

ASCS Color Transparency—8,500 Feet. Once a year a Cessna 172 chartered by the Agricultural Stabilization Conservation Service flies out of Preston, Minnesota, to make sure farmers match the crop plans they've filed with the government. Cruising a mile and a half above the ground, the pilot lines up with a big white cross painted on the highway south of Stewartville. Then the photographer, lying flat on his stomach, begins to click a 35-millimeter camera mounted on the bottom of the fuselage. He shoots square-mile sections of townships, but his true subject is the agricultural landscape.

The slides for sections 27 and 34 of Marion Township reveal a farm of traditional proportions: crops on the relatively flat uplands, pasture on the hillsides, and woods on the steep-sloped hollow. But it's the field patterns, the broad strokes of yellow and green, that catch the eye. The half-dozen rectilinear fields are laid out, more like a crossword puzzle than a quilt, to take advantage of slope and drainage. An ASCS agent running a planimeter along the image he had projected onto a white tabletop would find seventy-eight acres in corn, thirty-two in soybeans, and the rest in oats and set-aside. A modest operation by today's agribusiness standards.

Aerial Photograph—700 Feet. The iconography of farm photographs has shifted over the years from people to buildings and machinery, perhaps because there are so few people left.

This picture was taken last July as the pilot of a single-engine Cessna swooped over the farm at one hundred miles an hour. It is a hawk's-eye view of the place. Beyond the canopy of white oaks along the driveway you can see the circle of out-buildings, haphazard fencing around the corral and a vacant chicken coop waiting to collapse. Gone is the old, single-gable barn, replaced by a peeling, white, arch-roofed barn with six lightning rods along its spine and twin windows in the hayloft that give it a cryptic man-in-the-moon face. Gone are the horses and the machines they pulled. Gone is the hired man. Gone, in fact, is every human figure except my father-in-law. Born five years too late to make the 1915 photograph, Edward O'Neill is in the center of this picture, driving a blue Ford tractor with a silage chopper in tow. With a magnifying glass you can barely make him out on the tractor seat, steering one-handed, his face toward the sky. He squints not into the bright future but at a low-flying aircraft swooping out of the sun from the southwest, just above the trees.

THE DAY BEFORE Ed is to return from the hospital, I bor-row his four-wheeler and shovel and roar up the field road toward the hollow. Birdsong from hawthorns along the fence line trails off into a long, thin whine. I turn off at the creek and follow it through the tall wet grass to an old cottonwood with suckers growing vertically from its lowest limbs. Pulling on fireman's boots, I slide down the bank and wade into the creek where the old riding cultivator has been parked for who knows how long. Luckily the mosquitoes haven't hatched in any numbers yet. I go to work with the shovel to excavate the high, spoked wheels. The black muck at the bottom makes a sucking sound as it comes free and smells like rotten eggs. But even after I've dug out the front hitch, the cultivator doesn't budge. Feeling around with my boot, I discover why. Cotton-wood roots have woven through the spokes and won't let go.

In the afternoon I return with a pickup, a length of hay rope, a saber saw, and a brother-in-law. Together we saw through the roots, loop a rope around the hitch, and wrench the cultivator free of the creek bottom and haul it dripping wet up the bank. It's rusty and smells like swamp muck but is otherwise in good shape. The wheels turn and, with a seat added and a few gallons of 10-W-30, someone could use it— an Amish farmer, perhaps, or an antiquarian. I suddenly have no idea why the cultivator needed to be hauled out of the creek, except that it was something to do and now it was done. Loading our prize into the truck bed, we drive back down the field road to a shelterbelt of wind-stunted cedars where generations of harrows and hay rakes lay mothballed and carefully park the cultivator between an ancient fresno and a slightly newer grain wagon in a long, long row of rusting, useless machinery.

THREE

I met my wife in a bar called The Joynt. It's a narrow place with a straight-shot bar, a pool table at one end, and a jukebox at the other. One night during a long dry season I propped myself against the jukebox to check out the faces of women reflected above the bottles in the back-bar mirror, wondering which face might save my life or at least the rest of the evening. From this vantage point I thought none of the women could see me without turning around very suddenly, which one of them suddenly did. She had dark hair and pale-blue eyes and a mouth that turned down at the corners, and I had never seen her there before because I would've remembered. She tapped out a cigarette, looking me up and down while she lit it, and when she blew smoke in my direction I forgot anything clever I might have said and walked back to my table feeling I had lost something or maybe never had it. A few beers later I worked up the nerve to go looking for her, but she was gone.

She had a girlfriend, however, and whenever I saw this friend at the bar I'd ask, "Where's your pal?," figuring this would get back to her. And it did. A few weeks later she was sitting on the same bar stool. I brought two beers over and asked if she'd care to drink one. She said sure.

We had a few things in common. We were both newly divorced. We had both come through a long winter alone, and we were both on our way out of town. In a month I was flying north to spend the summer floating down the Yukon River, washing away the past, as it were; she had left a teaching job in a small town and was moving to the Twin Cities to begin her life afresh. So there seemed little risk in a brief, no-strings romance before our separate ships set sail.

Either nobody had ever told her that she was good-looking or she had not believed them because she tried so hard in other ways. She cracked jokes with other men and cried at movies and once threw a glassful of beer at some louts who were drowning out the jukebox with their fraternity songs. All this made her seem vulnerable to me in a way quite different from women I'd known who let me crack the jokes and throw the drinks. When one of the louts she'd soaked with beer pointed at the small woman sitting at the table I had just left and cried, "It's not you, buddy. It's her!" I was secretly pleased, never imagining what might be flung my way in the coming years.

At the end of that month, she saw me off at the airport with no promises made. I spent the summer adrift on a great river, freer than I have ever been in my life, moored to no person or place, and increasingly, unaccountably, despondent. Her letters arrived general delivery in Indian villages all down the Yukon, and at night I studied them by flashlight in my tent as if they were secret maps to the future, which, as it turned out, they were. By the time summer ended and she picked me up at the same airport from which we'd earlier parted, I had made up my mind to marry her.

Her father cried at the wedding. He looked like a man watching his own foreclosure sale, not the marriage of his thirty-year-old daughter. But afterward, at the supper club, Ed tore off his necktie so that his shirt collar flared over his baby-blue suit and asked the bride to dance. It was an even match. Of his seven daughters, Sharon most resembles him in temperament. She could be the most charming, the most headstrong, the most stubbornly bullheaded. As a teenager she had terrific arguments with her father about Vietnam, where one of her cousins was fighting. Storming from the house, she would ride horseback over the hills until the rage subsided. Even years later, watching them thunder across the dance floor on our wedding day was to witness a contest of wills.

At that time we lived farther from the farm than any of Sharon's sisters, a hundred miles away, and her homecomings were always tinged with the clear bitterness of the exile's return. She would rearrange her parents' furniture until it suited her and point out that the barn needed painting or a shed tearing down. She would talk of the changes since her childhood, the abandonment of certain jobs that no longer paid. "You don't know what this place was like then. How much it's changed. When I was growing up, it was just this hub of activity, this beehive of chores. And now . . ."

She was angry that the farm was not run as it had been thirty years before, when a whole extended family was bent to the task. She was angry that none of her sisters had married a farmer. But most of all, I think, she was angry at herself for having left.

As a schoolgirl, Sharon would throw a bareback pad on a horse and ride south through the fields and across her uncle's farm to a township road that led to the Root River, where her grandfather owned hayfields on a bluff overlooking the river as well as the bottomlands along a tributary creek. The tall bluff grass parted like water around the horse and sealed behind her. Afterward she galloped home to give the horse a workout, crossing the borders of first her uncle's farm and then her father's, convinced that the best part of the world had her name on it. Growing up with enough land to cover on horseback on a good afternoon is a dubious gift if it means believing the land is yours to keep forever. Even after the Root River land was sold to a doctor to settle her grandfather's estate, Sharon could sustain this insular view of the world and her place in it. The real change didn't occur until later, when she left the township school and was bused into Rochester, where her classmates were no longer cousins and neighbors but the children of Mayo Clinic specialists or engineers at IBM. It was like going from princess to frog.

Until recently, a single horse remained on the farm, a white-faced black gelding that Sharon had broken as a colt. Nobody had ridden him for ages, so the horse had switched allegiances and ran with the cattle. Sometimes you'd spot him standing alone on a hillside, aloof as a ghost. A few days before he was sold, Sharon walked into the pasture with a bridle over her shoulder and a handful of oats. She whistled twice and the horse cantered over the hill. He had a tail ratty with burdock and enormous eyes that moved independently in the sockets of his bony skull. When he bent down for the oats, she slipped the bridle over his head. Then she took hold of the horse's mane in both hands, swung herself onto his back, rode up the field road and disappeared over the rise like the Queen of the Cowgirls in search of her lost kingdom.

One afternoon we drive to a nursing home to visit Sharon's great-aunt, the barefoot girl on horseback in the 1915 photograph. The staff wear blue jumpsuits and bandolier-style harnesses for hefting patients out of bed. Their cheerfulness, along with the songbird atrium in the lobby and the hallway notices for birthdays and balloon volleyball, almost make you forget the smell of urine and the overwhelming hopelessness of such places. Patients sleep three to a room, but neither of the women asleep in the room we are pointed toward is Sharon's aunt. We find her in the TV room watching a Chevy Chase movie while other patients snore open-mouthed in the drowsy sunlight. She is a slight woman with a delicate, angular face and, once she recognizes us, a pleasant smile. She wears a red cardigan with her wristwatch pulled over one sleeve and the other hand strapped to the arm of her wheelchair. We wheel her down the hall to the library, where it's quieter.

"But I was always riding a horse back then," Aunt Catherine says when she sees the old photograph. "This boy in the straw hat isn't your uncle, though, but a neighbor boy who always came to help in the summer."

I've brought some photographs along to jog her memory but feel a bit brutal when her eyes well up with tears over a yellowed snapshot. It is a picture of herself as a schoolgirl in a checked dress and sailor collar standing in front of her grandmother and namesake, Catherine Esmond O'Neill, the old woman looming grimly behind her in widow weeds, her white hair done up in a tidy bun. "Oh my lands!" Aunt Catherine cries out, not from seeing herself young again but at recognizing a face that had long vanished. During the school year she had lived with her grandmother and the old woman's companion in a small white cottage in Simpson, two miles from the farm. After Sunday mass young Catherine would sit drowsily on a red-velvet settee with the other children while her parents visited with the two older women, the conversation buzzing overhead like a fly. Then her grandmother would nod at the bowl of yellow mints on a lace doily in the center of the round oak table and say, "You may each have one."

This is a long-lived family. Aunt Catherine is ninety-three. Her grandmother, who died in 1932, was born in Ireland before the reign of Queen Victoria. It strikes me that the collective memory of the people in this room easily spans two centuries and covers more lifetimes than anyone could care to use.

"She had her own way," Aunt Catherine says of the old woman in the photograph. "She did everything her own way. If she had an opinion, that was it."

I take a closer look at the faded snapshot. There are the same light eyes, the same down-turned mouth, and the same ironclad set to the jaw that I'd seen in the bar the night I met my wife. Well, I think, this explains a lot.

CATHERINE ESMOND O'NEILL was born the week before Christmas, 1834, near the village of Killena, County Wexford. She had fiery red hair and cold blue eyes. When her mother was buried three years later, the small girl wept bitterly. When her father remarried to a woman who bore him a steady stream of sons, she understood that the world was going to be hard on her.

In the landscape of Catherine's youth, the sun rose over St. George's Channel to be snuffed out at day's end by the dark rim of the Blackstairs Mountains. The moist lowland in between tilted toward the sea and was partitioned into a multitude of fields by hedgerows of gorse and whitethorn. The larger fields held wheat and barley. The smaller fields, especially the square rood behind mud-and-thatch cottages, held velvety-green potato plants and perhaps a pig. The potatoes came in many varieties: Rocks, Cups, Pink Eyes, Leathercoats, Irish Apple, Yam, White Kidney, and Sherry Blues. The most prolific, as well as the most vulnerable to disease, was the Lumpers, which had been introduced as animal fodder but became almost the sole diet of peasants, who roasted the spuds over a peat fire or boiled them in a common pot with buttermilk and ate them skins and all.

The summer Catherine turned eleven, a blight appeared on the potato crop just before harvest. The dark-green leaves and purple blossoms blackened as if scorched, and crumpled to the touch like ashes. Frantically, farmers cut away the blighted leaves and stalks to save the tubers, only to find them rotting in the ground. Piles of potatoes already picked and cleaned soon turned putrid. A carrion stench hung over the fields. It was the smell of famine.

The Great Famine resulted not only from successive failures of the potato crop but also from an agricultural system that concentrated ownership of the land among a few wealthy, often absentee, landlords. Owners of large estates presided over a rickety pyramid of subcontracts by leasing their lands to farmers and middlemen, who subleased to cottiers or rented potato patches by the season to the landless peasants who made up half the population of the country. To meet rising debts, gentry and strong farmers began to consolidate their holdings by evicting tenants and converting tillage to grazing lands to raise cattle for export to England. Caught between exorbitant "rack" rents, tithes, and taxes, tenants relied almost exclusively on the potato for their own sustenance, as a single acre could feed an entire family for a year except for the "hungry months" of midsummer between the end of one year's potato supply and the harvest of another. When the blight appeared in 1846, caused by a fungus in a shipment of American potatoes, the "hungry months" stretched into four years.

The west of Ireland was hit hardest by the famine. Entire villages disappeared, and those who didn't starve outright died of typhus, scurvy, cholera, and dysentery, or "the bloody flux." Coffins sold at county fairs were sometimes fitted with a hinged bottom to make them reusable. During the famine's second year, Parliament amended the Poor Law with the "Gregory clause," named for the Irish landlord who proposed it, forbidding public relief to any household head who possessed a quarter acre or more of land unless he relinquished it to his proprietor. Cottages were leveled and their former inhabitants set loose upon the countryside, their eyeballs swollen out of their sockets, the taut skin over their skulls the same pale greenish hue as the nettles they ate. To keep from catching the fever, farmers rolled a few spare potatoes downhill to the ghostly figures begging at the gates. Even in the breadbasket of County Wexford, a shopkeeper wrote that "young and old are dying as fast as they can bury them, the fever is rageing here at such arate that there are in health in the morning knows not but in the Evening may have taken the infection." More than a million Irish died during the Great Famine, one out of every eight, while landlords managed to export tons of food-stuffs across the Irish Sea. For every corpse laid in the auld sod, two chose to emigrate. One of these was sixteen-year-old Catherine Esmond.

The decision to emigrate could not have been difficult for a young woman in Catherine's position. If she left, she could always find employment as a domestic; if she stayed, she would remain the unpaid servant of her younger brothers. On the eve of departure, relatives often threw the one who was leaving a parting spree called an "American wake" because the emigrant was traveling west, like the souls of the dead, and wasn't expected to return. The wake lasted from nightfall until dawn and, like its namesake, combined grief with a final good time. Family and relatives gathered by the hearth to dance reels and sing ballads and eulogize the emigrant for the difficult journey ahead, the older women sometimes keening in shrill voices as the mood turned somber. The next morning a crowd accompanied the emigrant to the docks or train station to say so long, the tears and wailing beginning again until the de-parting person felt as if he were going to his own funeral. So many of the young were leaving, a newspaper observed, that the entire country seemed "one vast 'American wake.' "

Catherine traveled with her relatives, the Sinnotts, who paid her passage. They crossed the Irish Sea by steamer to Liverpool, then, after a cursory medical inspection that con-sisted of showing their tongues to a doctor, boarded a sailing packet with four hundred other souls to be towed down the muddy Mersey to the Atlantic, where the real journey began. The ocean crossing took six weeks, longer than usual because a violent gale blew the ship back almost to Ireland. What would a young girl remember of such a lengthy voyage? The green, receding coastline of home? The terrible stink in steerage, where she and other passengers were berthed like bales of cotton? Or the sight of an old woman's corpse bound in sail-cloth and weighted with shot as it splashed into the cold, gray deep?

The ship sailed up the Delaware River and dropped anchor beside a forest of masts that were the docks of Philadelphia. The city had a sizable Irish population, but Pennsylvania was also the land of the Know-Nothings, mostly Scotch-Irish descendants from an earlier migration, who had burned down three Catholic churches in the city's Irish neighborhoods the decade before, fearing that cheap foreign labor would undercut their own wages. Jobs were scarce for men, but women could always find work as servants. American women looked down on domestic work, but Irish women preferred it to the sweatshops and mills because it offered room and board and a chance to put away a little money. Bridget the ill-tempered Irish servant girl was a figure of fun in the popular imagination, a priest-bound lass who shattered the crockery and threatened to quit on the spot if anyone criticized her terrible cooking.

The tide of mick-hating didn't begin to subside until the nation was embroiled in a greater conflict and thousands of Irish emigrants volunteered or were conscripted into the Union army. When the war began, Catherine was working in the Coates Street mansion of a Philadelphia carpet merchant and his family, remitting a portion of her wages to her father back home. In off hours she retired to her small room and clipped accounts from Irish-American newspapers detailing the exploits of New York's Thirty-seventh Regiment, the Irish Rifles, at Bull Run, Manassas, and their near-annihilation at Fredericksburg. With so many Irishmen under arms, hopes were raised that when the war ended an army of veterans would recross the Atlantic with the green flag flying at the mizzen-peak. Among the lithographs of General McClellan and exiled Fenian leaders Catherine pasted into her scrapbook was a speech entitled "The Downfall of England," delivered to "loud cheers" before the Brotherhood of St. Patrick, that concluded:

> Unite, and by the famine graves,
> By your sires' sacred dust,
> You shall not, will not, long be slaves.
> You'll break your chains accursed.
> The tyrant Saxon soon shall quake
> At banded million's might:
> The time is nigh—arouse! awake!
> For Ireland's sake unite.

When Robert E. Lee's army invaded Pennsylvania in the summer of 1863, local farmers and shopkeepers too old to have been called up earlier hastily formed a regiment of state militia known as the "emergency men." Among them was an Irish-born dairy farmer from the Schuylkill Valley named William O'Neill. He stood five feet four inches tall with blue eyes and brown hair, and had a sandy complexion. Assembling in the heat of morning, the volunteers formed ranks and marched down the pike toward the seat of war, rumbling through covered bridges and receiving cheers in every village they passed. By the next morning, the men awoke from their bivouac feeling jolted and sore, but they reached Reading in good time. On the third day the sky poured rain, but they warmed themselves with the news of Gettysburg. For the final leg of the journey they boarded railroad cars to Harrisburg, where they received uniforms and an assignment: ferrying horses to regular troops. They never once glimpsed a secessionist, dead or alive, and spent the remainder of their tour guarding the Potomac River and dreaming, one summer soldier later recalled, "of soft beds, new-made hay, and orange harvest-fields and not the girls, but the kindly housewives we left behind us." A month later, Lee's army having retired to Virginia, the volunteers were mustered out and returned to their wives, except for bachelors like William, who had left behind only his parents and their large brood.

The O'Neills also came from County Wexford and were related to the Sinnotts. Like other emigrant families, they tended to duplicate in this country the society they had left behind, so it was perhaps inevitable that Catherine and William were brought together after the war. By then she was neither young nor especially pretty, except for the blue, unwavering eyes, but she was strong and furnished her own dowry. He had taken the pledge, so she knew he had potential. When they married at St. Matthew's Church, he was forty-two years old and she was thirty-four. Both thought their lives were starting over.

Catherine had taken a name grander than her own, a chieftain's name. It fit her like a glove. Every Irish child knew the story of *Nial Noï'igiallach* (Nial of the Nine Hostages), who divided Ireland in two and set his younger sons to rule over the North. The Red Hand of O'Neill is the symbol of Ulster and derives from an even older legend. As a fleet of longboats neared the Irish coast, the invaders engaged in a race, having agreed that whoever touched the land first would be its ruler. Whereupon a certain O'Neill drew his sword, lopped off his own right hand, and flung it ashore. The story was apocryphal, but nicely illustrated the lengths to which an Irishman will go for a bit of land.

William and Catherine rented a dairy farm outside Plymouth Meeting, just north of the Schuylkill River. While her husband and the hired man worked the crops—corn, oats, and hay—Catherine and her sister-in-law Margaret attended the small herd of milch cows, since the dairy was as much a woman's domain as the kitchen. Catherine was a wet milker. She always squirted a little milk on her hands so they would slip better on the teats, though it meant grit in the milk. Then she'd press her head against the cow's warm side and pull, listening to the hiss of milk against the pail. The women carried the milk to the springhouse, skimmed the cream from the top, and fed the skim to the hogs. Afterward Catherine poured the cream into a butter churn and began throttling the plunger as if she had the devil by the throat.

Cone-shaped limekilns dotted the countryside, where the quarried stone was burned to make lime for sweetening the soil. The massive bed of limestone underlying Plymouth Meeting made it some of the most fertile soil in the East. But land was too expensive for William and Catherine to consider buying their own farm, so they continued to rent. Shortly after the birth of their second son, a cousin of Catherine's living in Minnesota, another Civil War veteran, wrote of cheap land there and the fine opportunities for an experienced farmer on the rich black soil of the prairies. For the second time in their lives, they decided to leave family behind and move west.

A few days before Christmas, 1875, Catherine watched as the auctioneers, M. Pester and Son, sold off everything they owned in what seemed another version of the American wake. The auctioneer quickly moved the crowd through each item: twenty-one head of fine young cows, one bull, two horses, a mule, a colt six years old, fifty pairs of chickens and thirty geese. Also: a two-horse Dearborn wagon, one-horse sleigh, hay wagon, falling-top wagon, cart, harnesses of all kinds, two mowing machines, two-horse thresher, telegraph cutter, windmill, plow, hoes, forks, shovels, chains, and dairy fixtures consisting of cans, churns, and the like, as well as the household furniture. Catherine kept an auction notice as a reminder of all they had given up for the prairies.

On the swaying train ride west, Catherine nursed the baby and kept the older boy from running up and down the Pullman with an occasional yank on his ear. When they pulled into Rochester and Catherine surveyed the muddy streets and wooden storefronts that ended abruptly in prairie, she must have thought they had arrived at the bat's end of the world. William had come out earlier to make arrangements, but at

$40 to $50 an acre, farmland wasn't cheap, and they still had to purchase stock, machinery, and seed for the coming year. So they rented a ramshackle place north of St. Bridget's Church from Paddy O'Neil, who was no kin to them. The barn was falling down, and the house just short of a pigsty. The house stood on a bench above a willow-lined creek and wind blew through cracks in the door frame until Catherine hung a quilt over it. The winter just ending had been a mild one, and tolerable except for the howling of wolves in the oak breaks. A March thaw uncovered the brown hills, and showers washed away the last signs of winter. Then rain turned into snow and a northwest wind brought the worst blizzard of the year. The roads drifted over and canceled the St. Patrick's Day celebration they had been looking forward to attending. A month after the snow melted, William plowed and harrowed the fields and planted spring wheat, barley, oats, and potatoes.

By summer 1876, things looked better. The tall grass bloomed with wild plum, prickly pear, bergamot, oxeye daisies and wild indigo. Neighbors buzzed with news of gold strikes out West and some young bucks even left for the Black Hills, but the real gold was in wheat. On the Fourth of July, all of Rochester turned out to celebrate the nation's centennial with a parade led by a golden chariot. The procession of brass bands and temperance societies marched down Broadway to the park. After a choir sang the "Anvil Chorus," an orator from St. Paul praised the nation's hundred years of progress and called upon God to "bless this land, that it shall be perpetuated through the ages as the home and sanctuary of the downtrodden of the earth." The speaker was Dillon O'Brien, secretary of the Minnesota Irish Immigration Society, so Catherine had a pretty good notion of whom he meant by the "downtrodden." The expansive mood was dampened a few days later when the *Rochester Post* carried news of Custer's annihilation at the Little Big Horn. The slaughter, the newspaper concluded, was "a terrible commentary on the peace policy of the Eastern philanthropists and every soldier killed is an argument in favor of Indian extermination."

The wheat began to ripen in early August. The plague of grasshoppers that had devoured most of the crop in the western counties stopped just short of Olmsted, pushing the price of wheat to a dollar a bushel. All William had to worry about were midges, black stem, stem rust, wheat smut, steamy weather, and chinch bugs. Chinch bugs were the worst. The size of winged bedbugs, they would descend on a field of wheat and literally suck the plants dry.

In a letter to the Sinnotts, Catherine wrote: "We have sent money to my father twice since we come out here. It was only gone a few days when we lost a cow. He rote again to us saying he had rote to them all and never thought it worth answering his letter. It was the winter Will was sick and when he was able to get out he sent some more . . . The crops is looking very well if the chinz bugs don't distroy them. They are more numerous than any year yet. Whether they will work on the grain or knot we cannot tell yet."

By the summer's end, the wheat fields had turned yellow-white. When the grain heads dropped and the kernels tasted doughy instead of milky, the grain was ready for harvest. Three times a day during the reaping, Catherine set a full table for the hands, mostly neighbors, but she didn't like being at the beck and call of every tramp that followed the wheat harvest and hired men soon learned to take any disputes to the farmer and not his hard-eyed wife. From the house she could hear the rattle and whir of the reaper as the horses walked it clockwise through a field of wheat. The reaper's rotating rakes pulled the grain into the mower blade with the churning motion of a paddle wheeler against the current. Men and boys followed in the reaper's wake, binding the wheat into sheaves and standing them in tentlike shocks until the mowed field resembled an encampment.

Four years after moving to Minnesota, William and Catherine quit Paddy O'Neil's place to rent another farm a mile and a half to the south along the Dubuque Trail. Half of the 120-acre farm was still in woods, but the land was higher and better drained than what they had been farming. It was underlaid with limestone, the white rock poking through like bone in places, yet on the level uplands the soil was deep and rich. There were two springs, a five-acre meadow, and a small frame house in the lee of a hill. Walter Brackenridge, a lawyer for the railroad, drew up the lease.

Nearly all the tillable land on the new farm had been planted to wheat the year before, with only five acres in oats for the horses. But the wheat belt was moving farther west, out to virgin prairie where land was cheaper and successive plantings hadn't exhausted the soil. The wheat craze ruined a lot of farmers, who had nothing to fall back on if their single crop failed or prices fell. Progressive agriculturalists at the Olmsted County Farmer's Institute preached crop rotation and year-round dairying. The O'Neills kept a small herd of Shorthorn-Durhams that foraged on wild hay and provided milk and butter as well as beef. Twice a day Catherine walked around the woods north of the house to bring in the milch cows.

In the summer of 1887, William suffered a stroke and lay paralyzed in bed for a year before dying. At his wake, he looked no different than he had for twelve months past, except that his eyelids were sewn shut. Catherine buried him in the cemetery beside St. Bridget's and for the rest of her life, another forty-four years, wore only black. The brunt of the work now fell upon her teenage sons, Edward and John, but Catherine ran the place. It was she who haggled with bankers each year and kept abreast of the latest developments in agriculture. Her point of reference in these matters was a thick, often-mended volume entitled *How to Make the Farm Pay*, whose preface was a stirring call to action: "Enterprising young men of good abilities are putting their hands to the plow, and the plow to the furrow, resolved to leave the mark of improvement on the work of the farm. The labor of the farmer is thus elevated. What has always been claimed by a few, will soon be acknowledged by all, that the prosperity of a country depends upon the intelligent cultivation of the soil."

The years sped past. Catherine seemed to shrink with the passage of time and took to walking with a stout cane that she called her gad. In 1898 Kate Sinnott, the last surviving daughter of the family, sold her millinery shop in Philadelphia and moved to Minnesota. Her siblings had all died of bad hearts and, rather than live alone, she elected to care for her aunt in old age just as Catherine had cared for her as a child so many years before. Kate was a tall, thin-lipped spinster with the annoying habit of clacking her false teeth against her gums. But she was generous. When Catherine decided to buy the farm, it was Kate who lent her the money for a down payment. For the first time in her life, a piece of land had Catherine's name on it.

Her sons grown and married, Catherine moved with Kate into a small white cottage at the end of a street in nearby Simpson. They had a beautiful flower garden, and Kate started another millinery business. The two women convinced Catherine's son John to send his three oldest children to school in Simpson to live with them during the week. The children slept in one bedroom, their grandmother and Aunt Kate slept in the other. They were very religious. When the children ran home for lunch, they would find both women on their knees beside the kitchen table praying the Angelus.

One of Kate's vocations was ministering to the sick and dying, an endeavor in which she was often joined by a neighbor known as Death-Watch Mary, another old maid with greatly arched eyebrows and a face like a sigh. If Kate and Mary showed up at someone's door, the end could not be far off. Before a wake the two women prepared the body for viewing, then helped feed the steady stream of mourners. Mary's brother, who lived in a shack in the woods across from the church, would sit up all night with the corpse and tell stories. As Catherine was, by then, in her eighties, Kate certainly imagined performing this final courtesy for her aunt. But Kate's heart failed, and it was she who was laid in the ground first.

Three days before her own death, Catherine chased off a flock of white geese that had wandered down from the pig pasture to the farmhouse lawn. After selling the cottage in Simpson, she alternated between her sons' homes, spending winters in Willmar with Edward and summers at the farm with John and Mame. At the latter, she moved into her old room, the west room, which had been the original house until her son added another wing and raised the roof. In Irish farmhouses, aged parents traditionally retreated to the west room once they had relinquished control to a son and daughter-in-law. But Catherine took over the household as if she had never left, shaking her gad at grandchildren if they didn't get out of her way quickly enough. She moved surprisingly fast for a woman of ninety-eight.

The first of May found the lilacs and flowering crab beside the house in full bloom. Catherine was angry about something all through breakfast and hardly ate a bite. After drying the dishes she turned and hurried toward her room. One of her bedroom slippers caught on the throw rug in the doorway, and she fell to the floor with a muffled crash. An hour later, the doctor arrived in his Ford to examine the patient propped against the headboard of her bed. He sounded her chest and felt her limbs, then pronounced her hip broken. But she was slowly drowning with pneumonia, her breath coming in quick gasps. For three days, as her lungs filled with fluid, she floated in and out of consciousness. Waking once, she looked out of the window of the west room to see the white geese regrouped in the yard. Her hand reached for the gad. . . .

OF COURSE, I'm imagining this last part. Who knows what the old woman was thinking about at the end? In the library at the nursing home, another patient has sat down at the piano, and she thumps out show tunes until we gull a nurse into silencing her, but it's too late. The racket has jolted Aunt Catherine—all of us, really—out of the past and into the drowsy present. She looks at her wristwatch and confesses to feeling tired. We wheel her back into her room and admire snapshots of her grandchildren's children before making our getaway. On the drive back to the farm, I innocently ask why Catherine Esmond O'Neill was so angry the day she fell, had been angry, it seems, all her life. My wife shoots me a look as if I hadn't heard a word.

FOUR

Driving through Simpson on the way to 10:30 mass, my father-in-law points out the scenes of his youth. Haney's grocery store, blacksmith shop, Bennet Hotel, Farmers and Merchants State Bank, lumberyards, Winona and Southwestern Railroad depot, cheese factory, the twin-towered white schoolhouse his older sisters attended. This is an exercise in conjuring, as none of these places remain, except for the bricked-up former pool hall where Ed learned to roller-skate. There is no town anymore, only converted storefronts and overgrown lots with cars for sale and horses grazing on the ragged outskirts. "Whatever they built in Simpson," Ed says, "always burned down."

Set on a small rise, St. Bridget's is a lovely old church of buff-colored limestone with lancet windows, a Gothic belfry, and a cornerstone that reads 1859. Above the door to the vestibule stands a statue of Saint Bridget, cloaked and wimpled, a shepherd's staff in one hand and a stone cow at her feet facing several live Herefords across the road. The walls are three feet thick and keep the church cool as a fruit cellar. The names on the stained-glass windows—Griffin, O'Brien, O'Neil, Campion, Convoy, Burns—are the names of the people in the pews around us.

The 10:30 crowd has gotten smaller as the service got longer. The old priest had stripped the mass to the essentials, replacing the choir with a cassette player on the altar so he could punch a button and release the deep, purling voice of Tennessee Ernie Ford. He retired two months ago with heart trouble, returning only once, like Christ from the dead, on Pentecost Sunday. His face looked doughy and pale; he made a crack about changing his permanent address to the hospital's, and halfway through communion he ran out of wafers. "That's it!" he joked. "Come back next Sunday. We've run out of supplies!" But he seemed flustered by the mistake and I felt sorry for him, wondering how much longer he'd be around.

The new pastor is a younger man in his fifties, an ex-Floridian who does double duty as chaplain at the federal minimum-security prison outside Rochester. Father Santos brought the choir back and restored the mass to its original, uncut length. Walking up the aisle in an emerald-green chasuble, he sings the entrance hymn—all three verses—in a clear voice.

Unlike his predecessor, a one-man show, Santos seems anxious to extend the mantle of parish work. "I don't want an all-woman worship committee any more than I want an all-male finance committee." His homily contains fewer jokes and more information. He begins with a quiz, asking how many parishioners know when Saint Bridget's Feast Day is. No hands go up.

"It's February first. Of course, I asked that question to embarrass you. I didn't know the answer until I looked it up. There are two Saint Bridgets, one from Sweden and one from Ireland. We're interested in the one from Ireland. She was born in four-fifty A.D. Her parents were baptized by Saint Patrick. Her mother was a slave. Her father was a chieftain. The Irish were converted at that time, but not necessarily civilized."

The priest goes on to explain that in Ireland the feast of Saint Bridget marks the end of winter and the beginning of the agricultural year. He suggests that the parish should plan a celebration to honor its patron saint. Santos studied in Ireland for two years and says the countryside is similar to Minnesota's, except that the fields are smaller and bordered by stone walls. I don't know the significance of any of this but recognize in the priest an outsider's interest in a past that is clearly not his own.

I love being here. I love singing with strangers and the part where we shake hands and say "Peace be with you" or usually just "Peace," and I love being exhorted to do good rather than evil, which is a wake-up call I could use every morning. But mostly I love hearing stories that I've heard all my life and still wonder what they mean, what bearing they could possibly have on any of us when, at times, their language is so archaic it's hard to know what to think.

On this thirteenth Sunday of Ordinary Time the lector, a man whose nylon jacket advertises aluminum siding, struggles through a reading from the First Book of Kings. "The Lord said to Elijah: You shall anoint Elisha, son of Sha-phat of Abel . . . uh . . . Abel-me-ho-lah, as prophet to succeed you." Despite the funny names, the rest of the reading proceeds smoothly because it is grounded in the everyday tasks of farming, which is what most Old Testament characters did when they weren't smiting Canaanites. When the prophet finds his man, Elisha is plowing a field behind twelve yoke of oxen. He promptly slaughters one pair for a feast and uses his plow for the cook fire. The breeding and slaughter of livestock, the sowing and harvesting of crops, lend themselves to expressing the kind of human verities that, say, retail sales cannot. But as the farm population dwindles and we move farther from that life, these references become increasingly mysterious, like fragments of a lost language.

After mass, Ed and Fran stop on the front steps to compare illnesses with Jim Sheehan, a lifelong neighbor who has been diagnosed with farmer's lung. Both men are the same age, though Sheehan stands a head taller and has grown pale and thin these past few months.

"I'm fine," he says, "so long as I don't *do* anything."

"I heard you were in the hospital," Helen Sheehan says to Ed. "But I see you're doing better."

"And how are *you* doing?"

"Well," she says, momentarily at a loss, "I'm here."

"That's the important thing, isn't it? That you're here!"

SITTING AT the kitchen table, Ed takes a hit from a nebulizer and then finishes braiding a length of rope into a lariat. He twirls the loop between table and kitchen counter. "When I was thirteen I could put out a forty-foot rope. But I could never jump through it, what they call the Texas hop."

He throws the loop across the room and lassos a passing grandchild. The child bursts into tears.

Earlier in the morning Ed brought the cattle up from the orchard by spreading hay in the corral and calling "COME BOSS! COME BOSS!" from the cab of his pickup until twenty-five white-faced Hereford cows, each with a calf in tow, were strung out in a long line behind him. They moved slowly up the lane and around the barn to the corral. That they came so willingly says something of the relationship between farmer and cattle, an implied contract, biblical in nature, that says, "I'll fatten you and then you'll return the favor."

All year the cows range freely over the pasturage and, after harvest, will have the run of the stubble-fields as well. Their calves, three months old, already weigh a couple hundred pounds. They have never been separated from their mothers and are in for a bad day. Rounding up calves is the one event for which Ed requires more manpower and not just another machine. It's also my only chance to play cowboy, although this is Minnesota and nobody rides a horse.

The cattle are bunched at the far end of the corral, looking edgy and confused, as if they realize some tacit understanding is about to be broken. The first order of business is to drive the cows out of the corral. Ed opens the gate while the rest of us form a skirmish line to move the cows through the gate without letting any calves escape. As with any herd animal, if one goes through, the rest should follow. A few quickly canter back to the cow yard and waiting hay. But when a calf tries to sneak out between two cows, we rush forward and the whole crowd gallops to the end of the corral.

"Don't give the little shits time to think!" Ed rasps from the gate. "Keep 'em moving."

The cattle whirl in a circle, each trying to melt into the center, a vestigial defense against predators. Because we're on foot rather than horseback, the roundup feels less like wrangling than crowd control; it's Pamplona in reverse. I'd sooner yodel than yell "Yee-hah!", so I improvise with cop-show dialogue, urging calves along with "Hey you!" or "Where do you think you're going?" or simply "Move it, asshole!" The stick I carry is more a symbol of authority than a billy club, but when a piebald cow lowers her horns at me, I give her a little tap and thank God the bull was sold off last fall. For the most part, the cows know the drill and soon there are only a few holdouts among the pack of nervous youngsters. We get them running and block the calves until the last cow lopes into the yard and Ed slams the gate shut.

The idea now is to run the calves into a holding pen, where they can be sorted by sex and the young bulls castrated. Steve parks the tractor parallel to the fence and wires a gate section to funnel calves into the pen. This business of moving them into smaller and smaller areas of confinement resembles the sequence of waiting rooms one is led through at the doctor's office before the threshold of pain is finally crossed. Amazingly, all the calves run into the pen on the first drive, except for a solitary stinker, a reddish bull calf that wheels around at the last second. We chase him around the corral, working up a sweat and getting nowhere. After the fourth lap, Ed, his face reddening, says, "Get the lariat."

Inside, the barn is dusty and dimly lit, its great vaulted roof and heavy crossbeams resemble nothing so much as an inverted ark. The stanchions are empty and the barn smells more of gasoline than manure, but there's a floating population of barn cats and pigeons, not to mention the woodchucks tunneling under the foundation. I find the lariat hanging on the wall beside a tangle of bridles and saddles from the farm's premachine age, when the roundup was done on horseback in a pole corral at the north end of the hollow and steers were made with a pocketknife.

The bull calf is holed up in a corner of the corral, eyes big as fried eggs. Ed coils the rope in one hand and pitches the loop with the other. He misses. Finally Steve catches the calf with a flying tackle and the two of us wrestle him into the holding pen.

We've been too busy to notice the ginger-haired man, elbows hooked over the corral fence, watching this clumsy exhibition. He's a cattle breeder out of Lanesboro, name of McCabe. He scratches his head. "How'd you get the rest of them in there?"

McCabe has come to drop off this year's bull, though he's a week early. Ed has leased the bull for $300 plus all the grass it can eat. Farmers who keep a bull in the pasture tend to raise beef and handle their cattle only a few times a year, not twice a day. The few dairy farmers who still breed their cows with a bull instead of by artificial insemination seem reluctant to remove the element of risk. Like a bear in the thicket, the bull's presence keeps the land wild with possibility. A few times in the past, one of my other brothers-in-law, a Medevac nurse on the Mayo helicopter, has been set down in a pasture to retrieve the body of some farmer whose rib cage has been crushed like an accordion by his own bull, usually a Holstein that was only biding its time.

McCabe backs a stock trailer into the cow yard to unload this year's model, a blunt-nosed, neckless, two-year-old Black Angus with a yellow tag in his ear. Spotting the bull, the cows momentarily forget their calves and rush him as a group, not out of panic or desire but to check out the stranger in their midst. The bull stands his ground, impassive as a heavyweight at a weigh-in, allowing the throng to examine his great bulk.

"We've got the bull," Ed says after McCabe drives off. "Now let's make some steers."

There are three ways to make a steer: cutting, pinching, and banding. We've used them all over the years, and they all result in an animal that is more docile and gains weight more rapidly. The surest method of emasculating a bull is by cutting off his nuts, but this increases the risk of infection, especially with free-ranging cattle. Pinching the sperm ducts with what looks like a giant pair of pliers is bloodless but less certain, since the bag remains. Ed opts for banding, which is the least painful and nearly foolproof, although this cannot mean much to the bull calves.

I cut a bull calf from the bunch and drive him toward a gate we've rigged like a squeeze chute. As the calf runs for daylight, Steve pins him between gate and fence while Sharon slips a loop over his head to snub him down. Reaching through the gate, I take hold of the calf's tail and bend it backward over the spine, immobilizing him so he can't kick Ed in the face when he puts on the band. Ed fits a thick green rubber band the diameter of a Lifesaver onto a handheld spreader and, kneeling behind the calf, fits it over the bag. When he lets go, the band retracts, cutting off the flow of blood so that the testes eventually wither and fall off. As each calf is released, Ed scratches a chalk mark on the fence post.

"Watch that red calf," Ed shouts. "He's goofy!"

A goofy calf, apparently, is one that doesn't want to lose his balls. Having watched the previous calf made into a steer, the reddish calf bolts, kicks, and jumps halfway over the fence until Sharon snubs him with a rope. She's dressed in sleeveless white shirt, bandanna, and jeans with a big rip in the leg. When she braces against the fence, I find myself staring at a patch of brown thigh and getting ideas.

"Well, I'll be!" Ed says, reaching between the calf's legs. "Unless he's only got one nut, I'd say the other one rode up."

Once the errant testicle descends, Ed slips the band over it and Sharon unties the rope. The reddish calf doesn't move even when the gate swings open. Hesitant, he looks as dazed as an accident victim, slow to leave the scene of pain and uncertain of the damage done.

By now the cows, having filled up on hay in the cow yard, realize their babies have been taken. They stretch their necks and bawl, a deep trombone slide of remorse. The calves, massed in the holding pen, strain at the other side of the fence. Between them, a terrible bellowing fills the air.

The concrete floor of the pen is slick with manure that deepens with the calves' rising panic. In the crush, one of them mounts a heifer, his forelegs riding her flanks in a gesture that will soon be meaningless. To see him standing there man-like is to recall why pint-sized Picasso liked to draw himself as a Minotaur. And the barnyard joke about making steers comes out of the nervous recognition that sex, along with death, is what we have most in common with animals: It's when we're in a lather, down on all fours, moaning and groaning, no longer certain who we're supposed to be.

Last fall we castrated the bulls with a knife, and the floor of the pen was speckled with blood and pale prairie oysters. A few of the younger children wandered over from the house to spy on the proceedings from the barn, and one of them, my youngest niece, was in tears. Her father told her to get home. "I can't!" she cried. "I'm too scared!" She looked as fearful of him as of the cattle, and I wondered if it was the transformation of the familiar moo-cows into bellowing beasts or the sight of our own methodical cruelty that had frightened her. In bedtime stories children understand animals as a kind of stand-in for themselves, based on their mutual dependency, and my niece may have concluded that the bulls were being punished and somewhere down the road she might be next.

"A farm is such a carnival of birth and death," the Scottish poet Edwin Muir wrote, "there is no wonder it should frighten a child." We no longer live off the labor of animals as we did less than a century ago, although we still eat their flesh. What's changed is the way we choose to think about them or not to. The Amish, who live most closely with animals, don't allow their children to read stories with talking animals, not just because such a thing is unreal but because it sets up an impossible relationship. Like most farmers, Ed doesn't kill his own livestock. The work is compartmentalized, and his calves will be passed along at auction to another set of hands to be fattened on corn until they weigh twelve hundred pounds and are sold again. Then it's on to the slaughterhouse and death on the assembly line, as removed from the farmer as from the consumer who buys his steak in shrink-wrapped increments at the supermarket.

The only blood spilled today is Ed's. He's gashed his elbow on a nail sticking out of the fence, and the blood flows bright and watery because the anticoagulant he's taking makes his skin as thin as paper. His forearms are a map of bruises and bandages.

"See how nice they are," he says of the steers, "once they've been fixed." By afternoon there are thirteen chalk marks on the fence post for steers and another twelve for heifers. With the calves back with the cows, we head across the yard for home. Last year there were twice as many calves, and the day ended in a rainstorm.

"We can't be done," Steve exclaims softly as we cross the yard for home. "It's not pitch dark and we're not soaking wet."

AFTER SUPPER Ed goes off on the four-wheeler to check on the cattle, especially the new steers. He comes back looking pleased with himself. "McCabe said his bull would need a few days to settle in, but I just saw him breed two cows down in the pasture."

He takes a well-thumbed "Ready Reference" booklet out of the closet and pages through it until he finds the gestation index for cattle: 283 days. After a little finger calculation, he announces, "First calves around April ninth."

Sharon and I sleep in the guest bedroom, our children in sleeping bags on the floor. This isn't the house she grew up in—Debbie and Steve live in the old farmhouse—but there's still the strange sensation of knowing her parents are in the next room. It's as if we're dating again.

Early the next morning I awake to the bellowing of the bull outside our bedroom window. The sound is deeply resonant, a mixture of sexual urgency and pain that rends the soft morning air with its unmistakable longing. Through the window I watch the cattle move at a dreamlike pace through the orchard and into the lower pasture, heading for the creek. The bull's massive humped back floats above the others like a dark cloud. The steers bringing up the rear take short, mincing steps, and I can't help but wonder what, if anything, they remember.

FIVE

I spent an afternoon tearing down a fence, three strands of rusty barbed wire strung between oak posts to keep cattle out of the orchard. I wore heavy leather gloves to coil the wire, which was brittle and kept breaking. One strand disappeared into a pine bole that had healed over it like an old wound, so I snipped the ends with a wire cutter and started a new roll. Dismantling the fence, like lowering a flag, signaled a shift in the land's meaning, namely that these ten acres were no longer an orchard but part of the lower pasture, a fact the cattle have known for some time.

Even without the fence, a border of pines remains to show that the hillside had been set aside for something special. Only a few apple trees are left, mostly wind-bent Greenings, to cast circles of shade in the afternoon heat. Now it's open ground covered by oxeye daisies, patches of white clover, and sun-baked cow pies. The orchard is my favorite place on the farm, maybe anywhere, because it's one of those half-wild places where the intentions of people and nature overlap, like an overgrown lilac hedge that marks a farmstead gone to woods. The land falls away to the west to overlook Sheehan's cows grazing on the opposite hillside, their black-and-white hides patterned like Mercator maps of the world. To the east, along the section of fence I took down, there's a sunken lane running between the orchard and Night Pasture that Ed's cows walked down every morning after being milked and then walked up again every evening.

Apple trees were the blaze marks of civilization. Government surveyors laying out Jefferson's grid upon the prairie often planted apple seeds to mark the section lines, knowing the settlers to follow could distinguish an apple tree from a wild plum or a thornapple. It wasn't the settlers themselves but the next generation who planted orchards and ornamental shrubs around the farmhouse to show that the break with wilderness was complete.

I can guess the varieties John O'Neill planted from a map of the orchard that he sketched across two pages of a ledger sometime around 1906, each tree marked by a pen scratch in columns as even as figures on a balance sheet. The trees were a long-term investment, an act of faith that he and his descendants would be around for some time to harvest the fruit of his labors. He favored Russian varieties like Duchess of Oldenburg, Tetofsky, and Hibernal that could survive a short growing season, but he also planted the Iowa Beauty and the Wealthy, a variety developed by a Minnesotan who crossed a cherry crab with the common apple. The orchard held a dozen varieties in all to provide apples at different times of the year and for different purposes. There were Duchesses and Patten Greenings for cooking and pies, sweet Anisms for sauce, Whitney Crabs and Longfields—a yellow apple with red stipples —for pickling, Strawberry Crabs, which threshers called a harvest apple because it ripened early during threshing season, and finally the tart, hard-skinned Wealthy to close out the season. Whether John O'Neill drew his map after he finished planting or sketched it as a blueprint of things to come I'm not sure, but the orchard was his small-scale Eden, his clearest proof of order upon the land. When it was done, he pressed a lady's slipper between the ledger's pages as if to remind himself of what had been replaced.

"Some of those old Patten Greening trees were twenty-five to thirty feet high. Ma always wanted perfect apples, so I'd climb the tree and throw them down to her through the branches. She'd catch them in her apron."

Ed and I are pulling fence posts. I slip a chain around the post, hooking it to the bucket on the Bobcat. Then Ed raises it up until the fence post dangles like a hanged man. The oldest are white oak, furry with lichen, cut from the surrounding land as it was cleared for the plow. We stack them by the salt block for firewood.

"We had an apple shed out here that was like an outhouse with bins. Ma would come down and sit and sort apples. Some night when it was going to get good and cold we'd haul apples into the basement. We had a hard red apple that wasn't any good till winter. About February they were damn good apples."

A FARM with a lot of fences is one that recognizes different kinds of land and different possibilities for them. A fence announces our designs upon the landscape; it imposes limits. Before fence laws were enacted in the last century, farmers fenced their crops to keep them from being trampled by horses and cows and hogs. Cowboys may have sung "Don't Fence Me In," but certainly not anybody who had corn or wheat in the ground. The first fence laws coincided with the development of cheap barbed wire, so that livestock could be fenced in rather than out, and owners were liable for any damage their animals incurred while running at large. The state's current fence law defines "at large" as "to stroll, wander, rove, or ramble at will." Before that, it was every swine for itself.

The fence lines on this farm were laid out by an agent of the Soil Conservation Service during the thirties, when much of the northern plains was blowing away in dust storms. Civilian Conservation Corps crews in blue denim outfits and floppy hats fenced off the hollow, put marginal land in permanent pasture, and divided big, square fields into long, contour strips to follow the slope of the land. The field pattern was designed when the farm was more diversified and horses still did much of the labor. As machinery continues to get bigger, many farmers tear out fences to enlarge their fields until they resemble vast seas of soybeans or corn, undoing the conservation measures of an earlier generation. Ed has maintained most of his fence lines because they allow him to see the land in segments, to fine-tune it accordingly, even though the layout can seem daunting.

One day a man from the grain elevator in Stewartville came to spray the corn with herbicide. The sprayer was mounted on the back of his pickup with a fifty-foot boom that folded up like the wings of planes on aircraft carriers. He had never been here before and studied Ed's crop map as if it were a jigsaw puzzle. "I think we got enough to do her, but you never know. Depends on how the fields are laid out. Yesterday I sprayed for this woman down in Predmore. She had a lot of fields like this." He made a triangle with his hands. "I ran out six rows short of finishing."

A Depression-era attitude about money lingers on the farm, nothing being purchased new if something can be reused, so fence building often starts with a salvage operation. When the corral needed replacing, we began by tearing down an old sheep shed that anchored one corner of it. The shed was of indeterminate age, having been skidded to the site from a neighboring farm in the twenties. It had housed sheep, then hogs, and more recently a transient population of raccoons, along with lumber salvaged from St. Bridget's church hall. Built in the 1870s to house a local chapter of Father Mathew's Catholic Total Abstinence Union, the hall had waited thirty years for us to resurrect it as a corral. Some of the rough-sawn boards of yellow elm were thirty inches wide with no knots. Nails melted when we tried to hammer them into the boards, so we used spikes instead. When the new corral was finished we chainsawed the palings to a uniform height and burned the ends in a bonfire in the middle of the cow yard. Cows are immune to history and could care less if their corral once sheltered temperance meetings and church socials, but for us the fence is a reminder that nothing is lost forever. A tree becomes a shed, becomes a fence, becomes black smoke rising through tree branches into an everlasting sky.

SOMETIMES THE FARM IS so cluttered with the past that a bonfire of old things seems refreshing. But if the past is inescapable, the future remains a distant cloudland of possibilities. Sharon spends a lot of time imagining different scenarios for the farm in the event it stops being one. Some days she favors a pick-your-own strawberry patch, other days a hardwood tree farm, a bed-and-breakfast, storage for boats and RVs, a riding stable—any ruse she can think of to keep it intact. All this seems so much pie in the sky. You only have to look at the houses being built across Highway 52 to see the future.

One miserably humid afternoon a car with Iowa plates rolls up the driveway and parks in the shade. The driver, a soft-spoken man wearing yellow-tinted shooting glasses, gets out to introduce himself. He's a businessman scouting locations for new Sporting Clays courses and likes the farm, he explains, because it's close enough to Rochester for members to get in a round of shooting after work. He's brought his wife and daughter along for the ride, but they remain in the car, immured against the heat.

Sporting Clays is the sport of simulated hunting, the man explains, something like golf with a shotgun. Shooters walk through a course laid out with different stations, where they shoot at clay pigeons thrown to duplicate the flight of a particular game animal. The sport originated in England but is gaining popularity in this country, combining as it does the American affection for firearms with our propensity for turning anything elemental into a competition.

"Do you know the first thing General Schwarzkopf did when he returned from the Gulf war?"

I did not.

"He shot a round of Sporting Clays."

A championship shooter himself, the man asks to look around, so Sharon agrees to give him a tour, beginning at the south end of the farm on an old township road that dead-ends in a canopy of oak trees. Leaving the car, we hike through the woods and over a cattle gate to the narrow end of the hollow. No cattle have been pastured here this summer, and the hollow is waist-deep in tall grass, blackberry brambles, and stinging nettles. The man bounds ahead, pointing out potential shooting stations, while his wife carries their little girl on her hip and swats deer flies tangling in her hair. The air is gelatinous and thrums with insects.

"It's not like trap or skeet," the man says, "because every station is different."

The shooting stations are often elevated like backyard gazebos and named for the quarry they are meant to suggest. For instance, at Springing Teal the clay targets are launched almost vertically to match the flight of teal off a pond; at Bolting Rabbit, the targets bounce along the ground like scared bunnies; and at Fenceline Quail, they snap up like a wild covey. All the shooter needs is a shotgun and a vivid imagination.

Near the spring, the ground turns squishy and sends up clouds of gnats. We hike up a cow path out of the hollow and into a cornfield, which the man announces would make a good site for the clubhouse and parking lot. He's still laying out stations, but I stop listening once I figure out that the course would sound like a small war. (Maybe that's what Schwarzkopf missed—the rattle of gunfire.) I had dreamed up any number of scenarios for what the farm might become, but here was

an unimagined future—a happy hunting ground where shooters ride golf carts through the fields after work and blast away
at imaginary creatures.

As we walk along the edge of the cornfield I nearly step
on a tiger salamander. Striped yellow and black, the salamander is hunting earthworms in the exposed soil. The tip of its
tail is missing, as if the salamander had been hunted recently
itself. Despite this, it doesn't spring or bolt or run away, but
just lies there, a Stationary Salamander, and no sport at all.

WHAT WILDLIFE EXISTS on the farm thrives, for the most
part, on the edge of things, along the borders between fields
and woods, between the cultivated and the wild. Fences bridge
the gap between one world and the other. Leave a fence long
enough, and a line of trees will grow along it. Like an ocean
reef, a fence provides a foothold for plants and animals that
would not otherwise survive the monoculture of cropland. The
trees and bushes growing along it furnish nesting and food for
songbirds, cover for rabbits and woodchucks, and a corridor
for deer traveling from woods to cornfields. Ed tolerates the
trees until their branches shade his crops or threaten to knock
him off his tractor; then he gets out the chainsaw and cuts
them back, because if he doesn't they'll eventually take over.
Cultivation is not a permanent state. A cornfield will revert
to a meadow, but it never works the other way around.

When I rolled up the barbed wire that had enclosed the
orchard, I uncovered a linear prairie of weeds: gooseberries,
purple vetch, milkweed, Canadian thistle, wild mustard, cat-
nip, Queen Anne's lace, and wild grape—its twists and coils
approximating the barbed wire it had replaced. Some of these
species are native but many are not, such as cocklebur, which
Ed never noticed until he combined a neighbor's oats during
the sixties and the seeds hitched a ride back in the hopper.
Eventually the cattle will graze or trample these plants to get

at the grass, but for a moment I had a glimpse of what the land might have looked like before it was a farm and how it might look again if we just walked away.

Pioneers were too busy plowing the prairie into furrows to take inventory of what their moldboard plows turned over. If they noted anything, it was usually the bowl of blue sky or how the wind rippled the grass into sea waves. One of the most evocative and detailed accounts of the tallgrass prairie before it was plowed was written by Henry David Thoreau, who traveled to Minnesota in 1861 on the longest and last journey of his life.

Thoreau was forty-three at the time, and slowly dying of tuberculosis, when a doctor advised him to "clear out" to a more salubrious climate and recommended the West Indies. But Thoreau decided to try the air out West. Then, as now, Easterners came to Minnesota for their health; the new state had been shamelessly promoted as a health resort for consumptives. Thoreau left Concord in early May with a seventeen-year-old companion, Horace Mann Jr., and traveled by train to Niagara Falls, Detroit, Chicago, and East Dubuque, Illinois, where they boarded the steamboat *Itasca* for the trip upriver. Because he was obliged to stop and rest frequently, the journey progressed more slowly and in greater comfort than Thoreau was accustomed to. As they steamed up the Mississippi River, he coughed incessantly and wrote in his journal, along with descriptions of bluffs and Indian wigwams, how the *Itasca* always whistled its approach to a town before striking its bell six times "funereally."

Disembarking at St. Paul, Thoreau and Mann carried their carpetbags, coats, and an umbrella to the American House, where they ate breakfast, then traveled nine miles by stage over the prairie in the rain. They settled into a hotel within sight of St. Anthony Falls and made daily excursions into the countryside to botanize. Thoreau's method with wildflowers was to stoop and pluck the blossom, vigorously inhaling its fragrance before pressing it into his plant book. He also carried a compass, a notebook, Gray's botanical guide, insect boxes, twine and cards, a dipper and water bottle, and several handkerchiefs. He made extensive lists of birds and flora, freely mixing common names with the Latin and sometimes guessing outright: "Here on the prairie I see the plantain, shepherd's purse, strawberry, violet sorrel (?), common red sorrel, *Ranunculus rhomboideus*, *Geum triflorum* (handsome), phlox (as on Nicollet Island), *Druba nemorosa*, with black pods, a scouring rush by a slough, low grass and sedge. But here the prairie is fed over by horses, cows, and pigs."

Two weeks later Thoreau and Mann took a small steamboat up the snaggy Minnesota River to the Lower Sioux Agency at Redwood Falls to witness the annual treaty payment to the tribe. They watched as "half-naked Indians performed a dance at the request of the Governor, for our amusement and their benefit," and Thoreau noted that buffalo were said to be twenty-five miles away. In an earlier journal, Thoreau copied down what the Swiss naturalist Edouard Desor had told him about the Indians' lack of names for wildflowers, "that they had a particular name for each species of tree (as the maple), but they had but one word for flowers. They did not distinguish the species of the last." In fact, the Sioux had many names for individual flowers, such as the pasqueflower, which they called *hoksicekpa* and used for medicine, as opposed to flowers in general, or *wahca*. (On the trip, Mann gathered quantities of pasqueflower to send to his uncle, Nathaniel Hawthorne.) Through interpreters, Thoreau listened to speeches by the Sioux chiefs, including Little Crow, the most prominent, who, a year later, would lead his tribe in a bloody uprising that resulted in the death of four hundred settlers and the total negation of the Sioux's claim to the land. But by then Thoreau himself would be dead of tuberculosis.

What conversations Thoreau might have had with settlers in Minnesota can only be imagined, because he wrote so little about them except that their houses were set half a mile apart on the prairie and their fences were built of sawn boards. But in *Walden* there is a memorable scene in which Thoreau, off on a fishing trip, escapes a rain shower by taking shelter with an Irish farmer, his wife, several children, and assorted chickens. While rain drips through the roof, the Irishman explains how he makes a living "bogging" for a neighboring farmer, turning meadow with a spade for $10 an acre and the use of the land and manure for a year. When Thoreau, transcendentalist and Yankee bachelor, regales the family with his own experiments in thrift, telling the poor bog-trotters that if they only worked less they wouldn't be inclined to eat so much, he sounds like a college kid home from the commune. "If he and his family would live simply, they might all go a-huckleberrying in the summer for their amusement." The Irishman heaves a sigh, and when the shower moves on so does Thoreau.

We've all gone a-huckleberrying of late, though our lives are hardly simple. Every schoolboy knows that the worst way to make a living is by physical labor. Leisure has been turned into an industry that even Thoreau would find unrecognizable, and the places we hold in highest regard are the scenes of our vacations, not our workaday lives. This public affection for wilderness often seems a way of pretending not to notice the wholesale destruction of our cities and countryside. If *Walden* remains a disturbing book, it is because the author advocates preserving the wild not by setting aside a few roadless parcels of land but by incorporating it into one's own life.

So I was interested when I heard that a pair of doctors who had bought an old farmstead between St. Charles and Chatfield were restoring part of it to tallgrass prairie. True prairie is made up of three-hundred-plus plant species, some of which have been lost forever, so a restored prairie is essentially a landscape of imagination. Re-creating a prairie ecosystem on a few acres of unmowed pasture may be no more possible than bringing back the herds of buffalo, but it's a landscape I wanted to see, and imagination didn't seem a bad place to start. "To make a prairie," wrote Emily Dickinson, a stay-at-home who certainly never saw one, "it takes a clover and one bee."

> One clover, and a bee,
> And revery.
> The revery alone will do,
> If bees are few.

Steve Hanke and Nancy Peltola are family physicians who work in St. Charles and Chatfield, respectively, and bought their farm ten years ago because it lay equidistant from their separate practices. Hanke gave me directions over the phone, explaining that if I passed the Amish school I'd gone too far. The Amish farms are easy to spot. There are always workhorses in the field, and no satellite dish. On the porch of one farmhouse I passed, an old woman was laying out quilts, her chalky face framed inside a black bonnet like water at the bottom of a well.

Overshooting my turn, I circle around at the one-room schoolhouse and backtrack to find the doctors' farmhouse at the end of an unmarked gravel road—and nobody at home. I hike up a grassy ridge past a windmill and a ruined cistern. The ridge is bright and windblown as it curves above the valley and the white road I came in on. At the end of the ridge, in the heat-wavering distance, two people stand in a swarm of horses.

Nancy Peltola sits in the spring seat of an ancient Farmall-M while her husband unrolls a spool of fence wire from a wagon hitched to the back of the tractor. They are stringing a new paddock for their horses, who drift around us like smoke. A fawn-colored foal keeps inserting her muzzle between us, and the mare doesn't mind; but when a sorrel gelding gets too close, she kicks him in the ribs.

Of the hundred acres the doctors own, roughly half are tillable and have been rented to a neighboring farmer; the rest is ridgetop and impossible slopes, a kingdom of sunlight and wind. The farmhouse had stood empty for years when the doctors moved into it. Friends suggested they bulldoze and start fresh, but they gutted the walls and rebuilt the house along its original lines. Not long after the renovation, a man came to the door and announced that he had been born in the back bedroom in 1927. His grandfather had built the house, and the man was surprised to find it still standing. Walking past freshly painted walls, he followed his memory to the scene of his birth and found, instead, a music room. Now the doctors are restoring the landscape along its original lines, burning hillsides in springtime and sowing the seeds of prairie forbs and grasses so that at least some of the land will remember its past.

"Before we came here we didn't know anything about prairies," says Steve Henke. "We were mostly interested in woods. If you asked Nancy or me ten years ago if we'd want to live in a place with few trees, we'd have said no."

Trees are the death of prairie, the climactic stage in a biological succession that in the wild was circumvented by drought and fire. True prairie has only one tree per acre. The only prominent trees in view here are a stand of Norway pines, the remnants of a windbreak behind the farmhouse. The doctors had planted maples along the south end of the ridge to provide cover for wildlife, but the saplings succumbed to last summer's drought and now poke leafless and wandlike from the grass.

While Nancy walks back to the house to fix lunch, Steve gives me a tour of the back side of the ridge. The terrain is dry and rolling, covered with only a thin layer of sandy topsoil, a good place for a prairie remnant to have escaped the plow. Steve stoops beside a fernlike clump of silvery green leaves.

"These are leadplants. And when you see leadplant, it's a pretty good indication the land has never been tilled. Once its seedbed is disturbed, leadplant doesn't do very well."

It's hard to tell the native plants from the aliens, and the most pristine meadow of wildflowers may prove to be a gathering of immigrants. Steve points out the lupinelike blossoms of a prairie turnip, which is native, and yellow goat's beard, or prairie dandelion, which isn't but performs the neat trick of closing its petals at midday like a long wink. He finds a pasqueflower past its bloom. This was the first prairie forb he learned by sight and name, and it sparked his interest in the restoration project. One morning during their first spring in the farmhouse, Steve and Nancy looked out of a window and saw scraps of white paper littering their hillside. Taking a break from remodeling, they climbed the ridge slope to discover that the pale scraps were hundreds of pasqueflowers in bloom. Last year they harvested one-third of a pound of pasqueflower seeds to trade at Prairie Moon Nursery outside Winona for prairie seeds they didn't have. The mixture of wildflower and grass seed had been gathered from virgin prairie farther north, near the town of Fertile.

Steve wears sandals, white running shorts, and a big straw hat. When the wind ruffles the brim of his hat, it reveals a red bandanna knotted pirate style around a receding hairline. Wandering through the tall grass along the ridge, he tosses names over his shoulder as if introducing guests at a dinner party. "This is pussy toes . . . buffalo pea . . . harebell . . . wild rose. . . . Here's one of my favorites, prairie smoke. It looks like a puff of smoke. . . . This is . . . nope. That's wrong. We'll have to look that up in the book at home. . . . You know what this is, don't you?" He gestures toward a particularly lush, three-leafed plant growing by a sandstone outcropping. "Poison ivy."

Certainly the first act of restoration must be memorizing the individual names of flowers and grasses that would otherwise blur under the general heading of "weed." In Genesis, naming is Adam's only task in creation, and it seems a measly chore, the one we give children when we bring home a pet; except that without names there can be no personal connection, and there is no love in the abstract. The common names for plants—like "prairie smoke" for *Geum triflorum*, for instance—are memorable precisely because they're metaphoric, nicknames based upon prior associations rather than the cold logic of Linnaean taxonomy. They are terms of familiarity, and walking through a meadow calling the plants by name is like entering a room of friends instead of strangers.

When he comes across a spiny-leafed plant bowing under the weight of a purple flower head, Steve hacks off the stem with the heel of his sandal. He does the same thing to the next one, and the next. "If you don't control them, they'll take over a field. There's an Amish man down the road, and half his pasture is thistles. Even a goat won't eat them."

The Canadian thistle is an ornamental accidentally introduced from Europe when it was mixed with crop seed and quickly got a foothold in overgrazed fields. Like many native prairie plants, it's a perennial that can propagate not only by seeds from its purple flower head but also by its creeping root stock, or rhizomes, so that new shoots will soon replace the ones Steve has hacked off.

"The true management of thistles is pasture management. They like disturbed soil, so if you don't let your animals crop the pasture too low, they can't get a start."

In May, Steve and Nancy bought six bred Holstein heifers, which they plan to sell in September. The cows are summer guests and represent a paradigm shift in the doctors' original notion that the prairie could simply restore itself. The cattle are stand-ins for the wild herds that once grazed here.

"When this was tallgrass prairie, it didn't sit idle. There were animals and burns. We learned that for the health of the land it has to be grazed. There was a man down in Iowa trying to rejuvenate prairie, and he wasn't having much luck until he borrowed a neighbor's herd of cattle. It sure speeded up the process."

Buffalo kept the prairie grasses green by feeding on their competitors, by fertilizing the soil with their manure, and by preparing a seedbed as they tore up the thatch with their hooves. Domestic cattle do all those things, but they do them to excess. Buffalo herds ranged across the open landscape like the weather itself, but the livestock that replaced them were confined by fences into smaller and smaller quarters and eventually grazed the prairie to death. The doctors' solution to that problem is more fencing. Using lightweight Polywire, they strung a grid of eight paddocks across their pasture and moved their Holsteins to a different paddock every three or four days. Rotational grazing imitates the effects of migratory herds without the complications of loosing buffalo among the cornfields.

We climb a barbed-wire fence into a grassy swale that looks like a neglected meadow except for the intense, pointillistic green blades rising among the brown tangle of weeds. This is a mesic prairie, midway between dry and wet, better suited to native grasses than wild forbs, so there is less phlox and bergamot but more porcupine grass and clumps of little and big bluestem. We watch wind currents moving through the grassheads on the far hillside like waves of light. A bobolink flutters overhead, singing like a hysterical music box.

"This is the area we burned last summer. We did roughly twelve acres. Two weeks later you couldn't tell it had ever been burned."

Prairie restorationists use controlled burns to set back the cool-season grasses introduced by Europeans—timothy, bromegrass, and orchard grass—so there's less competition for native hot-season grasses like big and little bluestem. Unless it is disturbed by periodic fires or grazing, the accumulated thatch grows so thick that the prairie eventually suffocates much of its variety or is invaded by forest. Fire does no permanent damage to the prairie plants, whose underground root systems resemble the tributaries of a great river system and allow the plants to conserve moisture, making them virtually immune to drought or fire. It was the constant growth and decay of these roots that formed the rich, chernozem soils of what would eventually become the corn belt. The thickly woven mat of roots was so interlaced that it broke the pioneers' wooden plows and awaited the development of John Deere's steel moldboard plow.

Indians set the prairie afire for a variety of reasons. A wall of flames was useful for driving game, eluding enemies, greening up horse pastures, or just cutting down on summer insects. The fires were great natural spectacles. A Methodist circuit rider described one such encounter in 1835: "The last twelve miles we traveled after sundown & by firelight over the Prairie, it being on fire. This was the grandest scene I ever saw, the wind blew a gale all day, the grass was dry . . . In *high* grass, it sometimes burns 30 feet high, if driven by fierce winds. By light of this fire, we could read fine print for ½ a mile or more." Of course, the spectacle could prove fatal if the observer was caught without a swift horse. One writer advised settlers to light a backfire to delay the inferno's advance, then "ride madly before the wind." If that failed, the settler could always disembowel his horse and climb into the cavity until the flames passed.

Maybe what the countryside needs is a good conflagration now and then to cleanse it, an annual rite of purification by which we torch the old growth and then "ride madly before the wind." Afterward we'd return to find the land uncluttered again, and could sustain for a little longer our belief in its endless possibilities. Not a bad idea. We'd get to see the landscape as the Sioux or Thoreau did, its wide-open horizons the perfect screen on which to project our daydreams. The only catch is that we'd have to be willing to travel light, nothing more than could fit onto a travois or a prairie schooner. Not long ago, one of the immense new houses south of Highway 52 caught fire when a rag soaked in paint thinner ignited spontaneously in the garage. The blaze spread quickly and the house burned to the ground; but it must have had tough rhizomes, or good insurance, because a few months later it had grown back, bigger than ever, squatting on the hillside and ugly as a toad.

When Steve and Nancy burned their twelve-acre swale, they could have jumped over the flames. The Minnesota Department of Natural Resources, which issued the permit, stipulated that the winds on the day of the fire should not exceed five to ten miles an hour, or the humidity be less than 50 percent. The permit was issued for the first Saturday of the month—May Day, as it turned out. A crew of friends used torches dipped in a mixture of gasoline and diesel fuel to ignite the north end of the swale so the fire would burn against the slight breeze. The flames may have been small, but the green prairie grasses sent up a billowing screen of smoke. Sparrows and meadowlarks shot ahead of the blaze. The crew, carrying five-gallon piss packs, contained the fire except when sparks from an old cedar fence post ignited the edge of a nearby field and the flames had to be swatted out with rakes and brooms. A neighboring farmer, drawn by the smoke, came up to watch the doctors burning their prairie. "Oh," he said dryly, "I see you're making a clearing for thistles."

WHEN SONS-IN-LAW get itchy to drive your tractors, you put them to work repairing fences because it's nearly impossible to wreck a post-hole digger. I spend the morning straightening metal T-posts on a section of fence over east, staggering them with pressure-treated wooden posts that the frost can't heave. Unless I feel like chipping through limestone, it's necessary to find the old post holes. The digging is tolerable where the fence line dips into shade, but in open ground the sun beats down like a hammer. I roll barbed wire off a spool in the bed of the pickup and, after it's secured at one end, use a fence tightener to pull it taut. A good fence is horse-high, hog-tight, and bull-strong. It's also a way of keeping faith that the land will remain a working farm.

Driving past the old orchard, I stop to pick a prairie bouquet for Sharon: bergamot, oxeye daisies, wild phlox, Queen Anne's lace. The cows haven't cropped the grass along the fence line yet, and I wonder what her grandfather would think of his bare hillside now or how he'd feel if it was diced into view lots or restored to tallgrass prairie. Either way, a kind of betrayal.

SIX

On the first day of summer, after three bone-dry weeks in the eighties, the temperature fell below freezing. Ed awoke the next morning to find his front lawn turned white as some distant dream of winter.

Frost had descended unevenly across Olmsted County, wilting some fields and sparing others. A farmer across Highway 11 rode a hay binder through his cornfield to lop off the brown leaves, confident the stalks would still grow as long as their inner core hadn't turned to mush. Inspecting his own fields, Ed pronounced the soybeans "questionable" but said the corn looked okay except for the singed leaf tips. If the corn doesn't tassel he can always chop it for silage, and the cows won't care as long as there's plenty of hay. Hay is the one crop that never leaves the farm. It's a farmer's hedge against the vagaries of Midwestern weather, the slimmest of margins against loss.

All summer long, Ed moves from machine to machine—cutting hay, baling it into quarter-ton loaves, stacking those bales against the certainty of winter. After a first cutting, he has fifty-eight round bales curing in the sun or already stacked; last year he had twice as many and used every one. "Make hay while the sun shines" is the fable of the grasshopper and the ant played out on a thousand farms every summer. There's a synchronicity to most farm work, nobody getting very much ahead or behind his neighbor without pushing the envelope of weather, so while driving from Plainview to Rochester, I could look on either side of the road and see a dozen different machines—mowers, windrowers, cut-conditioners—all busy as ants, engaged in the singular task of laying in hay for winter. Mowing weather means hot days and blue skies on the order of heaven, cloud-flecked and extending forever. Skies so expansive that you forget the reason for haying, which is that nothing lasts forever, least of all the weather.

Today the sun doesn't shine so much as blaze across the bowl of sky. The humidity makes the air silvery, and the limestone yard beneath our feet appears to shimmer. Revving up the Hesston 55 windrower, Ed raises its twelve-foot cutter head and advances upon the open gate. Shaped like a flying wedge, the three-wheeled windrower has neither steering wheel nor brakes. Its differential steering system, operated by hand levers on either side of the cockpit, responds to Ed's levering with such violent enthusiasm that his movements are largely compensatory. Past the machine shop, Ed pulls back on the right-hand lever and the machine whips around on its axis like a Tilt-A-Whirl. The gate opening is only slightly wider than the cutter head. Working both levers and the foot pedal that raises the cutter head, he threads the windrower through the gateposts with inches to spare.

Then we lurch up the field road and head east past the Night Pasture. Riding charioteer-style on the concrete ballast stacked above the tail wheel, I hold on to the back of Ed's seat and try not to be thrown by the windrower's lumbering side motion. The Night Pasture holds nine bales of June grass and weeds the color of broom straw.

"Ain't much for feed," Ed shouts above the clamor, "but it's better than a snow bank."

We scrape through a gap in the line of hawthorns and wild plums dividing the north fields from the south. The latter could have been laid out with a ruler, while the north fields are wavy contour strips that follow the tilt of the land as it slopes down from the wooded rim of the hollow. The rise in elevation is slight—the land is twelve hundred feet above sea level—but when I look back, I'm looking down on the barn roof and the sky seems to have dropped a few feet. Even on this slight slope, alfalfa acts as a brake, slowing down the erosion caused by more exposed row crops like corn and soybeans. A runoff depression runs down the middle of the fields in such a way that the contour strips form a chevron, two deep-green stripes separated by a belt of blue-violet blossoms. Next to the row crops, the hayfield looks as pretty as any wild meadow.

Ed lowers the cutter head two inches above the ground and engages the sickle bar. The scissoring motion of its triangular, serrated teeth adds a new dimension to the clatter, the *snick-snicking* of a thousand knives being whetted. On our first pass, the windrower travels counterclockwise around the field, shearing off its edges. As the revolving reel of the cutter head plunges into the surface of alfalfa, its tines rake the plants forward so the sickle bar cuts the stems off at the base. The motion of the reel is hypnotic, like watching waves break, as we sickle through alfalfa, white clover, and bromegrass, not to mention several varieties of butterfly, mostly viceroys and sulfurs. A horizontal auger running the length of the cutter head pushes the cuttings to the center, where they disappear into the machine's innards. The rest is sheer mayhem. Heavy rollers crush and crimp and otherwise mangle the cuttings as they pass through the windrower so they'll dry faster in the sun and become, in the process, hay. Craning my neck, I watch a shining wake of cuttings churn from the windrower's stern.

Alfalfa is the only perennial on the farm, the only crop that winters over. This field is in the last year of a four-year cycle beyond which alfalfa tends to poison itself. In the fall Ed will plow the field under, and next summer it will be something else. The rotation is as follows: four years alfalfa, two years corn, one year soybeans. The sequence duplicates over a short period of time the diversity of wild plants that would otherwise grow here. Since each crop feeds a different appetite for minerals and nutrients, planting one continually would soon deplete the soil's fertility. Alfalfa is a heavy feeder on potassium and phosphorus, but it's also a big tipper, taking nitrogen from the air and fixing it in the ground by means of a bacteria called rhizobium in the small nodules attached to the plant's root hairs. Next year's cornfield will green up on the nitrogen-rich grave of this summer's alfalfa.

Reaching the end of the field, the windrower swivels around violently and begins another pass.

After the first cutting Ed spread several loads of manure on the hayfield, an installment payment on a long-term loan of potassium and humus he'd taken out of the soil in crops. The spreader loads represented a winter's worth of manure scraped from the cow yard and, before that, the protein and nutrients in a poleshed's worth of hay that the cattle had consumed during the cold months to the tune of a round bale a day. What wasn't returned to the soil as manure had ridden a stock truck to the auction barn in Lanesboro as beef on the hoof. People sitting down to a pot roast or a T-bone somewhere were eating increments of this field, blissfully unaware they had the taste of limestone and brown dirt on their tongues. "All flesh is grass," says Isaiah, "all the goodness thereof is as the flower of the field."

A red-tailed hawk, alert for flesh on the run, hangs behind the windrower like a kite on a string. Ahead, seven long swaths of cuttings divide the field into as many lanes. An acre remains to cut. The hawk has been watching the windrower play solitaire with the field, turning it over a strip at a time. Breaking cover, a cottontail tunnels through the alfalfa just ahead of the revolving reel and disappears into the comparative forest of cornstalks. The hawk sails away.

Beneath its false floor of blossoms, the field looks level but isn't. There are hidden moguls and clear evidence of gophers, whose fan-shaped mounds are scattered about the field as if someone had dumped buckets of loose dirt at random. Deer may eat more corn, but gophers wreck more farm machinery. Backing away from a mound, Ed raises the cutter bar a few inches, then guns the windrower up and over, sideslipping on the moist cuttings and filling the air with diesel fumes and the sweet-sour fragrance of freshly cut alfalfa.

The soil in the gopher mound is Waucoma loam, a well-drained, grayish brown soil laying over bedrock. Cut a wedge of field and you'd have a layer-cake view of its history. Forty inches or so below the surface is a mantle of buff-colored Galena limestone, the fossil bed of an Ordovician sea, pitted with sink-holes and riven by underground streams. Above this are alternating layers of sand, silt, and clay laid down as the windblown loess of glacial dust, although the stratification also suggests alluvial deposits from the Root River overflowing its ancient banks. Mixed into this slurry are microorganisms, the charred grasses of countless prairie fires, and little more than a century of crop residue and fertilizer—the living and dead heaped up year after year to form this mulch on which everything depends.

Four rods short of finishing, the windrower breaches a particularly large gopher mound, dirt spraying up from the reel. The machine clatters louder than ever. Ed stops in mid-field and raises the cutter bar. With the engine running, we jump down to scrape clots of mud and grass stuck to the sickle bar. Even at rest, the triangular steel blades give off a bad karma. Ed disappears under the reel, while I hover just beyond. "Sickle's broke," he says ruefully. "That's a hundred bucks right there!"

The drama of used machinery is when will it break and how much will it cost. Back at the yard, Ed parks the windrower by the machine shed to see if he can weld the break. He lays a scrap of tar paper on the ground to hold his tools. Then he removes the two bolts holding the sickle bar in place and slides out the broken section. It's six inches long and split at the rivet. There's nothing to weld.

Ed telephones an implement dealer in Chatfield to see if he has any sickle bars in stock. He doesn't but can get a new one in about ten days. Ed holds the phone while the dealer looks up the price.

"I wish you'd quit putting money into that machinery," Fran whispers in his ear, " 'cause you're not going to be using it in another year or two."

MINNESOTA MUST BE the only state in the Union that still pays a bounty on its official mascot. A nineteenth-century Indian agent named Henry Schoolcraft once observed that "white hunters . . . frequently avail themselves of the labours of the gopher by planting corn upon the prairies that have thus been mellowed." As early as the 1850s, settlers in Minnesota debated whether the new territory should become the Gopher State or the Beaver State. Proponents of the latter objected to the gopher's puny size and destructive nature, while partisans of the former countered that not only was the gopher more numerous but the connection was already widely known. A popular ballad of the time relates the westward journey of a Buckeye who sets off across the Minnesota prairie and discovers more than just good land:

> The Gopher girls are cunning,
> The Gopher girls are shy,
> I'll marry me a Gopher girl
> Or a bachelor I'll die.

The issue was finally settled a year before statehood, when a St. Paul newspaper carried a cartoon that ridiculed a $5 million loan to the railroads by showing a trainload of legislators being pulled by nine gophers. The nickname stuck. But if Minnesotans identified with a solitary, hardworking rodent that spends its entire life grubbing in the dirt, they still had no qualms about trying to eradicate it.

Time was when every farmer hung a bottle of strychnine-coated corn from his cultivator to sprinkle on any gopher mounds he passed. A few days later, he might return to find the body of a gopher, or maybe a dead woodchuck or the neighbor's dog—or worse: Sometimes a youngster found the poison bottle in the barn and got himself laid in the ground instead.

My wife, like generations of Minnesota schoolchildren, once earned pocket money running a gopher trapline, which was harder work than poisoning but more selective. Just before a rainstorm was a good time to set traps because that's when gophers dig fresh mounds, plugging the openings to their burrow to equalize the barometric pressure. Squatting by a mound, Sharon would dig away the loose dirt until she broke through to the tunnel entrance. She used long-spring traps, nothing larger than a number one-and-a-half. She'd set the notch under the pan, then slip the trap into the hole, carefully replacing the dirt so the gopher wouldn't know anyone had opened its front door. In the morning, she'd return. If the stake was askew, the trap had been sprung. She would take up the slack, pulling in the chain until she felt the weight on the other end. Gophers dig with a breaststroke motion, pushing dirt ahead of them, and will practically swim into a trap; so the jaws closing around the upper torso won't necessarily kill the animal. And the gopher might emerge hissing at the end of the chain, yellow teeth bared, its jowly banker's face animated with rage and pain, then . . . Whap! A knock on the head with the stake and he went limp as a sock. Next came the hard part. Sitting on her heels, Sharon would cut off the oversized forepaws with a jackknife, stuff them into her back pocket, and bury the gopher in its own hole.

Sharon kept the forepaws in a glass jar inside the family freezer until they could be redeemed for the bounty at the town hall, the old one-room Burr Oak School. At that time, Marion Township paid twenty-five cents per gopher and ten cents for the smaller, thirteen-lined ground squirrel, or "streaky." The township treasurer was Edward J. O'Neill. Whatever money his daughter didn't bank, she threw away on carnival rides at the Viola Gopher Count.

ON THE WAY to this year's Viola Gopher Count, we pass a blue Adopt-a-Highway sign proclaiming the next two miles of pavement under the care of "WOMEN OF EYOTA." The graveled shoulders of road look clean enough to eat off. Cars are parked along the highway from the old creamery at the bottom of the hill to the silver grain elevator above the town of Viola. Abandoning the car to the heat, we join the others hiking along the shoulder of the road through open farmland, each of us with a child in tow, toward an island of shady streets ahead and the distant throbbing of a marching band.

A dinky carnival has been set up at the north end of the town square, a grassy lot circumscribed by the town hall and a steepled white church. A historical marker commemorates the first Viola Gopher Count held at a lemonade picnic in Wendall Vine's pasture in June 1874: "As the years passed and the destructive gopher was no longer a menace to the farmers, the hunters turned the day into a community celebration and offered prizes and later bounties for gopher tails . . . the only event of its kind in the world." If Sharon is measuring the carnival rides against her childhood memories, it's hard to see how they could have shrunk any further. There's a kiddie train running on a tight loop and a merry-go-round so small our four-year-old is too self-conscious to ride on it. She's more interested in the parade anyway, since the people riding on the floats pelt her with candy.

We sit on the grass and watch a high-school band blow past in plumed hats and maroon-and-yellow buccaneer outfits, followed by a caravan of old, two-cylinder John Deere tractors that go farting down the road. The parade is short but seems longer because it comes around twice, like summer reruns. Most of the floats alternate between the twin pillars of small-town life, commerce and religion, so staggered between Dairy-land Beef Producers and Throndson LP Gas is the Eyota Methodist Church Study Group ("Growing in Faith"). The Viola Gopher Gals' float features a quilt to be raffled at to-night's dance. And four altar boys from Holy Redeemer Catholic Church share the bed of a pickup with a tilting, life-size plaster Jesus, arms outstretched as if to catch Himself. When the Eyota Volunteer Fire Department's lime-green engine rolls past, sirens screaming, the bearded fire chief (another brother-in-law) leaps from the tanker and sprays bystanders with water from a pressurized canister. It feels pretty good. The Olmsted County dairy princess slides past in a red convertible with her court, runner-ups who lack the princess's blond pizzazz but seem more reliable, more the sort you end up marrying. The girls look young enough to enjoy riding on the backseat of a red convertible but old enough to understand that once you've been paraded down Main Street in your prom dress there's nothing much left to do except leave, so their stiff-armed waves seem as much farewell as greeting. A short gap in the parade and a silvery float hoves into view, bearing a white-haired couple, the king and queen of the Viola Gopher Count, on what appears to be a scaled-down version of the Parthenon. Their placement at the end of the parade, so close on the heels of the youthful dairy princess and court, seems deliberately ironic, a comment on the relentless march of time or a before-and-after picture of our lives, until I realize that the parade has simply come around again and this is not the end but the beginning.

Drifting away, I watch three men sitting behind a table counting gopher paws. A clarinet player still in uniform pulls a plastic bag from his pocket and empties a dozen gopher forepaws and fifty-two of the smaller streaky paws on the table. The first man counts them, the second makes out a claim check for $9.50, and the third sweeps the grublike paws into a plastic bucket. The towheaded boy who follows has kept his paws stored in a Mason jar all winter. When he unscrews the lid, the men at the table jerk their heads back.

"Keep 'em in a sock," says the next in line, an old man with gray stubble and blue suspenders. "They dry out and don't stink."

He dumps the contents of his sock on the table—gopher paws, a piece of chewing gum, a penny, and . . . no smell.

"When I first started catching them, fifteen cents was a high price," he says, as if to bridge the generations. "Lot more gophers now. There aren't enough people to trap them anymore."

Behind the counting table I run into a stringer for the *Los Angeles Times* who's here on assignment but hasn't decided whether to serve up the Viola Gopher Count to readers back home as local color or a more sinister version of *American Gothic*. When another sack of forepaws is poured out, he and his photographer wink at each other as if they've landed among the pygmies.

IN THE SUMMER of 1946, Edward O'Neill, recently discharged from the Army Air Corps, escorted Frances Bruski, late of Denver by way of Wibaux, Montana, to the Viola Gopher Count dance. She had arrived by plane that afternoon and this was his first chance to show off the bride-to-be. They drove to Viola in a blue, bull-nosed Chevy and stepped into a velvety night still steaming from afternoon thundershowers. A crowd of grinning, sunburned men in open-necked shirts loomed ahead on the town-hall steps. Too late, Frances realized she was overdressed for the occasion. As she made her way toward them, her three-inch heels sank deeper into the rain-soaked ground with every step.

"She sure made an impression," Ed recalls, pausing for effect, "in those high-heel shoes!"

He and Fran are baby-sitting tonight, and he offers this comment as we head out the door for the dance. As if to make a point about parallel lives, heavy afternoon showers have again soaked southeastern Minnesota and brought a lot of farmers in from the hayfields. When we reach Viola, the carnival area is dark except for a streetlight above the only concession still operating, a ring-the-gong contraption that's attracting more moths than customers. A beer garden beside the town hall, ringed with a snow fence, is awash in mud.

A woman at the door to the town hall takes our $2 and stamps the back of our hands with an ink pad. The hall is all knotty pine inside with a large glass display case of 4-H ribbons won by the Viola Victors and photographs of previous Gopher Count royalty. And the place is packed, every table staked out with purses and raincoats and plastic cups of beer while their owners whirl on the dance floor. It's only after we find seats back by the bar that I realize we are the youngest people in the room. We might as well have strolled into a bingo parlor. We drink beer until our legs get loose, then work our way through the crowd. As soon as one song ends, the band attacks another with accordion and saxophone, so once on the dance floor, you're there for the duration. Sharon and I dance a couple of waltzes, making underarm passes and twirls, fancy moves that have the effect of clearing a small space on the floor. In high school, I'd hold up the gym walls all night waiting for a slow dance. Sometimes the song began slow, then underwent a violent mood change to become the jerk or boo-ga-loo, and my legs would turn to stone. I'd tell the girl I'd left my car lights on and disappear. Now I'm a dancing fool, if only because marriage moves one beyond such simple humiliations. Still, when the band announces something called a circle schottische, I feel the old paralysis take hold.

Before I can head back to the table, two circles form on the dance floor, men on the inside, women on the outside. Standing behind Sharon and slightly to the side, I take her hands in a pose that suggests the finale of a figure-skating act.

"Okay," she says, plunging into the music. "One-two-three steps to the left. And one-two-three to the right. Kick out. Then twirl your partner, and one-two-three forward, pass her on to the next dancer. Got it?"

Not really, but the circles begin to revolve in opposite directions, sweeping my wife away and presenting me with a succession of older partners. The inner ring of men all have short-sleeved checked shirts and sunburned necks, the outer ring of women a softer, ampler version of its hub. After each twirl and exchange, there is a slight adjustment to the new partner's height and girth and, since I'm mostly watching my own feet, the sensation of passing a perfume counter. We hold each other at arm's length, avoid eye contact, and smile as we maneuver around the room. The band sings along to the tune of "You Can't Get to Heaven."

> Oh, you can't go swimming
> *Oh, you can't go swimming*
> In a baseball pool,
> *In a baseball pool,*
> And you can't do a schottische
> *And you can't do a schottische*
> To a rock 'n' roll band.
> *To a rock 'n' roll band.*

This is clearly no rock 'n' roll band, but there's a blustery insistence to their oompahs, and, despite the open windows and ceiling fans, I'm sweating pitchers of beer. Round and round we go. One-two-three, kick and twirl. I've almost got the steps down when a hard-eyed woman in a frilly western skirt, sparkly belt, and white boots twirls twice and throws me off. But, strangely enough, I'm enjoying myself. Dancing has never seemed so courteous, more of a social contract than a free-form performance art. This is the place where my father-in-law chose to introduce his fiancée to the Midwest, and some of these dancers may have been here that night; some look as if they never left. Like the parade, there's a ring-of-time aura to the dance, a sense of life's brevity as you're passed from one creased face to another, but also, in the simple repetition of movements, the sweet notion that nothing really changes, that we're all in this together and might as well enjoy it. Gradually we come full circle, like the hands on a clock, and arrive where we started, back to our original partner, as the song ends and everybody applauds.

"Those old guys," Sharon says, "really know how to dance."

I stumble into the warm night, music spilling through the hall's open windows, and lean my forehead against an outhouse wall. The voices from the beer garden carry farther than those from inside the hall, but the laughter sounds less buoyant, more like barking. A crowd has gathered around the hammer-and-bell concession. Steam rises from the wet pavement and the air feels inert and slightly charged by the unspent sexual energy that hovers on the outskirts of small-town dances. I fumble in my pocket for a dollar bill.

There's a trick to swinging the mallet so its weight does the work. You extend the mallet directly over the button, then let its own momentum carry it past your legs and overhead in an arcing swing that comes smashing down . . . right on the money! But I waffle somehow, and there's no gong, no cigar, no nothing. Next in line is a sweaty character in a muscle shirt who slams the mallet down so hard that when the gong rings we all take a breath like a crowd at a fireworks display. Bolstered by this, he tries swinging one-handed and fails. As the weight falls back to earth, the crowd exhales a sustained hiss. He looks at the mallet as if he's been double-crossed. Then he pulls out his wallet and buys three more chances. Halfway up the steps to the dance, I hear another hiss.

The woman who checks my hand to make sure it's stamped is listening to a biker with a Fu Manchu mustache and a breathless manner. "Well, I was there," he says, narrowing his eyes and casting them to either side, "and it ain't no joke!"

A FEW DAYS after the dance, Sharon's younger sister Rita calls to say she has a gopher problem. She lives in a new subdivision a mile north of the farm. When we arrive, four fresh mounds are clustered by the driveway.

"I don't mind if they stay in the woods," Rita says. "It's when they dig in the lawn that I mind."

Sharon kneels beside the largest of the fan-shaped mounds and digs with her hands for the tunnel, which always exits at the stem of the fan. The soil is sandy and as freshly sifted as flour, but even when the loose dirt is swept away the tunnel remains hidden. Finding a stick, she prods the ground until at last it caves in where the gopher has plugged the entrance with clay. The tunnel isn't much wider than my fist and slants downward, as much as five hundred feet in length with a network of chambers and lateral shafts linking the mounds, all belonging to a single animal, since the gopher is a solitary, territorial creature that will fight to the death over its burrow. Before Sharon slips the trap inside, I wriggle my fingers inside the tunnel and wonder if they might not look to the occupant like a many-headed earthworm. And here's what else I'd like to know: Do gophers carry a memory of the surface? And if the next time they emerged it was to the lush new grass of a subdivision instead of a hayfield, would they care?

I've been reading up on gophers, since their lives remain such a mystery. Like us, they don't hibernate but put up their own hay in underground storage chambers to last the winter. They live an almost entirely subterranean existence, venturing above ground mainly at night to forage on grasses and legumes, rarely moving more than a few feet beyond the tunnel entrance, nervous wrecks out of their element. If they view the surface the way we do the dirt, as a nasty place and a potential burial plot, it's because every predator has gopher on the menu. Foxes and coyotes dig them from the ground; bull snakes slither down their tunnels; hawks and owls carry them aloft to pick their bones from treetops. With death at every turn, the gopher hugs the earth and emerges reluctantly to feed. Only when the urge to mate becomes overpowering does he risk remaining above the surface for any length of time. Then he throws caution to the winds and travels cross-country on low-slung legs, usually at night but sometimes in broad daylight, in search of a mate, heedless of the danger, stopping to sniff every burrow, bloodied perhaps from encounters with other males, until at last he smells the cachet of the other sex and descends into the darkness, hopeful but alert, a fool for love.

SEVEN

When my father-in-law asks for a hand, he means it literally—as in, "Hand me another draw pin."

"This one?"

"Nope. It's larger."

Language fails me, and I scoop up anything that might be a draw pin from the toolbox behind the tractor seat for Ed to peruse. He selects the longest one. He has already unhooked the hydraulic hoses, power take-off coupling, and drawbar connecting the Ford 7700 to the baler parked in the machine shed so he can attach a hay fork to the tractor's three-point hitch instead.

"Raise the drawbar."

"?"

"The black knob above the right fender. Ease it back."

Ed, full of bon mots at the Legion, is so taciturn at work it's as if he thinks too many words will muddy his intent. Work is something you do, not talk about. For me it's always been the other way around. But the farm has its own vocabulary, and one reason I'm not much help around here is that even the simplest tasks require translation into language that is both wordier and less precise.

With the fork attached, Ed drives the blue Ford up the field road while I stand on the tractor step, one hand on the rail, watching the rear lug tire revolve a few inches from my face. We turn south through the gap in the hedgerow to the alfalfa field Ed cut last week. Walled in by standing corn, it looks like an empty lot. Twenty-eight round bales, weathered to a dirty oatmeal color, lay sideways on the mown field, casting deep shadows in the morning light.

Ed parks downhill from the nearest bale, shows me reverse, then proffers his seat. The only tractor I've logged any time on at the farm is a three-cylinder, English-made Dexta, the Morris Minor of tractors. By contrast, the big Ford 7700 has a hundred horsepower, sixteen forward gears, and could eat the Dexta for breakfast. Still, moving bales is the simplest of jobs; it's the chore farm kids are given before they get their license to learn how to drive. I lower the hay fork and put the tractor in reverse, impaling the bale on the tines. Then, raising the drawbar, I shift into forward gear and head for the barn, the tractor's shadow looking like a huge anthropod with an egg sac as it scuttles across the field. There's a tricky dogleg around the pole shed where I have to swerve to avoid a gate post, but, managing this, I bring the tractor around smartly, lower the tines, and deposit the first bale at the barn's upper door. Ed will stack the bales in the hayloft with the Bobcat later, but for the moment he's gone off to rake windrows in an alfalfa field to the south that's on a different timetable.

After a few bales, fifth gear seems too tame for the straightaway along the hedgerow, and I shift into sixth, which feels much livelier. I haven't switched on the fender-mounted radio yet because I am deep into the romance of tractor driving. I like the elevated view of the fields and the deep-throated throb of the diesel engine and the way the moisture cap on the exhaust pipe stands at attention. Seventh gear is better still, and slipping briefly into eighth, before the spring seat can catapult me, I can feel those hundred horses galloping over the hills. Unlike other nonverbal jobs I've had—cannery work and the assembly line—farm work is interesting because you see the whole process and understand the connections between crops and animals and the task at hand. Slowing down, I catch a glimpse of Ed emerging from a draw on the other side of the hedge. He's pulling a side rake behind the older Ford 5000 and doesn't appear to be enjoying himself half as much as I am. There's little risk of my becoming the prisoner of routine; on the contrary, repetition is my best friend at the moment, allowing me to concentrate on the shuttle between field and barn. Maybe I'll play the radio if I do this tomorrow, and maybe, if I move bales for the next twenty years, I'll wonder if I haven't wasted my life.

When Sharon drives up on the four-wheeler to announce lunch, twenty-seven bales are ready for inspection in front of the barn. Smiling like a boy at farm camp, I roar off to retrieve the final, outermost bale. It's wedged into a corner of the field between woods and standing corn and, worse, tilted at the wrong angle. Nudging it into position with the tines, I spear the bale without popping the twine and bring it home. Pulling the tractor into the machine shed, I sit there covered with glory until it dawns on me that I don't know how to turn off the engine. I'm still sitting there, my foot planted on the brake, when Ed strolls down for lunch.

"Maybe I should've explained," he says, talkative once more. "You have to pull the red lever under the dash. On a diesel, you have to shut the fuel off before you can switch off the ignition."

WORK TOO COMPLICATED for sons-in-law can be contracted to specialists, such as the man from the elevator in Stewartville who sprays the corn or the two-man combine crew that arrives four months later to pick it. They own their machines or work for an outfit that does, and can finish the job in a day, moving on to the next farm with no more than a hello. They aren't hired men, in other words, and neither am I; and though we might perform some of the same tasks, we lack the hired man's tragic stature. In westerns the hired man is always a retired gunslinger who rides down from the mountains, bearing his loneliness like a shield. He grubs out stumps and eyes the farmer's pretty wife, and when he rides back to the mountains at the end of the picture, we know nothing more of his past or future, only what he is leaving behind. What remains poignant about the hired man, other than that he has vanished from the rural landscape as thoroughly as panhandlers and poor farms, is that his rootlessness could be mistaken for freedom, and even if he couldn't be fashioned into a tragic hero, at least he could be tragic.

Sometimes an obituary in the newspaper sums up sixty years of the deceased's life by noting that he had done "custom agricultural work" for area farmers and is survived by an aging sister. Unlike the character in Frost's poem—"And nothing to look backward to with pride / And nothing to look forward to with hope"—most hired men went on to other lives and may, in fact, have looked back at their tenure on the farm with something like pride. Some were neighbor boys just biding their time between high school and the day they could enlist. Others were grown men, set adrift by hard times or some personal failing, who had come to live on the periphery of family life when that was the only safety net between themselves and the poor farm. If they seemed boyish or instances of arrested development, it was from having been detained on that uncertain ground between adolescence and manhood. Farm work was not a stepping-stone to anything, so there was no chance of advancement; on the other hand, neither was there the stress of being mortgaged to a quarter section of land, forty cows, a wife, and several children. Typically, the hired man performed the most routine of chores, like the endless back-and-forth of cultivating corn, freeing the farmer for more interesting tasks. Or, if he was the convivial type, the hired man might become a paid sidekick, working beside the farmer and guffawing at his jokes. For his labor, the hired man earned room and board and enough money for tobacco and a Saturday night drunk if he was a drinking man. He slept in the family's home, sometimes sharing a bed with one of the older boys, and sat at the farmer's right hand at the supper table, as if to make a point about vassalage. If tensions arose, they were usually between him and the farmer's wife, not from romantic stress but because the hired man's presence meant extra work for her, another mouth to feed and, if he was her husband's crony, a voice to rival her own in managing the farm.

The hired men who came to the farm arrived on necessity's timetable but left on their own, staying for a few days or a season or off and on over a lifetime. When they are remembered these days, it is for a certain skill or peculiarity, those often being the same.

Clyde Ames was hired every May during the thirties to shear sheep, arriving in a Model-T pickup with a little gasoline engine in the back to run the shears. He castrated young rams by snipping the bag with a pair of hand shears, pulling the nuts, then biting down to seal off the bag despite having no teeth. A constant stream of stories as well as tobacco juice came out of Ames's toothless mouth, his voice just loud enough to be heard over the puttering engine. He worked shirtless in the heat, and the front of his bib overalls was smeared black with lanolin. Setting a sheep on its butt, Clyde would bend its neck under his arm then start shearing at the sheep's hocks, peeling away the thick wool so the fleece came off in a single piece like a dirty union suit.

Shearing was a three-man operation. One guy caught the sheep, another sheared it, and the third tied the wool up in a burlap sack. At the end of a day's shearing, young Ed rode over east looking for the only sheep left unshorn, an old buck ram that he found in the hollow. The ram had the broad, knowing face of an old seducer. He lowered his horns and stamped his hooves as Ed dropped a lariat over his head. When the ram balked on the way back, Ed kicked his heels into his horse and the ram's feet went out from under him. He was still dragging the ram when they pulled up in front of the sheep shed. Ames walked out from under its shade with a pair of hand shears and snipped the ram's ear. The ram never moved. "He's dead," Ames said. "Dad's gonna skin me alive!" the boy cried. Ames said nothing, only dragged the ram by the legs into the shed and sheared him anyway.

Cecil Batchelder was hired in 1940 and stayed on the farm until he was drafted. He earned $35 a month and had a budget for cigarettes and clothes he ordered through Spiegel's catalog. Yet he's remembered as a bit of a simpleton for never changing his clothes and wearing overshoes when he dragged a field. "It'd be hotter than hell," Ed laughs, sifting through a stack of old snapshots at the kitchen table, "and he'd be walking that soft ground behind the drag in those damn five-buckle overshoes!" When the army took him, he sent a photograph of himself in uniform back to the farm. The Cecil in this picture is a handsome, almost fastidious young man in a khaki shirt and slicked-back hair. Only the mouth, wide in the extreme, seems slightly goofy, curling as it does in a smile that stops just short of a horse laugh.

Brad Phillips was hired on July 6, 1935, outside a Rochester liquor store at the corner of Third and Broadway. He came from Alabama and spoke with a soft, southern inflection that, along with his dusky good looks, made him seem vaguely Indian. John O'Neill put him to work cultivating corn. Right away it was clear he was good with horses, so he drove a bundle wagon on the threshing run. One morning after a barn dance at Francis O'Connell's farm, half the crew was hungover with half a day's threshing still left to do. They dumped the grain in any old bin and spilled the hay wagon on the long slope from the field to the barn. About noon, somebody found another gallon of alcohol. By the time they broke for supper, Brad was standing in the middle of the yard, all wrapped up in his own harnesses. But otherwise he was a hard worker, and when he left at the end of the season it was with the understanding that he would return.

Brad came back the following summer to pick up his old job. One evening a taxi rolled up in front of the farmhouse and a young woman got out and knocked on the door. She announced that she was Brad's wife and set to work convincing John O'Neill that a husband had to take care of his wife, which, of course, he couldn't deny. The Depression was in full swing and the newlyweds "didn't have two cents to rub together," so the family put them upstairs in the northwest bedroom. Mae Phillips was small and dark and flat-chested, a southerner like her husband. She smoked a lot and wasn't any good at cooking or cleaning but excelled in public displays of affection, which the family found as strange as her accent. "Oh Bradford!" she'd sing, throwing her slender arms around his neck and smothering him with kisses. Sometimes she'd carry a jug of water out to Potter's field, where Brad was cultivating corn, and ride in his lap while he steered the two-row cultivator with his feet. Or she'd sit in the shade loving him up while young Ed took the reins and caught glimpses of the happy couple between the rows of corn. When winter came around, the love birds flew south and never looked back.

Agnes Clark was a neighbor girl hired on threshing days to help Mame with the enormous midday meals. She was a big, stout young woman, the oldest child of a large family, who "was always looking for a man but never got one." When a crew of carpenters moved into the farmhouse in the spring of 1927 while they built a new barn, Agnes moved in as well. After supper she dried the dishes while the carpenters played sheepshead at the table. Later she strolled through the orchard, a fog of white blossoms hovering over the hillside, the fragrance of a hundred apple trees filling the night air. She'd return to the house refreshed and sit at the other end of the table from the carpenters. If they began to file from the room,

Agnes would drop her knitting. "Wait, boys!" she'd call with a kind of urgency. "Don't run away!"

Berne St. George was hired off and on for sixty years and, like the sad case in Frost's poem, returned late in life to claim a bed by invoking the past. He was Mame's cousin, a short, round-faced bachelor, always jovial, "a jack of all trades and no good for himself." Berne and his brother owned a portable sawmill, and whenever they needed money they sold an interest in it to John O'Neill, then bought it back when they got ahead. A genius with machines, Berne was a first-class steam engineer and an experienced sawyer. But these were professions that didn't weather the years well. He was an old man the last time he moved back, when he would drive tractor with a bottle of Four Roses in his lap; yet even after he plowed through fences, John wouldn't fire him. In the winter Berne ran a boiler for the highway department. He'd ride home at night from the Roxie Bar in a taxi, dump his tar-stained clothes for Fran to wash, then sit up in his room and smoke. Mornings he'd rouse the house with his coughing. Fran, who had babies and aging in-laws to care for and no debt to the past, finally put her foot down. "If you can afford to drink and take cabs," she told him, "you can afford to wash your clothes in town!" He moved out the next morning. That this task should have fallen to Fran, who has more patience than anyone I know, is the most surprising part of the story. Even now, recounting it forty years later, Ed seems surprised, as if he'd just learned of some unexpected strength in his wife. "It was Fran that got rid of Berne," he whispers across the kitchen table. "She run him out."

Stan Strama was hired in August 1924, at the end of a week's boxcar tour of the Midwest with three pals. He was seventeen years old. Threshing had begun, and as soon as the morning dew burned off, Stan and the other two boys were put to work pitching bundles. He'd lift bundles of oats at the end of a three-tined fork to the driver of the bundle wagon, who caught them at the end of his own pitchfork and stacked the bundles head-in so the grain wouldn't jostle loose. Slowly the wagon moved down the row of shocks. Stan followed beside it, building the rack man-high, until the driver turned the team around and headed for the separator chuffing in the distance. As the morning heated up, Stan took off his leather jacket and folded it neatly beside a stack. When he came back at the end of the day, the jacket was gone.

By early October, threshing season was over. Pug Jenkins, who had been homesick all along, went back to Wisconsin; Bart Dixon took a job as pastry chef at the Koehler Hotel in Rochester, and Stan Strama stayed on at the farm. He shared a bed with Bill O'Neill, who was a year older and would wait until Stan had warmed the sheets before climbing in. The boys became fast friends. They milked cows twice a day and wrangled cattle by horseback, once driving a herd as far as the railroad siding at Plank's Crossing. The most monotonous job was riding a single-row cultivator through a cornfield be- cause the rows had to be cultivated crossways as well as length- wise and ten acres could take all day. They "plowed corn" the first half of the summer and threshed the second half. After a day's threshing, they caught horses and rode down to the Root River to wash off the chaff and dust, warning any timid souls in bathing suits to clear out before they jumped in. On Saturday nights they drove to dances at the church hall at St. Bridget's. But the Irish girls were clannish and none would dance with Stan until they had been properly intro- duced. Between dances, he and Bill would step outside on the pretext of using the outhouse and fortify themselves with swigs of Bill's homemade wine.

In winter the boys cut red oak to be sawed into lumber for the new barn, snaking the logs from the hollow behind a team of horses. Berne St. George was chief sawyer and taught Stan to run the steam tractor that powered the sawmill. He'd stoke the firebox with wood until the needle on the pressure gauge rose above forty. A steam engine, Berne told him, is like a living thing because it has its own steady pulse, and as long as you have steam, you have power. If he caught Stan with a low head of steam, Berne would saw even faster and make him pour on the wood.

At the end of August 1926, a month after his twentieth birthday, Stan told the O'Neills that he would be moving on. He had lived under their roof as someone more akin to son or brother than a hired man, but he also understood that there could be no future for him there. He had a sister in Chicago Heights, Illinois, and that was where he was headed. Bill drove him to the depot in Simpson, where he boarded the train with $100 in back pay and a free ticket since he was accompanying a carload of cattle to the Chicago stockyards. Then the train pulled out, and Bill drove back to the farm.

AFTER MILES of dairy farms, Highway 64 cuts like canyon through the white pine and lake country of northern Wisconsin with only a slot of blue sky above the pavement. At Fuzzy's General Store and Bait Shop, I stop to ask directions, which are simple enough: Drive west for a mile and look for the mailbox. Stan Strama's mailbox is hard to miss, encased as it is in welded steel bars against the onslaught of the county road plow. Up the driveway a trailer house is set back in the woods next to a small sweet corn and tomato garden with aluminum pie plates dangling from strings to scare away the deer.

Stan Strama comes out on the front steps to wave me inside. He's a compact, square-shouldered man in a gray sports shirt open to the chest, dark trousers, and no shoes. Except for the tentativeness of his walk—padding around in his socks—he looks as solid as a bridge support for someone who has just celebrated his eighty-seventh birthday. The trailer is paneled and cozy inside, with a grandson's high-school photograph on the TV ("It's nothing for him to score two or three touchdowns a game"), a cuckoo clock, a framed print of the Sacred Heart, and a picture window looking out on a hummingbird feeder. Josephine Strama, fixing *cotto* salami sandwiches in the galley kitchen, asks, "Do you want the peppers left in or out?"

After he quit as hired man, Stan went on to work as a construction worker, welder, diesel mechanic, and machinist. His jobs took him to Greenland, Okinawa, the Yukon and Northwest Territories, places his former employers on the farm could only have dreamed about. Despite his absences, Josephine managed to raise nine children, including one they adopted after she returned from her sister's funeral with an eight-day-old baby. A photograph on the wall shows Josephine surrounded by children.

"She sent me that when I was working on the Alcan Highway," Stan says, "to remind me I was married."

Since he was only twenty when he left the farm, his memories of it remain vivid, a traveler's impressions shaped by two years rather than the blur of a lifetime. It is the pre-Depression agriculture of men and horses he remembers. But I'm more interested in the parts of the story I don't know, the trail of events that led to the farm and away from it.

Strama's parents were born in the crown land of Galicia, as the Austrian-controlled portion of Poland was known, and emigrated to the United States. His father ran saloons in Detroit, Chicago, and Chicago Heights, where, on the Fourth of July, 1906, their first son was born. When the government opened up Rosebud County, Montana, to homesteading six years later, his father quit the saloon business and went out to claim a half section of land, 320 acres of dry gulches and rattlesnakes. He built a cabin, then sent for his wife and five children by train. The next year, while working for the railroad, he came down with typhoid and died. Stan's mother, who received a monthly widow's pension of $12, elected to stay on the homestead. She had to haul water three-quarters of a mile to keep the garden going. Most of her neighbors were bachelor emigrants from Norway and Sweden, and when she gave them clabbered milk, they returned the favor by bringing the family a hindquarter of antelope.

On Friday afternoons Stan—the oldest child, at seven— would sling an empty flour sack over his shoulder and walk five miles to the nearest town of Ingemar. He stayed overnight in a tar-paper shack where the family spent the winters. The next day he went down to the train depot to sell the newspapers and magazines dropped off for him by the morning flyer: *Saturday Blade, Chicago Ledger, Saturday Evening Post, Ladies Home Journal, Country Journal*. He did better business on the days when the sheepherders came to town, once selling the whole bag to a lonely sheepman desperate for something to read. With the money, Stan bought the list of groceries his mother had given him and then walked back on Sunday.

Stan's mother sold the homestead in 1917 after she proved up on it and moved the family back to Chicago. When Stan became a teenager, she sent him to live with his grandfather on a farm in northern Wisconsin. One summer he was working in a sawmill with two friends, Bart Dixon and Pug Jenkins, and decided to take a hobo vacation. Each had $10 and an identical leather jacket when they hopped a freight as it slowed through town and hid in an empty gondola. Safely into the countryside, the boys stretched out on the roof of a boxcar to sun themselves until someone noticed a warning net suspended above the tracks, and they scrambled down before the boxcar snaked into a tunnel. The train paralleled the Mississippi River all day, then crossed it into Iowa, and the boys jumped off at Independence, where Bart had a sister. A few days later they moved to a hobo jungle outside town to await another train. The tramps invited the boys to join in their mulligan stew if each would steal an ingredient. Assigned to bring back an onion, Stan was too polite to raid a garden, so he knocked on the farmhouse door and asked if he could buy one instead.

When they finished dinner, the hoboes licked their tin cans clean and hung them on tree branches for the next 'bos to come passing through. The boys then caught an empty boxcar and rode it east to the big railroad yards at Oelwein, where they treated themselves to pie and ice cream at the station café. They hopped a northbound local to Minnesota, the brakeman letting them ride as long as they helped unload freight, and reached Simpson that night in a cold drizzle. After unloading freight, the boys crossed the road to Claud Haney's General Merchandise to buy a can of beans. By now the cold nights and bad weather had taken the shine off the boxcar tour and the boys asked Haney if there was any work to be had. The storekeeper made a telephone call and twenty minutes later a lantern-jawed farmer, lean and leathery, drove up in a Model-T truck and hired all three of them. They rode back in the bed of the truck and spent the night in John O'Neill's farmhouse. The next day Stan lost his leather jacket.

The farm job was a last fling before settling down to marriage, and, not surprisingly, the memories of a hired man that remain most lucid are not so much of work, which was constant, but those moments of exuberance that mark anyone's youth.

"I liked to dance when I was young. That's why my knees are worn out. Circle two-step, waltz, two-step, Charleston contests, and there was that other . . . Mother, what did they used to call those old barn dances?"

Josephine looks up from folding laundry. "Square dancing."

"Sure. Square dancing. How dumb can a guy be?"

I asked if he remembered Agnes Clark.

"They used to kid me about her."

A year after Strama boarded the train to visit his sister in Illinois, he met Josephine and married her. They lived in a flat in Cicero until they decided it was no place to raise children, and bought a farm in Wisconsin. Running it while her husband traveled the world in seven-league boots was too much for Josephine to handle alone, so she wrote him a letter asking what to do. He wrote back: Sell the place. The farm had been south of Highway E. I must have passed it on the way that morning, but Stan says there's nothing left to see—no buildings, the whole place gone to woods.

Stan returned to the O'Neill farm only once, ten years after he'd left, to find Bill married and the place a little thread-worn from having weathered the Depression. Hard times all around.

We walk outside to my car, stopping to inspect the garden. Too late, I realize I have asked nothing about my wife's grand-parents, John and Mame O'Neill. Hoping for details, I ask him what his former employers were like, but the question must seem strange to him, coming from someone connected to the family, and his answer feels a bit like a rebuke.

"They were good people."

EIGHT

The moment John O'Neill stepped outside the front door of St. Bridget's Church on a raw morning in November 1899, friends pounded him on the back and wished him and his bride all the luck in the world. Their buggy was brought up from the horse shed, the team breathing clouds of frost. He took the reins and they set off briskly at the head of a long black line of buggies winding north past the church hall and the cemetery, where snow lay in small drifts against the limestone slabs.

The wedding breakfast was held at the bride's house. The St. George place was set in a square of oak trees beside a three-story barn built into the hillside. Sheep were pastured on the lawn, so guests had to climb a stile over a picket fence to reach the front porch. Leaving their gifts in the parlor, they walked through French doors into the dining room, where a cut-glass chandelier hung over the table. Dark landscapes in gilt frames decorated the walls, and from the parlor came the tinkling of an upright piano. All the St. George girls were musical and took turns playing for the guests except Mame, the oldest, who sat beside the groom and greeted everyone with a smile and terrified blue eyes.

The bride's sister had sewn the wedding dress, a heavy-ribbed gown of silk faille with fitted sleeves edged in lace, and now Mame sat as stiffly as if she were still being fitted, her new life held together with pins and needles. She met the groom at a skating party at Flugel's millpond on the Root River, although they had seen each other at mass for years. Then he seemed boyish and shy. Now he looked dapper in a winged collar and cutaway coat with a Hibernian pin in the lapel, full of talk and assurance, acting as if the only thing on his mind was breakfast.

The guests bowed their heads while Father Condrun said grace in a slight brogue. Then the dining room swelled with chatter and the clinking of silverware as the guests broke their fasts on smoked ham, scrambled eggs, oysters, rolls, hot coffee, and bowls of fruit brought up from the cellar. The mothers-in-law eyed each other across the table. Mary St. George towered above her counterpart. She was a big, robust woman with a quick laugh and the nervous habit of twiddling her thumbs in reverse when her hands weren't busy. She had emigrated from Belfast and once took her parasol to a clump of tiger lilies in St. Bridget's cemetery because they reminded her of Orangemen parading through the streets of her youth. It was from her father that the bride inherited her long, handsome face and a reserve that some mistook for haughtiness. The St. George family had preempted the farmstead in 1856, two years before statehood, and were certainly better fixed than the O'Neills were.

The groom's older brother rose to propose a toast. A head taller than his younger brother and more garrulous, Edward wished the newlyweds long life and happiness. The guests clinked glasses and drained the fruit punch. The groom's family belonged to Father Mathew's Catholic Total Abstinence Union, but the same could not be said for some of their new in-laws.

After breakfast John and Mame changed into traveling clothes and loaded their bags into a buggy for the ride into Rochester to catch the eastbound train for their honeymoon in Philadelphia. When they came back, it would be to a new life. Three weeks before the wedding, Catherine Esmond O'Neill had made the first mortgage payment on the farm the family had rented for the previous twenty years. Edward, the oldest of the children, had shouldered most of the work since their father died, so it was natural that he should take over the place. Besides, John had other plans. On the eve of the twentieth century, he did not intend to go into the future as a farmer. The country was filled with farmers.

When the newlyweds returned from their honeymoon, Mame was pregnant. They moved to Oelwein, Iowa, where six railways converged in a hub of steel track, and one of them, the Chicago Great Western, was building the largest railroad shops in the country. John took a job in the roundhouse and found a room for Mame in a nearby boardinghouse. It was the first time either of them had lived in town.

Every morning John set off, lunch pail in hand, to join an army of machinists, boilermakers, and blacksmiths high-stepping across rails in the train yards that spread out beneath a redbrick smokestack. Freight trains rolled into the switch-yards by the hour to be uncoupled, then reassembled in a different sequence of boxcars, and sent on their way again. The roundhouse was a walled city unto itself. Inside, loco-motives and rolling stock were drawn into stalls around a central turnstile to be repaired or rebuilt from the ground up. A battery of boilers powered the generator that drove the machines. The clangor of metal on metal was deafening. When a locomotive was finished, the hostler signaled for the door to open and a small yard engine would haul the locomotive out of the dim roundhouse and into a sunlit, weedy area that railroad men called "the farm." The shops ran twenty-four hours a day, seven days a week, and this was what the new century looked like: a great machine that ran on coal and never tired.

Exhausted and grimy, John crossed the yards at the end of his shift and walked back along Frederick Street to the boardinghouse, where Mame sat swelling beneath a white cotton dress. She was used to chores on the farm, but now had nothing to do except sit in the room or on the front porch and sew while she waited for her husband. At supper they sat down to a table of strangers and soon learned that if there was pie for dessert you ate that first or it disappeared. Nights seethed with the shunting of locomotives in and out of the yards.

The baby was born at the end of a sweltering August and named for John's mother, although her angular face and corn-silk hair favored the St. Georges. She was colicky at first, and made the short nights even shorter. Then, as the baby improved, John fell ill. At first he thought it was just the lack of sleep, but his head ached and the air in the roundhouse felt parched and unbreathable. The next morning he couldn't get out of bed. His legs throbbed and he couldn't hold down any food. Mame gave him sponge baths to bring down the fever, then wrapped him in quilts to stop the shivering. Later he would describe his affliction as "spotted fever" or "river fever," but the symptoms clearly pointed to typhoid.

In the winter they returned by train to Simpson and moved into his mother's farmhouse so that two women could look after him. Convalescing in the west bedroom, John often heard the women's mingled voices, one high and wavering, the other firm and unrelenting. He could hear as well the baby daughter he was too sick to hold. Always slender, he had grown gaunt and hollow-eyed, and his skin hung loose on his bones. The cold rose up through the floorboards and he couldn't get warm unless he was sweating out a fever. To come full circle, to lie in the very room where, as a child, he had watched his own father languish for a year before dying, convinced him that he would die here.

But by spring he had gained back his appetite and some of the weight he'd lost. He dosed himself with beef wine and iron and took long walks in the fresh air. The earth looked green and freshly made, and in the lower pasture that year's calves were running circles around the cows. The illusion of spring is that the world is unchanging, that you can go away and come back to find everything the same because the seasons repeat themselves unerringly. But nothing is ever the same; it's only replaced by something that looks identical. He had come close enough to dying to know that the days do not form a circle but are separate and irredeemable, and that he would never leave this place again.

As it turned out, he didn't have to leave. His brother Edward preferred the lumberyard in Simpson to running the family farm. The lumber business was booming as farmers cleared their land, and the work was cleaner and not a gamble with the weather. Edward viewed his brother's unexpected return as a second chance for himself, and when the lumber business moved to Moorhead, so did he.

WHEN COLD WEATHER put an end to crop work, John traveled by buggy from farm to farm selling nursery stock for the Wedge Nursery of Albert Lea, Minnesota. He carried a leather-bound stock book that fastened with a hasp and held color lithographs of ripened fruit that looked like tropical sunsets. Fruit trees and ornamentals were important to his customers, most of whom were second-generation farmers like himself who viewed a border of hollyhocks or a small orchard as evidence that they were no longer scratching out a living. The frontispiece of the stock book presents just such a tableau, two farms that could be illustrations for the twin gates of perdition and paradise. "As It Is—AN UNPLEASANT HOME—Before Patronizing the Nurseryman" shows a one-room shanty, shutters askew, hogs rooting among broken fences, and a slovenly farmer perched on what appears to be a hogshead of whiskey. In the second scene, "As It Will Be —A PLEASANT HOME—After Patronizing the Tree

Dealer," the shanty has been replaced by an Italianate mansion with a cupola and elaborate gardens through which a pair of ladies stroll beneath parasols.

With a kind of fervor, John set about remaking his own farm. He kept cutting back the line of trees to the east, grubbing out stumps with the hired man to extend his pasturage. He added a new wing to the house and raised the roof twice to accommodate his growing family. And he fenced off ten acres of west-facing slope above the lower pasture and planted an orchard. As soon as the saplings arrived from the nursery, he puddled their roots in a mud slurry and planted them in rows thirty-five feet apart. When the trees blossomed he rode a stoneboat between the rows, spraying them from a wooden barrel of water mixed with arsenate and lead. In the fall he brought the sheep down to feed on the windfalls and destroy next year's worms. When the trees went dormant he pruned them so severely that a blackbird could fly between any two branches. Mame begged him to buy red peonies for her garden, but he always ordered another apple tree instead.

The life cycles of crops and animals were the great cogs upon which the farm year turned. Decisions about when to plant or turn out the bull could be delayed according to the weather, but not indefinitely because most farm chores were hitched to the timetable of seasons and the earth's relentless rotation. The start of spring planting was heralded with smoke and fire. On a windless day John set the pastures afire to clear away the thatch and add potash to the soil for the new growth of grass. He'd hitch a plow to a team and make a firebreak, sometimes plowing furiously over the hills just ahead of the flames if a breeze picked up. After a rain, the pasture would green up again as the grass resurrected itself from the ashes. When the fields were dry, he disced and plowed and dragged them to prepare a seedbed. By mid-April he had begun seeding his grain crops and finished off with potatoes and corn, recording in his ledger the date each task was started and completed.

1906

April	11	Sawed wood
"	12	began plowing
"	21	began seeding
May	17	planted potatoes
"	23	began planting corn
"	30	finished planting corn
Aug.	24	began threshing
		Oats 642 bu.
		wheat 200 "
		timothy 100 "
		flax 22 "
Sept.	27	began corn cutting
"	28	finished
Oct.	17	began plowing
Nov.	10	stacked corn
"	18	froze up
"	22	put up the pigs to fat

Livestock were not bound so much to the weather as to an endless round of breeding, birth, and slaughter; and while there was only one harvest for crops, the flow of eggs and cream, butter and milk, hogs and cattle, wool and poultry to market was spread throughout the year. Calving often coincided with the last blizzard of the season, and in early spring both skies and animals were closely watched. When a cow delivered her calf, John carefully noted the date she "came in," as if gestation were a long and perilous journey from which she had successfully returned. His rangy herd of Shorthorns provided both beef and milk. He would rope any cow with a big bag and lead her to the barn, placing kicking chains on her hind legs before sitting down to milk her. Mame ran the milk through a hand-cranked separator, cranking faster and faster until the thick yellow cream flowed from the spout. She then covered the five-gallon cans and sank them in the horse tank so the cream wouldn't sour before it could be taken to the creamery. Chickens ran loose in the yard and hid their eggs in the straw of the horse mangers. Once a week John took an egg crate to town and waited while the grocer candled the eggs. In late fall when the weather turned cold, John butchered a steer in the barn or a couple of hogs in the cellar, and for a few days they enjoyed fresh meat before Mame canned the rest.

Horses were exempt from the common fate of farm animals because they traded on their labor, not flesh, and seemed less brutish, falling somewhere between hired men and livestock in the barnyard hierarchy. So it was only natural that they were regarded as individuals and afforded names and personal histories. They could be as defiant as any man, which is why they had to be broken, but even afterward the horse knew you wanted something from it and expected something in return. Mame understood this implicit bargain, which is why she always carried a bucket of oats down to the pasture when she wanted to catch a horse, calling it the way she called the men in from work—a piercing whistle through a gap in her teeth.

John, on the other hand, never bargained with animals. He believed in spurs and a quirt and made the dirt fly when he galloped from the yard. But brute force alone didn't always work. He was driving a grain wagon back from Simpson once when one of the team balked. The more he pounded and swore, the lower the mare sank in the harness until she lay in the middle of the road, head down, and wouldn't budge. Finally John walked the half mile back to the farm to fetch Mame. "Come on now, Gyp," she said, patting the mare's hip. "Get up." The horse did, and pulled them both back home. If Mame was gentle with horses, it's because she saw them as poor

dumb beasts that lacked any hope of heaven and were deserving of human pity. These same distinctions, however,
made her more demanding of her children, because with them
she had to worry about both body and soul. And it was she,
not John, who took down the lilac switch that hung behind a
picture frame if the children misbehaved. "Right is right and
wrong is wrong," she'd say before the blows fell, "and there's
nothing in between."

Life on the farm wasn't all work. There were card parties
and oyster suppers at the neighbors', baseball games and ice-
cream socials at the park in Simpson, and leap-year dances at
the church hall. John's tastes in entertainment ran to circuses
and Wild West shows. More than the shows themselves, he
enjoyed the fanfare of their arrival by train, the elephants
pulling up the big top in Cook Park, and seeing the bareback
riders and trick shots out of costume. He admired the horse-
men for their expertise at doing in a complicated ritual for the
crowd what he did simply every day. Sometimes he returned
from a Wild West show with a new horse or a piece of tack
like the pair of goatskin chaps he bought from Bill Pickett,
the famous black cowboy and bulldogger with the Miller
Brothers 101 Ranch. He liked to give impromptu displays of
horsemanship, making Brownie or Old Colonel buck and sun-
fish in the yard until his mother cried out to stop before he
was killed. "That's okay," Mame told her. "He's enjoying
himself." His work outfit included a wide-brimmed sombrero,
leather cuffs for roping, a sheath knife, and he usually carried,
somewhere on his person, a small ivory-handled five-shot pistol. One winter, during the annual ice harvest at Simpson,
John helped load clear blocks of river ice through a trapdoor
to the cold-storage room to be packed in sawdust. While he
waited for the next block, a pair of heavy iron tongs dropped
through the trapdoor and narrowly missed his head. Upstairs,
someone giggled. Then it happened again. In an instant, the

little pistol was in Johnnie O'Neill's hand. "The next one who drops his tongs is going to be down here with me!" The giggling stopped.

Mame's social life centered around the church, but she also belonged to the Oak Valley Homemakers Club, whose members included Protestants as well as doctors' wives from Rochester. They printed programs for their monthly meetings at a member's home and followed the three-course luncheon with a featured presentation. She spent hours at the library researching a topic when it was her turn to give a speech. At home she kept a thirteen-volume set of *John L. Stoddard's Lectures*, bound in black leather with gold filigree; its breathless, tour-guide prose and halftone color illustrations of ruined castles and costumed peasants—"A Tyrolese Maiden," "Gate to the Sultan's Palace"—addressed her curiosity about the larger world, just as the circus and Wild West shows answered her husband's. Mame loved to sing, and when the organist played "Oh Jerusalem" on Sundays, her clear alto rang through the church. After mass they stopped in Simpson to visit her mother-in-law and Kate Sinnott. The children played in the garden or sat in a daze while their father and grandma drank tea and discussed the farm. They revived on the ride home in the surrey. After supper Mame played the pump organ and put everyone to sleep singing the latest sheet music.

> Rose of Kil-dare,
> Sweet flow'r of my care,
> No col-leen's so true
> As my Moy-a a-roo.

Every summer great thunderstorms blew in from the west, preceded by a sudden calm and yellow storm light. As the wind gathered, John would climb the forty-foot windmill that stood east of the barn to shut off its blades. There was a brake wire at the base that should have done this but didn't. So he climbed hand-over-hand until he reached the tiny platform.

The bladed wheel was as tall as a man and spinning madly as the vane shifted with the wind's direction. Far below, his wife, her dress pinwheeling, yelled up to him, "Johnnie, be careful!" He pulled the vane into the wheel and lashed it down with a lariat. Then he stood there for a few minutes with the wind billowing his shirt and admired his fields and orchard, an orderly landscape and the perfect complement to "a pleasant home." At night, as the storm rocked the house, the children awoke between lightning flashes to see their mother, a candle in one hand and a bottle of holy water in the other, sprinkling the corners of their bedroom, making her own bargain with God.

ON APRIL 22, 1911, John rode to the railroad depot in Simpson to take delivery of the Reeves twenty-horsepower steam traction engine he had ordered the month before from an implement company in Minneapolis. The tractor was as big as a locomotive and burned a ton of coal a day. He had taken out a chattel mortgage for $2,215 to buy it and go into the threshing business.

When the tractor was unloaded from its flatcar, Berne St. George stoked the firebox until he had a head of steam. Then John eased the clutch lever out and the tractor pulled away from the depot, chugging down the road at four miles an hour. The two men rode high above the roadbed on a platform behind the boiler, sheltered from falling sparks by a black sunroof. Behind them they towed a rattling wooden tank wagon. The Reeves' five-foot lug wheels gave the passengers an elevated view of the countryside. John steered with one hand on the wheel and the other on the throttle lever, keeping constant watch on the steam gauge. Boiler explosions involving steam tractors averaged two a day across the country—newspaper accounts always made a point of reporting the distance victims were thrown—but the biggest danger, due to the machine's great weight, was a bridge collapse, so drivers preferred fording creeks to crossing unfamiliar bridges. But there were no bridges between Simpson and the farm. When the Reeves chugged down the last grade and turned into the yard, scattering chickens, John tooted the shiny brass whistle and Mame and the children watched from the porch as the steam engine hissed to a stop in front of them.

Steam tractors were too slow and ponderous to replace horses at most field work, except for pulling stumps or plowing unbroken sod. When the eight-bottom gang plow John bought to pull behind the Reeves proved too heavy (a man riding on a platform above the plow had to raise and lower the shares), he gave it to the St. George brothers, who took it out to the Dakotas, where a farmer could plow a straight line into the next county. Essentially, the steam tractor was a portable power source for running other machinery such as a sawmill or a separator. John bought the Reeves to start his own threshing ring, which, like the nursery stock business, was a way of making money off the farm. Threshing began in late July and extended into October. The order of farms alternated, but there was always an urgency to the run because once the grain was cut a stretch of bad weather could ruin it. Now that he owned the tractor and separator, the threshing run would begin at home.

Early morning. The sky was pale and cloudless except for a smudge of black smoke rising above an oat field over east. The oats had been cut and bundled the week before, the bundles stacked in shocks and lined up in neat rows to dry. Now a dozen wagons slowly drove down the rows. At each shock the driver stopped, wrapped the reins around the wagon post, and began to build a load of bundles on the rack. Two blasts of a steam whistle signaled that the separator was working, and all over the field men and horses quickened their pace, all of them inextricably connected to a whirring machine whose appetite for grain never slackened. When the rack reached his own height, the wagon driver flicked his reins and his team clopped across the stubble field toward a black cloud funneling from the Reeves' smokestack.

The steam tractor stood hissing in the center of the field. Across from it was a canary-yellow Avery separator, a narrow, shivering contraption of sheet metal and wood with a long-necked spout at one end that shot a constant stream of straw and chaff into the air. The two machines were connected by seventy-five feet of whirring canvas belt that snaked between them like voltage leaping a gap. Wagons lined up along either side of the separator as drivers waited their turn to pitch bundles into the machine before heading back to the field for another load. Most teams were used to the noise and heat of the boiler, but even with blinders a new horse might shy if it caught sight of the belt streaking past or sniffed the unfamiliar tang of coal smoke and hot grease.

Berne St. George sat on the platform beside the firebox, chain-smoking and keeping one eye on the pressure gauge. If the needle fell below forty, he'd swing the fire door open, exposing his shins to a red-hot blast of heat, and chuck in another shovel of coal. If he ran low on water, he'd blow the steam whistle for the water monkey to fill the Reeves' side-mounted tanks. The whistle blasts were a kind of Morse code for communicating with the far-flung crew, so many toots for more coal and so many for more grain sacks. Neighbors who knew the code could tell what a crew was running short of just by listening for the whistle.

John stood atop the separator in a swirling cloud of chaff to supervise the unloading of bundles. It was the most important job, and also the dirtiest. A conveyor belt fed the bundles into a revolving cylinder with sawteeth that beat the kernels of grain out of the stalks. Inside the machine, separating tables winnowed grain from chaff while a fan blew the dust and straw out the wind stacker in a great rooster tail. A bundle tossed sideways or butt first onto the feeder would plug the cylinder and slow the belt until Berne gunned the throttle, the engine belching black smoke, but the grain would already be lost up the blower. When he wasn't astride the separator, John prowled around it, oiling the boxings and filling the grease cups, adjusting chains and pulleys, listening for trouble and trying to head it off. He checked the grain spout, where threshed oats poured into heavy linen sacks like a shower of gold. Three bushels to a sack. Before a sack was stitched and loaded onto a wagon to be driven to the granary, he dipped his hand inside, put a few kernels into his mouth, and chewed them to test their moisture before spitting them out.

Morning dragged on. The straw stack grew higher and higher, but the bundle wagons never stopped coming. When they stopped bringing oats, they went on to barley, wheat, rye, and flax. Oats were the easiest to thresh, flax the hardest, especially if there was any moisture. Chaff from the blower dusted the spike pitchers with minstrel faces that cracked when they smiled. The sun beat down with no shade but the tatters of coal smoke drifting overhead. Some of the threshers munched green apples filched from the orchard and washed the sour taste down with cool water from a crock wrapped in burlap. John pulled his Elgin out of his pocket with increasing frequency. When it read 11:30, he gave the signal to shut down. Berne blew the whistle, then eased back on the throttle so the belt sagged to stop without slipping off the flywheel. The spike pitchers stabbed their pitchforks into the remaining bundles and headed across the field for the farmhouse in a long, ragged line.

Hearing the long whistle blast, Mame told the neighbor girl to hurry and finish setting the dining-room table. With four leaves added to accommodate the threshers, the table stretched from one wall to the next. Both women's faces were flushed, their hair hanging in damp ringlets, as they pulled crockery from the warming oven above the Jewel cookstove.

They could hear the men washing outside from a pail of water set out on the lawn. Now the crew stepped heavily onto the porch, the screen door slamming as they filed into the dining room and sat shoulder to shoulder, men and boys in sweat-stained overalls, sunburned except for blanched foreheads, their faces wet and shining with anticipation. Back and forth the women rushed from the kitchen, setting down platters of fried chicken or roast beef with gravy, bowls of mashed potatoes and rutabagas, fresh green beans, thick slices of bread with sweet butter, and gallons of hot coffee. A thresherman's wife was judged by the table she set, because the men she fed were not just hired hands but friends and neighbors. Mame would never think of serving mutton, as some wives did, and on Fridays she bought tins of salmon, which even the Protestants liked. The men barely spoke at first, so busy were they shoveling food into their mouths. They emptied their plates, refilled them, emptied them again. They ate in shifts, and as soon as one man left another took his place. Mame set down a half-dozen apple pies with golden, fluted crusts and slices of Cheddar cheese. Within minutes the pies vanished. Slowly, the last men stood up, nodded to Mame, and staggered from the dining room to find some shade in the yard, leaving behind them the vast shambles of dinner.

Threshing continued into the evening until the last sack was filled or a heavy dew fell. Then the separator was hitched to the back of the tractor and hauled over the stubble fields and across the road to Sheehan's place. Some farmers wanted the straw piled in a field or blown into the barn, so the separator had to be placed accordingly and leveled. Berne would wheel the tractor around to face the separator, eyeballing it until flywheel and drivewheel were aligned to receive the belt. The last thing he did was bank the fire in the boiler so he could get up a head of steam the next morning. After Sheehan's farm, the crew moved down the road to Wileman's, Engles', McCoy's, St. George's, Portier's, Boardman's, Allen's, and

Ryan's. For three months, the men spent their days at other farms and rode home each night to sleep in their own beds, so the threshing run itself resembled a long journey of stops and starts. By November the crew had traveled widely across most of two townships.

Every summer during threshing a caravan of Gypsies camped on the school grounds north of the farm. They arrived in canvas-covered wagons and stayed until the urge to move again struck or the law ran them off. Sometimes the men would drift into the grain fields to trade horses or borrow a tool. They were swarthy men, very serious, and their horses were always very fine. The women came later. Wearing layers of brightly colored rags, they cordoned themselves behind a ring of snot-nosed children and begged unabashedly. Usually they begged grain for their horses and went away if they got it. Once a thresher refused and a short time later noticed a very fat Gypsy woman loping oddly from his grain wagon. He sent some boys running after her. As they chased her across the field, something the size of a small child dropped from beneath her skirts: a full sack of oats. The woman kept running.

The next morning the school yard was empty; the Gypsy caravan had struck camp, and, in a little while, so did the threshers. What would it be like, a thresher might ask himself as he rattled down the road to the next farm, to live that way, like a Gypsy, traveling all the time with no place to call home but the stars overhead and the great, wide world beneath your feet?

WHEN HE lined up his wife and children in front of the barn for a traveling photographer in 1915, John O'Neill was a man who owed the world nothing. He had paid off the note on the steam tractor in less than two years. Mame had given him five children: Catherine, Mary, William, James, and baby Theresa. He had crops in the field, forty head of Shorthorn cattle, a dozen horses, sheep, hogs, assorted poultry, and a barn full of mostly new implements. Having cleared most of its timber, he registered the farm by name and had it inscribed on his stationery: ~*Woodland Farm, John E. O'Neill, Prop.*~. His family and hired men referred to him as "the Boss," and when he wrote on the back of a photograph, that's what he called himself.

The Boss couldn't have known it then, but he was living through the golden era of American agriculture. In the decade since taking over the farm, he had seen farm prices double and the value of the land rise even higher. More important, these gains hadn't been offset by an even greater rise in the cost of the goods he bought in town. For the first time in his memory, a farmer's purchasing power was roughly equivalent to that of a grocer or a factory worker. This fair rate of exchange between town and country would come to be known as "parity"; and in later times, when it had vanished, farmers would hark back to the years immediately preceding World War I as the benchmark against which to measure their losses and gains.

The war itself brought even greater prosperity as farmers exported surplus grain to Europe and filled government contracts at home. When Tom St. George enlisted in the army, John bought his brother-in-law's Delco Electric lighting plant and had the house and barn wired for lights. The sixteen glass-jacketed batteries occupied two shelves in the basement and needed recharging every week, usually on wash day, from a kerosene-powered generator. He also bought a windup Victrola to compete with Mame's singing. A few cranks of the handle and an entire orchestra came growling through the speaker horn. A hired man walking back from the barn on a sultry summer night would have seen a farmhouse ablaze in electric lights and heard the syrupy voice of Aileen Stanley serenading the cows with "When My Sugar Walks Down the Street (All the Little Birdies Go Tweet-Tweet-Tweet)."

At the age of forty-two, Mame bore her last child, a son named after her brother-in-law Edward. In October of 1920 she wrapped the baby in a big gray shawl and took him to a meeting of the Friends of Irish Freedom at the Simpson village hall. Most of her neighbors were there, along with Father Brown from St. Bridget's. They heard a speaker describe the latest fighting in Cork, where the Lord Mayor was in the seventieth day of a hunger strike, and bought bonds sold for a nation that did not yet exist. A few months later, a big Irishman from the Hibernians came to supper and the talk naturally turned to the deadlocked Irish Free State. "By God, Johnnie!" the man shouted, pounding his fist on the table. "Where there's a will, there's a way!" The older people kept alive a keen bitterness over the land they had left. But times were good at home, and it was difficult for the younger generation to feel the same allegiance to a place known only through the fading memories of their parents or to identify with a people who had lost their country so long ago.

After the war, farm prices began to plummet even as the rest of the country enjoyed a dizzying wave of prosperity. With Europe at peace, exports shrank, and farmers had to plant more crops to keep pace with falling prices and their own rising costs. John borrowed heavily to buy two adjoining eighty-acre parcels, Potter's to the east and Stillwell's to the south, trusting that increased production would outrun any further decline in prices. He also hired Hans Jensen's crew of carpenters to build a thirty-four-stanchion barn so he could milk more cows. The new barn was designed with a concrete block foundation and an arched roof for more hay storage in the mow. It was framed in oak cut and milled on the farm and sheathed in pine. Double sliding doors at both the north and south ends allowed a man to drive a wagon through without backing up. For a month carpenters whistled from the scaffolding during the day and played cards in the farmhouse at night. When John led the cows to the finished barn, they wouldn't go in at first because they had never stepped on a concrete floor.

THEN EVERYTHING went to hell. After the stock-market collapse, farm prices fell lower than they had at any time since before the Civil War. Banks that had competed for the privilege of lending farmers money when times were good now began to call back second and third mortgages to keep themselves afloat. Farmers who had confidently taken out loans when corn sold for eighty cents a bushel could not repay those debts when the same bushel was worth only a dime. They either took whatever the stockyard or elevator offered or they returned home empty-handed. When the elevator in Simpson wouldn't pay him a decent price for a truckload of rye, John drove the Model T back to the farm and shoveled the rye onto the ground for the pigs to eat. When Bill St. George shipped a six-hundred-pound boar to the Chicago stockyards, he received a bill of freight instead of a check; the price of the hog hadn't even covered shipping. Farmers who had sunk their sweat and every dollar they owned into land, thinking it the only safe form of wealth, watched their farms go under the auctioneer's gavel.

On the evening of August 30, 1932, two young farmers from Kandiyohi County addressed a mass rally of "agriculturalists" beneath a starlit sky in Rochester's Mayo Park. Speaking from a platform in front of the band shell, the two men explained that they had come to organize farmers in a national movement, the Farm Holiday Association, pledged to withholding products from the market until a fair price could be obtained. One of them cited a welter of figures to prove what the audience already knew, that most farmers were operating in the red. The other speaker described recent events in Iowa, where striking farmers had blockaded highways leading into Sioux City, turning back livestock trucks and dumping milk on the pavement. Things would go smoother in Minnesota, the speaker predicted. "We will call a strike on perishables—butter, eggs and milk—if we find it is the only way we can get cost of production for our farmers. We trust, however, that such action is not going to be necessary." The audience pledged to withhold their farm products from the market if a strike was called and elected a seven-member board of directors. Among the seven men who heard their names called from the platform that night was John O'Neill.

Across the border in Iowa, the strike was in full swing. Farmers patrolled roads into market towns with pitchforks. In Council Bluff, an angry mob on the courthouse lawn stood off sheriff's deputies armed with tear gas and machine guns until the governor threatened to call out the National Guard. The strike astonished the rest of the country, not so much by its violence, which was endemic during the Depression, but that such events should occur in the Republican heart of the corn belt. "They sound like some far-off foreign country," a columnist for *The New Republic* wrote, "not like the Iowa of big red barns and small white farm houses." On board an ocean liner in the mid-Atlantic, J. P. Morgan dispatched a cable to his Wall Street offices: "What is happening in Iowa?"

The Farm Holiday Association was the brainchild of Milo Reno, a farmer-politician and retired head of the Iowa Farmers Union. A craggy-faced, Lincolnesque figure with curly gray hair and enormous ears, Reno was an old-fashioned, finger-pointing orator whose speeches were equal parts Scripture and personal invective. He wore dark, owlish spectacles and a flaming-red necktie and spoke with a clipped, prairie harshness that made people uneasy in New York but not in Des Moines. "Our organization is the last hope of the American farmer for independence," he told a newsreel audience. "It is fighting a battle that will determine the issue as to whether the farmer shall become a peasant, the menial slave of the usurers and the industrialists, or whether he will retain the birthright he inherited from his father." Reno came by his radicalism naturally: His father was a Granger, his mother a Greenbacker and a Populist. As a young man, he had campaigned for William Jennings Bryan and, like the Great Commoner, he understood that people will get behind a leader who offers simple solutions to complex problems. For Bryan, the rallying cry had been free silver; for Reno, it was cost of production. Just as banks had declared a holiday to preserve their assets, Reno proposed that farmers take a holiday by withholding their products from market until they were guaranteed a price that would cover the cost of production plus a reasonable profit. He envisioned farmers simply staying home, not a violent siege of market towns. Even Reno was surprised at the eagerness with which they took to the barricades.

By September the strike had spread to Minnesota. Campfires lighted the highways as pickets blockaded towns in the southwest corner of the state and the Hormel plant in Austin. A picket stationed down the highway would wave a red lantern as a truck approached the checkpoint, where striking farmers waited with pitchforks and clubs. As the truck slowed, someone would jump on the running board and ask the driver what he was hauling. If it was farm produce, he was told to turn around. If he didn't, the pickets threw a log or a "porcupine," a threshing belt studded with nails, into the truck's path. Most drivers, farmers themselves, turned around, but some armed themselves with hammers and pistols to run the blockade. The leader of the state Farm Holiday had promised "Gandhi-like" methods, but fistfights often broke out, and, two weeks into the strike, a twenty-five-year-old striker was killed by a shotgun blast as he stepped outside a tent near Canby. He was shot by a farmer who didn't like trespassers on his property. A week later a riot broke out between pickets and nonpickets at Howard Lake, Minnesota. The strike began to fall apart. It had been doomed from the start, precisely because farmers weren't peasants or yeomen or Bolsheviks but small businessmen, speculators in crops and livestock, who rarely agreed on anything except that the country had forgotten them.

The strike was suspended after Roosevelt's election in November, and the Farm Holiday Association turned its attention to the more immediate problem of halting foreclosure sales. This time cold weather worked to the farmers' advantage, as hundreds of idled farmers crowded into a barnyard for a sheriff's auction could be very intimidating. On a single day in January, Minnesota farmers halted three foreclosure sales. Sometimes all it took was a noose hanging from the barn door or a wall of grim faces pressing the sheriff into a corner to make him call off the sale. Other days, a holiday mood prevailed as the crowd bid pennies for everything and even the auctioneer seemed to be in on the joke.

"How much am I bid for this cow?"

"Two cents!"

"I'm bid two cents. Who'll make it higher?"

"Four cents!"

"Don't you men know," the auctioneer would say, grinning, "that I'm working on commission?"

When the bidding reached ten cents or so, the crowd chanted "Sell it! Sell it!" until the auctioneer brought his gavel down. The sale would proceed briskly, with horses selling for twenty-five cents and wagons for a dime. If an outsider raised the bid, he'd feel a heavy hand on his shoulder while a voice whispered in his ear, "Plenty high, ain't it?" At the end of the day the assigned bidders paid their loose change to the auctioneer and returned the property to the original owner.

Most "penny auctions" were bloodless, but Iowa was the exception. The governor declared martial law after an angry mob, having failed to halt a sheriff's sale earlier in the day, dragged a sixty-year-old judge from his courthouse and threatened to lynch him. When the crowd burst into his courtroom, the judge coolly told the men to take off their hats and stop smoking. At this, he was seized by the throat, thrown into the back of a truck, and driven to a lonely crossroads, where the mob looped a rope around the old man's neck and yanked it until he collapsed. When he revived, the judge was forced to his knees and made to pray for the deliverance of the farmer from his "present miserable condition." After deciding not to hang him, the mob removed the judge's pants and left him in the road with a hubcap full of grease on his head.

Incidents like the one in Iowa persuaded banks and insurance companies, which held the mortgages on most farms, to negotiate rather than risk confronting an angry crowd. Each chapter of the Farm Holiday Association had a Council of Defense to work out solutions between debtors and creditors. When John O'Neill discovered that five large insurance companies held the notes on more than half the farms in Olmsted County, including his own, he invited their representatives to meet with council members at the Union Hall on South Broadway. Later in the week, five hundred farmers showed up to protest a chattel mortgage sale south of Stewartville only to find that a deal had already been struck to leave the farmer most of his livestock and machinery.

In February, Minnesota's Farmer-Labor Party governor, Floyd Olson, signed a temporary moratorium on mortgage foreclosures. The state Farm Holiday Association had won a great victory and decided to press its advantage with a rally at the state capitol. Arriving in St. Paul by bus, automobile, truck, and special trains, twenty thousand farmers marched six abreast down Wabash Street to the capitol building carrying banners praising the governor and threatening legislators if they didn't vote to extend the moratorium. They listened to speakers from the steps of the capitol or chased down lawmakers in the chambers and corridors. Some of them wore clodhopper boots and barn coats as if they had just finished chores. But John O'Neill dressed formally for the occasion in a black fedora and double-breasted overcoat with a gray muffler wrapped around his neck. He was fifty-six years old and had just been fitted with a set of dentures. When a newspaperman snapped his photograph as he marched alongside a group of Grant County farmers, he resisted the impulse to smile.

ON THE FOURTH DAY of threshing, John O'Neill moved his rig to John Jacks's farm. Jacks, a short, hefty Irishman, was a Protestant from Ulster who had smuggled himself aboard an emigrant ship by hiding under his sister's skirts. He'd lost his own farm during the twenties and now rented this place north of the school yard.

There was a different rhythm to threshing since the steam engine had been replaced with a four-cylinder McCormick-Deering tractor that ran on gasoline rather than coal and never whistled. Otherwise everything was the same. John ran the separator while his oldest sons, Bill and Jim, operated the tractor and sacked grain. They threshed oats first, then moved on to rye and barley. As the temperature climbed into the eighties, the horses twitched beneath their fly nets. A bundle wagon of rye shocks had just pulled alongside the separator to unload when its team spooked and galloped toward an open gate. Stepping in front of the runaways, John grabbed at the bridles and one of the horses, a big sorrel, reared up and came down on his leg. He disappeared under the wagon. When his sons reached him, he lay on the ground, still conscious. The iron wheels had passed to either side, but a shattered bone protruded from his right leg. The boys lifted him into the back seat of the Ford, and Bill raced across the field to the road, his father moaning each time they bumped over another furrow.

John was laid up for six weeks in the basement ward of Colonial Hospital, his broken leg encased in plaster. Every day Mame came to talk about farm business and listen to his complaints about the pain from his leg being in traction. One evening the night nurse heard a heavy thud, as of an iron weight hitting linoleum. She walked down the ward with a flashlight and found the old man sawing at his cast with a sheath knife. He surrendered the knife but hid the pulley cord under his pillow and later fashioned it into a lariat for roping nurses and unsuspecting interns. He swore that the first thing he'd do when he got out of the hospital was shoot the horse that put him there. But he didn't need to. A few weeks before he was released, someone tethered the big sorrel to the back of a manure spreader, where, maddened by flies, it drove one of the spokes into its head.

The Ford didn't leave the garage all winter after an early blizzard filled the road cuts with snow. John hobbled around the house all day on crutches and kept watch on the snowfields from the windows. Sometimes he'd get restless and tell his sons, "Go put a saddle on Blue." They'd saddle Ed's roan pony, leading him to the front porch, where their father leaned on his cane. While the boys held Blue steady, John eased into the saddle, then sidled the horse up to the gate to lift the latch. A twenty-foot drift buried the bottom of Sheehan's hill, so he rode along the top of the pasture where the wind had scoured the snow. He rode down North Broadway to a grocery and waited on the horse until the grocer came out to take his order. Then he handed down a pair of saddlebags and a list detailing how to fill them. What a figure he must have cut on the streets of Rochester—bundled against the cold, hat pulled low, his pony stamping the icy pavement! Sometimes boys who saw the old man on his horse, his right leg splayed out, called him Hop-a-long behind his back because he looked like someone who'd ridden out of the Old West. And, in a way, he had.

John O'Neill had voted for Roosevelt in the previous year's election, and then waited to see what the New Deal meant for the farm crisis. During the campaign, the Democrats had flirted with two opposing farm bills whose basic differences were apparent in the organizations that supported them. The

Farmers Union and its more radical offshoot, the Farm Holiday Association, both represented small midwestern farmers and favored a guaranteed cost of production; the more conservative Farm Bureau, which represented large farmers and southern cotton growers, advocated government payments linked to acreage controls. Roosevelt chose the latter, and that spring his secretary of agriculture, Henry A. Wallace, unveiled the New Deal's latest acronym: the AAA. The Agricultural Allotment Act proposed to raise farm prices and cut surpluses by paying farmers the difference between the market price and the fair value, or parity price, for certain crops if they reduced their acreage voluntarily—pay them, in other words, for *not* farming. For a generation of farmers who had spent their lives clearing land and buying ever more powerful machinery, the Allotment Act was incomprehensible. And when the government bought and slaughtered six million baby pigs to eliminate an anticipated surplus of hogs at a time when people were still standing in breadlines, it seemed not only wrong-headed but wicked. Milo Reno called the secretary of agriculture "Lord Corn Wallace" and denounced the plan as an attempt to "sovietize" American farmers by putting them directly on the government dole. He called a new farm strike in October. Railroad bridges were burned in Iowa and strikers closed a packing plant in Minnesota, but there was little picketing. The public had grown tired of the Holiday's sporadic guerrilla warfare, and Citizen Protective Leagues sprang up to protect those who wanted to take their produce to market. In a few weeks the strike sputtered out as farmers began receiving government checks in the mail.

Whatever farm surplus the government's Allotment Act didn't eliminate, the next summer's drought did. That spring had begun with unrelentingly fair skies, and when dark clouds appeared from the west they brought not rain but windblown dust. On May 10, 1934, a great dust storm blew in on gale winds behind a cold front and lasted two days. By noon the countryside had taken on the violet-green twilight of an eclipse. People drove with their headlights on at midday and pulled kerchiefs over their faces to keep from being sand-blasted. Farmers who had just seeded their fields saw the seeds blow away in the wind. The storm coated buildings inside and out with a powdery gray dust. Surgical operations at the Mayo Clinic were suspended after the fine grit got into the instruments. Housewives placed wet towels on their win-dowsills to catch the dust, but it sifted inside anyway. Wiping their kitchen tables with a damp cloth, they reconstituted the dust into what it had been originally—the windblown topsoil of Great Plains farms.

What followed was the worst summer in Minnesota history for crops and livestock. By the end of May temperatures topped one hundred degrees. A field John had planted to oats north of the Night Pasture came up nothing but pigeon grass, which even the cows wouldn't eat. A barley crop that looked promising in July burned up in a few scorching days, just shriveled and died. Sometimes the wind didn't blow for days, and the stock tank ran dry. Stockyards in Rochester filled as farmers shipped their gaunt cattle to market at two cents a pound rather than watch them starve. The spring in the hollow never went dry but there wasn't enough grass to feed a hundred cattle, so John divided the herd, pasturing one bunch on rented land along the Root River and driving the other to a woods south of Chester, where they survived by stripping the leaves off trees. Jim and Theresa accompanied their father on the drive, moving cattle along both sides of the dusty town-ship road. The morning began hot and dry as usual, but on the way back a sudden rain shower caught the riders and they arrived home soaked to the skin. It would be the last rain for a long time.

Like most farmers, John O'Neill enjoyed a love-hate re-lationship with the government. He hated the college-educated New Deal Brain Trust and the kind of logic that paid farmers not to farm; on the other hand, he traveled to the state capitol several times to demand special concessions for farmers when other businessmen were going broke just as quickly. During the drought he sold a government buyer two aging milk cows for $5 apiece, then watched the buyer shoot them. He would have applied for Wallace's hog-reduction program if hog cholera hadn't wiped out his pigs the year before. When the newly formed Soil Conservation Service offered to lay out his fields in contour strips to keep his topsoil from blowing away, he welcomed the plan. Truckloads of government-paid CCC workers in denim outfits and floppy hats swarmed over his farm and further transformed it. They chopped down dead trees and planted black locust and pine to anchor the hillside against erosion. They built small check dams at the head of ravines and fenced off the hollow for a permanent pasture. And when a $7,000 note came due for the mortgage he'd taken out to buy Potter's and Stillwell's, he drove from bank to bank and found that none were lending to farmers that year, especially not to one so prominent in halting foreclosure sales. He was desperate and would certainly have lost the farm if the Federal Land Bank in Claremont hadn't loaned him the money.

On Sunday afternoons at three o'clock, John stopped whatever he was doing and tuned the radio in the living room to WOC-WHO to hear "The Golden Hour of the Little Flower." After the organ music subsided a deep, mellifluous voice said, "Good afternoon, my friends," and Father Coughlin would launch into that week's sermon, invariably a discussion of the causes or cures of the Depression, which the priest referred to as "our present sorrow."

Our present sorrow, Coughlin told his listeners, was the direct result of a "money famine" instigated by Wall Street and the nation's banking system. His remedies—the revaluation of gold and the remonetization of silver—and choice of villains were not far removed from those offered by Milo

Reno. And though he never mentioned the Farm Holiday movement by name, he quickly aligned himself with its followers. "Are you not apprised of what is happening in Iowa, in Illinois, in Ohio, in Minnesota, in Michigan, and in the Middle West generally? These men have rebelled against the dishonest dollar and those who attempt to use it. . . . We have had enough of evictions. We have been surfeited with confiscations. We have been scourged long enough at the pillar of obsolete contracts and mortgages."

Listeners were stirred not so much by the radio priest's arguments as by the sound of his voice. It was a soothing voice, heavy with assurance, that would rise to a strident pitch of righteous anger at least once before the end of the broadcast. A voice impressive for the sheer volume of facts and metaphors it could hurl at the listener. It was the voice of a newsreel without pictures in which Christ, J. P. Morgan, Ezekiel, Karl Marx, the Unknown Soldier, and the Braintrusters all linked arms and marched together down the Road of Time. For Irish Catholics, especially, the voice was familiar for the trace of brogue it retained, a voice that could trill with heartiness or descend to a hush as confidential and weighted as that other disembodied voice, the one that whispered from behind the confessional screen and knew the soul's darkest secrets.

At first, Coughlin had been a gushing supporter of Roosevelt, telling his listeners that the New Deal was "Christ's Deal," but he soon reversed himself and started attacking the administration's policies, especially the Agricultural Allotment Act for reducing crop production in the midst of hunger. Inevitably, Coughlin began to turn on the president himself, calling him "Franklin Double-Crossing Roosevelt," and told his audiences that though the money changers had been driven from the temple, "they landed in the White House."

There could have been no more loyal audience for the radio priest than John and Mame O'Neill. They belonged to the Radio League of the Little Flower and even in lean years sent donations to keep Coughlin on the air. A picture of Saint Theresa of Lisieux, the Little Flower herself, hung in an ebonized frame in their bedroom. When Coughlin broke from the Democrats and started his own political party, the National Union for Social Justice, they joined. And in the summer of 1936, when the party held its nominating convention, John traveled to Cleveland as a delegate.

Berne St. George drove John and two other delegates to the convention in the O'Neills' red Ford touring car. The twenty thousand people who jammed Cleveland Stadium for "three days of uninterrupted frenzy" were the tattered remnants of the decade's social protest movements: Dr. Townsend's old-age pensioners; members of Share Our Wealth clubs run by Huey Long's successor, the Reverend Gerald L. K. Smith; and, of course, the Coughlinites. Among the latter were members of the Farm Holiday Association, which had badly splintered after the death of Milo Reno. Reno himself had advocated a third party and cast around for someone to lead it. Since Long had been assassinated and Floyd Olson lay dying of cancer, Reno's hard-core followers pledged themselves to Coughlin almost by default.

The nominating process itself was perfunctory, because Coughlin had already hand-picked the candidate: William Lemke, a second-term congressman from North Dakota who had coauthored a bill for a national moratorium on farm foreclosures. He was a lackluster figure, but the crowd that filled the stadium had not come to hear him but Coughlin. For most of them, it was the first time they actually "saw" the Voice they had come to know so intimately from their radios. Coughlin sat on the platform in a high-backed, brocaded chair while delegates paraded their support for his candidate. When the moment came for him to speak, he approached the tangle of radio and newsreel microphones, nuzzling closer to them until his lips were no more than two inches away. He wore a very high Roman collar and rimless spectacles. "His face is completely lineless," a reporter wrote. "It is not properly fat, but rather appears perpetually swollen, with the hard, bright, crimson surface of skin just after an insect bite—possibly an indication of glandular unbalance." As he railed against Roosevelt and the international banking conspiracy, Coughlin became more strident, more plainly anti-Semitic, more desperate than ever.

Thirty delegates were picked from the audience to second Coughlin's nomination as president of the National Union for Social Justice. Most had never spoken to an audience before and addressed the microphone haltingly. One of them was from North Dakota—a tall, erect man with close-cropped hair and level eyes who said slowly and with great restraint, "I am a farmer. I've worked hard. I've raised a big family. Now I've got nothing."

On the way home, John and Berne drove north of Detroit to see Coughlin's newly built church, the Shrine of the Little Flower, with its impressive stone crucifixion tower from which the radio shows were broadcast. John bought postcards and a souvenir book. He also brought home something from the convention for Mame—sheet music to a campaign song called "Let's Get Behind Lemke." It was a march in four-four time. She sat at the pump organ, her fingers searching out the keys as she sang in a wavering voice:

> There was a boy named Lem-ke
> Who grew up out North West,
> Who ear-ly learned to look for caus-es deep;
> He said, "Why where there's plent-y should such a few
>   men feast
> And waste while mil-lions starve and weep?"

The tune was catchy enough, but the lyrics were depressing. After so many years of hard times, people wanted to feel hopeful again. They wanted to believe the worst was behind them. They wanted to sing "Happy Days Are Here Again," not a song that rhymed *deep* with *weep*.

Lemke received less than 2 percent of the popular vote, failing to carry a single state—even his own—as Roosevelt swept to victory in the greatest landslide in the nation's history. To farmers like John O'Neill, the election was a reminder of just how small a minority they had become in their own country.

NINE

Because his land is spread out in different corners of Marion Township, Dennis O'Neill spends a lot of time commuting between fields and often takes his three children along for the ride. After unloading a fence-post auger at Ed's, he drops the kids off to jump on the trampoline while he checks on the progress of his soybeans in Potter's Field. Patrick, the oldest, has the rusty hair and freckled face of a boy on the label of a peanut-butter jar. I ask if he's picked out a pig for the county fair yet.

"Yeah."

"What's his name?"

"Hasn't got a name yet."

Last year was the first time he showed animals at the fair, a pair of heavyweight barrows named Butch and Sundance, and took a red instead of a blue ribbon, which was disappointing. But what I remember was the load-up after the livestock auction when the hogs were loaded into a stock truck for a trip to the Hormel plant in Austin. The lateness of the hour, the bright lights, and high-pitched squeals—all conspired to suggest a roust and mass arrests. But when he prodded Butch and Sundance up the ramp to the waiting truck, Patrick seemed unmoved. "Piggies going bye-bye," he said, a ten-year-old ironist, and went back to cleaning out their pen. Only later, during the ride home, did he burst into tears.

Dennis and Bridget started crying too, even though they ship a thousand hogs to market each year; then the two younger children started in and the whole pickup was sobbing. "This year," Bridget vowed, "we're going to treat the fair hogs like any other."

ON THE OPENING DAY of the Olmsted County Fair, Dennis and the two boys chase their fair hogs out of the nursery and onto a hydraulic hog loader to be hosed off while Bridget records the scene with a camcorder.

"Don't spray their ears," she says. "They'll get water in their ears and end up with a tipped head. Make sure their feet are as clean as possible."

As the mud washes away, snouts turn pink, hooves and bristles glisten, and the hogs emerge as sleek as zeppelins, their hides fairly bursting with corn-fed bulk. The boys are showing hogs in each of three categories. Their names are Chinese, Orangie, Ham, Roan, Blue Roan, and the Terminator. The last two, heavyweight barrows, are six months old today.

Small farmers raise hogs because they are more efficient than cattle at converting corn into meat and require less land, although they do need a great deal more attention. Dennis and Bridget own fifty brood sows and farrow a dozen at a time. From birth until market, the hogs never leave the farm but are shuttled through a series of buildings and fenced yards arranged around a cluster of round corn bins. Piglets go from farrowing house to nursery and at fifty pounds graduate to the finishing yard, where they'll reach market weight at six months. The young pigs skittering across the finishing yard are all kinetic energy and run with the speeded-up motion of people in a silent movie. On the other hand, the brood stock—sows and gilts and three enormous boars that service them—lumber slowly through their open pens like stuffed pashas. One of the boars, a 550-pound Babcock with a pillow-sized scrotum, is named Needlenose.

"That son of a bitch would eat me if he could," Dennis says, dumping a bucket of feed over the fence. "He stalks me every time I get in the pen."

The hogs won't be taken to the fair until it cools off in the evening, so the kids and I watch *Wheel of Fortune* while Dennis takes a shower. In the kitchen Bridget fixes a quick supper of hamburgers. She wears tiny, pig-shaped earrings and a green T-shirt with white lettering that reads: "Irish girls are healthy, have great personalities, very sexy, tremendous lovers, extremely witty, dynamic in every thing they do, great cooks . . . and humble." Stacking dirty dishes in the sink, she says, "I'm not a home mom. Not this week anyway."

The Olmsted County fairgrounds is a mile south of downtown Rochester, sandwiched between strip malls and a metal recycler and directly across from the Crossroads Shopping Center. An article in the afternoon newspaper hinted that the fairgrounds had outlived its usefulness and would add substantially to the county tax base if developed. The article quoted the Rochester-Olmsted planning director as saying that the fairgrounds weren't used by many people outside fair time and didn't offer the same "aesthetic experience" as a city park. Yet there's also sentiment for leaving the fair where it is precisely because it's one of the few places where city and country come together on terms that approach anything like parity. School primers no longer include a section entitled "A Visit to the Farm" because the farm population has shrunk to the point that most people wouldn't know whom to visit, but a county fair offers city dwellers the same opportunity to wander through buildings smelling of hay and manure and see more animals than they would at a circus. And while the carnival rides and midway tend to overshadow the livestock barns, like a glitzy pleasure dome, the core of a fair remains flesh and bone.

The swine barn is a pole building on the outer ring of the fairgrounds, an obstacle to be passed through on the way to the screaming fun. Dennis waits in line to back his trailer up to the building. When he does, a slack-jawed fair employee jumps in to unload the hogs, pushing them roughly with his knees, only to be chased out by Bridget. "Would you *please* get out of there!" She is less worried about the hogs than about the possibility that the man might contaminate their trailer with germs from other animals. Swine, whose single-stomach anatomy resembles our own, are vulnerable to all manner of diseases, and an epidemic can wipe out an entire herd in a few days. She and Dennis and the kids wear designated "fair shoes" for the duration of the fair, disinfecting the soles every night with bleach, and will sell their hogs after the auction on Thursday night rather than risk bringing a disease back to the farm.

The hogs jump down from the lip of the trailer and trot down the aisle on forelegs that seem too short, swaying their heavy heads in that peculiar Captain Bligh gait. The first to reach the scales, the Terminator, weighs in at 294 pounds.

"Got to reject her, Bridget," jokes the guy doing the weighing. "Not big enough!"

At the fair, bulk itself is a virtue, but the reality of the market is that packers like Hormel pay less for hogs that exceed their set weight limits. Bridget was astonished last year when the judge awarded Grand Champion to a blimp of a hog that went on to flunk the carcass competition. "You should've seen him. He was so fat he could barely walk."

The boys steer their hogs down another aisle of pens to the Burr Oak Beavers section, where they'll spend the next few days, two to a pen, snuffling through fresh sawdust. The surnames above the pens—Sheehan, Clark, Griffin, O'Connell, Williams—read like a list of ushers at St. Bridget's. The O'Neills are the only ones in their 4-H club who raise hogs commercially; the others, mostly dairy farmers, buy a few piglets each year for their children to raise for the fair because they're an easier project than a Holstein heifer. Across the top of the pens are boards that hold brushes, feed, and water bowls. Bridget hands Shawn a plant mister. "They need some H-two-O, dearie." Hogs can't sweat to cool off, which is why they wallow in mud, so the boys take turns spraying them with the mister. When he's finished, Shawn climbs into the pen and lies against his two barrows as if they were bean bags.

After the hogs have been fed a ration of ground corn and soybeans, we stroll down the midway to get a snack ourselves. So much of a fair's attraction involves eating, and, as with the thrill rides, comfort is not the object. The choices include Chicago-style dogs, chili dogs, beer brats, corn dogs, foot longs, Polish sausages, pizza, tacos, gyros, fajitas, chicken wings, cheeseburgers, and a lethal-looking sandwich called an Italian beef bomber. Walking between food concessions on the left side of the street and livestock barns on the right entails a kind of balancing act between a person's hunger and the knowledge that one set of odors makes the other possible. We head straight for the Olmsted County Pork Producers trailer and order barbecue rib-ticklers, sharing a picnic table with another Burr Oak Beavers family. While the kids squirm to get to the rides, their parents know there will be three more days of this.

"I just love Four-H," the man says with less than enthusiasm.

"You look wore out," Bridget tells him.

He's propped his head up with both hands and stares across the table at her T-shirt. "Say, Bridget, what does that shirt say?"

She folds her arms across her chest. "It says Irish girls are humble."

While everybody else goes off for cotton candy, I wander over to Graham Arena, a hockey rink doubling this week as a 4-H exhibit hall. The displays are a cross between a science fair and a rummage sale: woodworking projects, homemade dresses, canned jams, model airplanes, instructions for building a pond, and the usual cornucopia of limp vegetables. Do children still do these things? The ribbons had been awarded earlier that morning. Patrick won a blue for a suet bird feeder made out of chicken wire that is simplicity itself. ("Tools needed—pliers.") Shawn took a red for "Trees of My Backyard," and Kelly, who's a Cloverbud—a junior division of 4-H—won a green ribbon for a refrigerator-door magnet. There is a sweet optimism to these projects, as if most of life's problems could be resolved with pliers and a little gumption. My favorite exhibit of all is an illustrated report entitled "My Cat Had Ring Worm."

The 4-H program (head, heart, hands, health), which began in the boom years before World War I as corn-growing clubs for boys and canning clubs for girls, was conceived as a means of disseminating agricultural information. Farmers are unique among businessmen in believing that innovations should be shared with neighbors rather than hoarded. As the organization evolved, it came under the extension services run by state colleges and administered by the U.S. Department of Agriculture. But it's largely a volunteer program, with the family as its organizational model rather than the military or corporation. Unlike scouting, 4-H has no uniforms, ranks, or funny handshakes. The emphasis is on work rather than play. Even the roster of clubs—Burr Oak Beavers, Pleasant Grove Producers, Maple Leaf Wonder Workers, Hickory Hill Hustlers, Eyota Willing Workers—promotes the old-fashioned notion of work as its own reward.

It's dark by the time I get back to the swine barn. The hogs are bedded down and the day's heat has gathered inside the metal building. The older kids sitting in lawn chairs outside the stalls look indistinguishable from their city counterparts and wear the same haircuts and rock-concert T-shirts, which may be the leveling effect of television or the simple fact that teenagers want to look alike. Their parents, those who grew up in the era of school consolidation, remember when the lines were more sharply drawn. Finished with chores, Patrick and Shawn stand outside peering through the cracks in the high wooden fence surrounding the speedway, where a trotting race is in progress. Above the fence looms the neon blur of Ferris Wheel and Zipper, and the whole glittering skyline of the midway.

THE NEXT MORNING I drive with Dennis and the boys to the Hormel buying station, a small white building on the backside of Chatfield, and herd eight hogs from the trailer into a wooden pen worn smooth by the passage of swine. These are the fair rejects—lightweights that are too light, gilts with bad nipple placement—hogs that didn't make the team. The floor of the pen is a giant scale. In an adjacent room, the buyer moves a counterweight along a calibrated bar until the bar levels off at 2,064 pounds, or 258 pounds per pig.

"What are these, fair hogs?"

Shawn nods and points out a roan hog named Jaws. "That one bites."

"We'll send him to the dentist."

The buyer docks Dennis a couple dollars per hundred weight because his hogs are eight pounds heavier than Hormel's ideal hog. "Forty-five dollars a hundred weight," he says, handing Dennis the check. "Not bad."

"It's already spent."

We drive west along the Root River on Highway 30, passing through a rain shower that will delay Dennis's plans for another cutting of alfalfa, until we reach the grain elevator at Stewartville. Dennis buys soybean meal, hog wormer, salt pellets, and four hundred pounds of sow concentrate pellets in fifty-pound sacks that we heave into the trailer. Each hog goes through four different ration plans from birth to market.

He and Bridget keep track of the feed costs, gestation periods, and litter size on a computer program called PigChamp developed by the University of Minnesota. The thousand pigs they'll sell this year represent a tiny fraction of the hogs slaughtered every single day in this country. To survive today's marketplace, small hog farmers like Dennis and Bridget must manage their herds intensely and sell their own labor dirt-cheap.

Raising hogs has traditionally been a "mortgage buster" for farmers because of the opportunities for profit. In the last ten years, however, half of the producers have quit as the business undergoes the process of *poultrification*, which is to say that hog farming is following in the same steps that transformed the chicken business from a barnyard of pullets on ten thousand farms to an industry dominated by a few large producers supplying the Colonel Sanderses of the world. In many cases, they are the same corporations. Tyson Foods—which revolutionized the chicken business through a strategy of vertical integration—controlling both production and processing—is the fourth-largest hog producer in the country and recently bought its own hog-packing plant. Murphy Family Farms of North Carolina, the nation's number-one hog producer, owns 180,000 sows, which means they market three and a half million hogs a year. Hog production has historically concentrated in the corn belt, but the current trend is to build mechanized farrowing units and packaging plants in the South and Southwest, where there are fewer anti–corporate farming laws. Instead of buying hogs on the open market, many of these corporations either contract out with farmers, who have no control over production and no share in profits, or else raise hogs themselves in great, mechanized confinement buildings overseen by technicians. Such plants are rightly called factory farms because they take their cue from the assembly line rather than the hog yard with its mud and stink. While the entire history of American agriculture has been a movement toward fewer and larger farms, the future promises to be its apogee: farming without farmers—indeed, without farms.

"Half the big farmers in this country do very little physical work," Dennis says as he loads feed sacks. "They're sitting in front of a computer watching what figures come out of the Chicago Board of Trade. There's a guy down in Spring Valley. He owns building sites but no land. He hires men to manage the farrowing and feeding. One of the largest hog operations in the country is in Colorado. That's *all* it is. Buildings. They have twenty-five to thirty thousand sows. They got a water-treatment plant that makes the one in Rochester look like peanuts. It's all a game, and we don't get to make the rules."

With the trailer loaded, Dennis circles a parking lot down the street where farm machinery has been assembled for an upcoming auction. He's looking for a Massey-Ferguson to add to his antique tractor collection, which includes a 30 Massey Harris and a 101 Jr. Massey Harris. Besides old machinery, Dennis has an abiding interest in family history and we often trade bits of information like "Did you know that Catherine Esmond O'Neill had red hair?" or "Did my dad ever tell you how as a kid he sneaked up on a KKK rally right here in Marion?" His interest stems in part from knowing that the family's continuation in farming, the unbroken link binding them to the same land their great-grandparents worked, rests largely upon his shoulders and, in the future, those of his children. When his grandfather John O'Neill was born, half the population of the United States made a living on farms, and now, only a couple of generations later, it's less than 2 percent and still falling. Nobody wants to be the last farmer.

As we head out of Stewartville, rows of corn strum past the window like spokes on a wheel. We recross the Root River and, just before the road ducks under I-90, Dennis waves toward a farmhouse. "Bridget was raised there. That's another farm the eighties did in."

DENNIS ENLISTED in the Marines the year he graduated from high school and a year after his cousin, also a Marine, returned from Da Nang. But the war was winding down and he served his hitch programming computers in south Philadelphia, not far from where his great-grandmother had worked as a domestic. When he got out of the service, he farmed with Ed until a dispute arose one evening and the partnership dissolved in a few words hurled over the stanchions. He was hired as a fireman in Rochester and spent his off days farming rented land west of Simpson. The land bordered the Brennan farm, and sometimes one of the daughters, a girl he'd seen growing up at church, came out to visit or ride along on the tractor. Bridget was ten years younger but knew what she wanted, and that included farming. She got Dennis's attention by riding her motorcycle past his house and popping wheelies. At her senior prom he was the oldest person other than the chaperones. After a few dances, he said, "Let's get out of here and get some beer." When they married, everyone said how lucky he was to find a young woman who didn't mind running a hog farm while her husband waited around the station for something to catch fire.

Dennis and Bridget bought their ranch house and fifty acres in Marion on a contract for deed. When the seller got into trouble in the farm crisis of the 1980s, he turned the contract over to Farm Credit Services, which turned out to be a stroke of luck, since they stretched the balloon payment out another ten years. Besides the home place, Dennis farms another 150 acres of cropland, half in corn and the rest divided among soybeans, oats, and alfalfa. Everything goes to feed their hogs except the soybeans, which they sell to offset the cost of soybean meal. Dennis grows the crops while Bridget manages the hogs, and they both work outside jobs.

THE MORNING of the judging, Dennis and the boys are at the swine barn six hours after having left it the night before. They've changed into dress shirts and stiff new blue jeans. Most of the kids are in the pens, brushing their hogs, cleaning their hooves, patting their bristled backs with baby powder. Some of the younger exhibitors are sword-fighting with the riding crops they'll use to direct their hogs in the ring. Huddled in a corner, Dennis quizzes Shawn.

"What's your pig's date of birth?"

"March thirteenth."

"What's he weigh?"

"Two hundred and seventy-two."

"What's his rate of gain?"

"Two point fourteen pounds a day."

"What breed?"

Shawn hesitates, looks at the floor. "Babcock?"

The science of judging livestock seems as mysterious and prone to quackery as phrenology, as judges attempt, by sight and touch, to divine how a living animal will look when it is flayed and quartered. The dairy competition the day before had been slow and methodical, the judge walking down a row of Holsteins turned out for inspection, lifting a tail to check one's haunches, stooping to check the set of her udders. The swine judging, by contrast, is pure chaos. A dozen or more youngsters swarm into the ring, attempting to steer their pigs past the judge with swats from their riding crops. From the bleachers, it's like watching a break shot in billiards, hogs of many hues zigzagging around the ring in an uncontrolled chain reaction. Two lightweight barrows square off with an ear-piercing squeal like a power drill on sheet metal. The judge, a slouching man with thick, pursed lips, keeps his head low, taking a hard look at the hogs while avoiding eye contact with their owners, who stare up at his impassive face for some clue. With a slight nod or a gesture, he makes his initial selection and directs a hog at a time into ten holding pens on the side of the ring. Shawn and his roan barrow have become invisible. The judge looks over, around, and through them until a single pen remains unfilled. Shawn and three other youngsters cake-walk around the ring until the judge gives the final nod to a girl's brindled hog, and that's that.

Before determining the order of blue ribbons, the judge explains why the others were eliminated. Shawn's barrow, he says, was "a little loose in the jowls, gives certain indications of . . ." His voice is lost in the reverberations of the PA system.

Parents at a 4-H livestock judging are as involved as any screaming fans in the bleachers of a Little League championship but less inclined to outbursts, since they are also the coaches; and though most parents don't expect their children to play in the majors someday, not a few here hope their kids will take over the family farm. Bridget, who's been videotaping from the bleachers, goes over the decision with Dennis.

"He never looked at the judge once."

"I don't think he knew who the judge was."

The lightweight barrows are released back into the ring to determine their ranking. Stalking flat-footed around the ring, paunch out, the judge prods the side of one hog with his thumb or lays his hand on another's rump to check for excess fat. He assigns them to the numbered pens according to their rank, beginning with tenth place and ending with only the grand champion still in the ring. He seems fussy but also willing to correct a mistake, shifting hogs from one pen to another to rearrange the order. When he takes the mike to deliver his summations, his language is formal and post-modernist; he could be deconstructing a painting by de Kooning instead of assessing a hog's back fat. "When you look at this particular hog, he shows some good expression of muscle and substance of bone. And while I like this other pig's width, he gives some indication, frame-wise, that he's about as big as he's going to get."

Patrick and Shawn both go into the ring to show their heavyweight barrows in the final set of competition. Shawn is more diligent this time at keeping his hog before the judge, who, nevertheless, manages to turn his back every time the boys sail past him. Then the curtain of invisibility parts for the Terminator and the judge sends Patrick's pig into a pen. Five youngsters remain in the ring, then four. Shawn is still treading water. Only a few pens remain unfilled. At last the judge gives Shawn's barrow the nod, assuring both boys a blue ribbon. Dennis, watching from the floor, takes off his cap, sweeps his hand over his hair, replaces the cap. "Now I can breathe easier."

THE CLIMAX of any county fair is the livestock auction on the final night. All the ribbons have been awarded and what remains is the business of farming. Like the stock-car races, it is a life-and-death ritual, though the life that's given up is not one's own. The tearful farewell between a youngster and his prize heifer remains a kind of bar mitzvah for farm kids, a rite of passage into the particular world of their parents.

After last year's auction, as the hogs were being loaded, rumors circulated in the swine barn that an animal-rights group was on its way. Improbable scenarios quickly came to mind. The protesters would link arms and blockade the Hormel truck. They would wear pig masks and throw whipped-cream pies at the fair queen. They would interject their bodies between the truckers' cattle prods and set the squealing hogs loose in the streets of Rochester to awaken the great, troubled conscience of a changing city. But they never showed up.

The progression of farm animals from birth to slaughter

was once a cycle as familiar as the change of seasons, but it is an idea with which we have become increasingly uncomfortable. What had seemed a good way to live now strikes many as unconscionably cruel. Even state agricultural agents advise farmers to be evasive about the ultimate end of their livestock by substituting the word "processed" for "slaughtered." But if farmers are tight-mouthed about the life and death of their animals, other voices aren't.

I once intended to write a book about the animal-rights movement because it raises questions that anyone who spends time on a farm eventually asks: What are our connections to these animals? What are our obligations to them? But the activists I met were less interested in the connections between humans and animals than in the expiation of a free-floating guilt. Many were reasonable enough, but others just seemed sad cases, brutalized themselves in some way, and overly morbid. They viewed animals as the deserving poor, which is not the same thing as viewing them with affection. I eventually tired of the latest fur protest, the latest rally for animals, the gloomy parades of protesters marching down city streets in black robes and skull masks as in some ritualized Feast of the Dead. It was all too depressing.

The last such spectacle I attended was the rescue of a lamb (it's always a lamb) during a 4-H livestock auction in Wisconsin. The organizer of the protest was a skinny, energetic woman in her forties who sat behind a table at the Kenosha County Fair handing out pamphlets on veal calves and animal testing. Her table was between a palm reader and a company that sold kitchen tiles, and she had borrowed some tiles to keep her pamphlets from blowing away in the breeze. She wore a MEAT STINKS button on her tanktop, and when kids walked by wagging hamburgers at her, she gulled them with a long, withering stare.

"Most of the stuff you buy in the grocery store is from factory farms. I personally wouldn't eat the meat from any farm. I wouldn't eat an animal that's been tortured from the day it was born to the day it's slaughtered."

She had lost all sentimental notions about farming after seeing a documentary film about chicks raised in a broiler factory. She saw no difference between the slash-and-burn agriculture in Brazil and the surrounding dairy farms, while the only connection I could see between rain forests and mid-western farms was that both were disappearing acts. Her pamphlets had been supplied by PETA (People for the Ethical Treatment of Animals), which had targeted 4-H livestock auctions that summer. One of their flyers, "Farm Projects Can Be Psychologically Damaging," reworked a study by Margaret Mead which found that adult criminals often had childhood histories of violence to animals to suggest that a similar pathology was at work at the 4-H clubs. "While selling an animal to be eaten is commonly socially 'approved' and watching an animal be tortured is not, the events have similar damaging effects on the developing psyche."

At the livestock auction that afternoon, a contingent of young protesters in MEAT STINKS hats sat beside the fair queen and her court, each group amused to be sitting next to the other. At first, nothing seemed to go right. A television crew, alerted to the protest, left before the sheep auction began. Then the activists' buyer forgot the cowboy hat and boots he'd been instructed to wear, but nobody knew he was a protester anyway. When he made the highest bid on a black-faced Suffolk ewe named Bumbles, the audience applauded just as they had for all the others. The protesters waved their hats and raced to see the sheep they had saved. They caught up with Bumbles as she was being led away by her thirteen-year-old former owner. "The sheep you raised is not going to be slaughtered," the buyer said in a portentous voice. The boy looked confused. They tossed him a MEAT STINKS hat and told him to put it on so they could take a picture. He tossed it back and disappeared into the sheep barn. Later, wandering among the labyrinth of pens, the woman who had organized the protest grew alarmed. "Where is she? I can't find her," she said. "Which one is ours?"

We found Bumbles at the end of the barn with her pen mate, another Suffolk. An older boy, not the former owner, sat in front of the pen with his arms crossed. The woman picked up some straw and reached over the gate.

"Don't feed the sheep!" the boy barked. "They don't eat straw!"

When I telephoned the next day, the woman was terribly upset. During the night, she said, a person "or persons" had spray-painted something on Bumbles's side. What was it? I asked. There was a pause on the other end. "Eat Me." (At first I thought she said, "Eat Meat," a message with fewer levels of meaning.) The barn supervisor had discovered it that morning and shorn the words off the sheep's coat, but they seemed permanently etched into the woman's mind. I suggested that whoever had done this might have felt insulted by the protest, but she dismissed this explanation. It was obvious, she said, that the kids were angry only because the sheep wasn't going to be murdered.

At the Olmsted County Fair livestock auction, bidders don't purchase the animal itself, just the ribbon. Hogs are too unruly to make personal appearances, so the youngster stands in the center of the ring holding his ribbon while the auctioneer speed-talks into the microphone and the crowd appears to be bidding not for the pig but for its owner. Most of the bidders are banks or implement dealers who buy the ribbons as a public-relations gesture, and the size of the bid depends less on how a child's animal ranked in the judging than on the amount of business his parents generate. The auctioneer begins high and, if the bids aren't forthcoming, starts over again, coaxing the price up while his assistants scan the bleachers, shouting "Yep!" and slapping their hands together to register each bid. When the gavel falls, there's a round of applause as much for the man fronting the money as for the kid walking back to the swine barn. Disappointment, if it comes, is more often the result of a low bid than the thought of saying good-bye to one's boon companion.

Patrick's ribbon for his heavyweight barrow, the Terminator, is bought by Olstad Implements of Chatfield, where Dennis buys most of his equipment. When Shawn takes his place in the ring, he holds two blue ribbons in one hand and keeps the other hand in his pocket. Stock cars are racing at the speedway next door, so the bidding is momentarily lost in the roar of cars rounding the nearest turn. Bids see-saw between Olstad Implements and Zumbrota Livestock Barn, but the winner, at $235, is the All-American Co-op at Stewartville. I stay on through the hot August night, and the moment I'll remember best is watching a girl in a black-and-white riding outfit grow flushed and teary-eyed as the clamor of bidding rose around her, not so much for her hog, whose fate was sealed, but for herself, knowing that the bids were a form of personal endorsement, and she smiled through the tears like a bride whose wedding gown is pinned with money.

After the auction, a stock truck blocks the entrance to the swine barn and I have to go around the back. Inside, the hogs bound for Hormel have been marked with spray paint—blue for gilts, mauve for barrows—in patches like great bruises. The livestock haulers smack winners and losers alike out of their pens and toward the waiting truck. Patrick, who has seen this before, watches from the doorway, but Shawn doesn't understand why he isn't loading his own hogs.

"That's okay," Bridget says, holding him back. "They'll handle it."

The boys and I walk around back and climb onto the roof of Dennis's hog trailer to watch the stock car races over the fence. The grandstand across the speedway is ablaze in lights, but the stretch of track closest to the fence is unlit and the cars bore through the darkness. It's too dark to see the drivers, so the cars themselves seem alive as they roar past, angry or aggrieved, depending on the pitch of their manifolds. We return to the swine barn to find the load-out nearly completed. Among the last to go is the Terminator, who, seeing the ramp, doubles back squealing until a hauler holding a wooden panel blocks his escape and turns him around. The hauler slams the door shut, and we watch the rear lights of the stock truck fade into the night.

TEN

After supper I like to stand on the deck and watch the kids jump on a trampoline set into the lawn between the old farmhouse and the folks' place. Tonight it's hard to tell which two are mine, since they're wearing clothes their cousins wore last summer. Up and down they vault like pistons against a blue sky turning black. When I call them inside, they pretend not to hear—such is the lure of weightlessness, of escaping even for a moment the downward pull of gravity.

"Got a minute?" Steve calls from the other side of the lawn. "I want to show you something."

His voice seems disembodied in the dark, coming as it does from a glowing cigarette tip and the outline of a gray sweatshirt. I follow him around to the other side of the farmhouse, where the lawn abruptly falls away to the lower pasture and ghostly cattle graze alongside the creek. We stop beside the west wing. It's the oldest part of the house, and all that was standing when Catherine Esmond O'Neill moved onto the place in 1880. It's where she died fifty years later. Shut off for a generation, the west wing has atrophied into hillbillydom, with sparrow nests behind the window screens and a two-by-four propping up the front porch roof.

"Now just watch." He points the glowing cigarette at the roof peak, but I can't see anything except bare patches where the shingles are gone. A dark scrap of something tears away from the roof and sails into the greater blackness. Then another and another, like shingles flying off in a windstorm.

"One night Deb and I sat out here on lawn chairs and counted sixty-two bats fly out of there. They live in the spaces between the eaves. Them and the squirrels and whatever else can wriggle inside. Last summer Deb was changing the sheets on our bed and almost tripped over a four-foot bull snake that had wintered over between the walls." Steve takes a long drag on the cigarette. "This whole place is falling down."

WHEN ED and Fran bought a two-bedroom ranch house and moved it onto the farm after the last of their children had moved away, they deeded the old farmhouse and five acres to Deb and Steve. The exchange made perfect sense. The folks got a resident handyman and someone to keep an eye on the cattle when they went out of town; the Raduenzes got a big, drafty house and a whole farm for their three children to roam. In its long history, the farm had never been childless for long; another generation was always in the wings, learning to drive the machines and raise the animals and just generally wait their turn. But unforeseen strings came with the house as well. Steve passed up promotions at work that would have meant moving to a store in another part of the state. Between his work and Deb's job at the clinic, they easily logged a hundred hours a week, and all they had to show for it was a hand-me-down house with a leaky roof and an extended family that watched their every move.

Last Thanksgiving we were sleeping in the folks' guest room when I awoke to a flashlight beam in my face and Ed shouting to get up. It was two o'clock in the morning. While I dressed he explained that Deb and the kids had fled the house after smelling smoke in their bedrooms. Now she was worried that Steve, who had stayed behind to look for the fire, might have been overcome by smoke. Throwing on a coat and boots, I crunched across the frozen lawn to the farmhouse. The kitchen was wreathed in smoke, and Steve was nowhere to be found. Then I heard him call from the cellar. He had the cowling off the furnace and was tinkering inside it. There was no fire. Leaking fuel oil had burned out the furnace motor and blown black smoke through the heating ducts upstairs. "If it wasn't this," he sighed, "it'd be something else." We spent the next hour hauling cord wood from the barn to a wood stove in the cellar to keep the pipes from freezing.

After the furnace died, Deb began to broach the idea of tearing down the farmhouse and replacing it with a new, modular home. The place was hers, free and clear, but she sought a consensus from her sisters. Most of them agreed or said nothing, since the house was a wreck and clearly needed either major renovation or a wrecking ball. But every time Deb even hinted at demolition, Sharon argued for restoring the house to its past glory. If it was her house, she'd gut it down to the studs, put in new wiring, and get rid of the paneling and cosmetic repairs the house had endured for decades. She'd hire a contractor to replace the roof and tuck-point the crumbling foundation. She'd nail up trellises and replant Grandma's morning glories and hydrangeas. Why, it wouldn't cost any more than building a new house and instead of some crackerjack box of a split-level, they'd have a classic prairie farmhouse, a family heirloom.

"Yeah," Deb said, "but we'd still have an *old* house!"

Their arguments kept missing each other, because they followed different trajectories. One was talking history and the other economics, as if they shared no common ground. An ice age descended between the two sisters, a cooling of relations in which criticisms were subtly masked within helpful suggestions and the true nature of the disagreement was never voiced.

The final decision on the house belonged to the bank,

which wouldn't loan money for a new house until the well passed inspection. Drilled sometime in the thirties, the well went down 183 feet to tap water flowing through joints, fractures, and solutions cavities in the underlying limestone. Pour a glass of water from the kitchen sink and it swirls with a snowstorm of dissolved rock. The first time Steve took a water sample in to be tested, it contained thirteen milligrams of nitrates per liter, only three milligrams more than the level accepted by the Environmental Protection Agency.

The nitrates were traces of fertilizer and manure that had percolated through the fields and into the groundwater. Water in the Jordan aquifer underlying southeastern Minnesota takes thirty-six years on average to penetrate the dense quartzose sandstone, but in the karst topography beneath the farm, rain or meltwater can travel through cracks and fissures in the porous limestone and into the well within a matter of minutes. Steve took the first sample in April after runoff quickly flushed nitrates into the water table. When the new test results came back in September, the well easily passed inspection.

After the bank approved the loan, Deb and Steve ordered a modular home from a manufacturer in Waseca, and the concern of the rest of the family shifted from the farmhouse to the loan itself; if it was ever defaulted, the bank would probably subdivide the property. "Now honestly, Steve," the loan officer asked as he handed over the check, "how many houses could you fit onto that five acres?"

The day Steve drove to Waseca to make the down payment, Sharon walked over to the farmhouse to return some dishes.

"So you're really taking the plunge?"

That set Deb off. She was sick and tired of older sisters butting into her affairs, telling her what to do with her house, her life. The bickering shifted from architecture to personalities. As Sharon stormed back across the lawn, Deb's son Joey called after her, "You're not taking our five acres!"

The final step was finding someone to demolish the farm-house so the modular home could be moved onto the property before winter. When two Amish men came into Fleet Farm, Steve cornered them in the hardware section and asked if they'd be interested in the job. The men, who looked like the Smith brothers in their youth, had recently torn down two houses in Stewartville for salvage. They said they'd have to talk the job over with an elder. A week later, a gray-bearded patriarch came into the store, and Steve asked what the lumber might be worth to him. The old man smiled and said it usually went the other way around. They might drive buggies and wear broad-brimmed hats, but they didn't work for nothing. Anyway, he wasn't much interested in old farmhouses. Salvaging hand-sawn boards and pulling square nails was too much trouble. "You really earn every board," he said, then left.

Time was running out. In another two months the ground would be covered with snow. The chief of the Rochester Fire Department drove out to look the boxy, white farmhouse over as a potential training exercise. "Okay," he said. "We'll burn it down."

ARRAYED ON the grass beside the trampoline as if for a yard sale are stuffed chairs, boxes of clothing, a sofa, an upright piano, stoneware crocks, a musty carton of agricultural yearbooks and western novels, a console TV, the trunk to a 1936 Ford touring sedan, and a pie cupboard. Maybe it's the unseasonably warm October weather or the inevitability of the move, but there's been a thaw in the glacial epoch between sisters. Deb is packing kitchen utensils into cardboard boxes while Sharon carries up crates of Mason jars from the cellar to be loaded onto the pickup truck for storage in the haymow and granary. Slowly the farmhouse yields up its burden of the past. The wildlife prints that hung in the living room are propped against a dusty box of religious pictures they replaced—two distant views of paradise. As family members step forward to claim things, there's the same sense of dispersion one feels at auctions when a house's belongings are scattered among strangers. When Ed says, "I wish I had a nickel for every time I had to fill that damn wood box," it's hard to tell whether he wants the thing back.

The fire department won't torch the house until the end of the month. In the meantime, Steve wants to tear down the old west wing to excavate a basement before the ground freezes. He has already dismantled the front porch and chain-sawed a jagged line through the roof to sever the wing from the rest of the house. This should have been done years ago but now seems redundant, like amputating a limb after the patient has been diagnosed as terminal. The wing has been closed off for years and smells dusty and rank inside. There are bat turds on the floor and a ring of brown paint around the edges, as if the painter hadn't bothered to take up the rug. The wallpaper is silver rosettes against a light-blue background. When I try to picture Catherine Esmond O'Neill dying in this room, all that comes to mind is the wallpaper.

I pry up the mop boards with a wizard bar, then smash through plaster and lathe to the studs. When the studs are exposed, Steve slips an iron bar attached to a logging chain behind a sill on the south wall and hooks the other end to the back of the tractor. Ed slowly pulls the Ford 7700 forward until the chain draws tight. A lace curtain flutters in the upstairs window. As the south wall groans and buckles, hundreds of walnut shells spill from beneath the eaves, followed by an ominous, high-pitched screeching.

The second floor has tilted forward, but one end is snagged against the north wall. Unhooking the logging chain, Ed circles around to the other side of the house and inserts the iron bar against the sill. Then we all stand clear as he remounts the tractor and prepares to finish it off. In all the discussion over the farmhouse, Ed has said nothing either way. And to watch him methodically going about its destruction, you would hardly guess that this is the place where he was born.

The tractor pulls ahead and the north wall collapses in a wave of stale air and dust. As the roof pitches forward onto the lawn, small brown bats tumble from its nooks and crannies. They lie stunned on the grass, blinking in the harsh sunlight or hobbling grotesquely across the lawn on leathery wings. The dog pounces on several before we can call him off. Reviving, the bats flap into the air, weaving through sunlit columns of dust, scattering us with their low, erratic flight. A whirlwind of bats. Disoriented, some alight in the blazing yellow branches of walnut trees while others continue to circle aimlessly above the splintered wreckage of the house.

"IT SEEMS to me we always had a horse," Ed says as he sweeps up the cards and shuffles. "The only time we didn't was after I got rid of Blue. He was over in the hollow with the cows and he couldn't eat anymore."

We're playing five hundred around the kitchen table. Cards fly out in cardinal directions until each of us has a hand that opens like a fan. Sharon inkles diamonds. Fran passes. I bid a cautious seven diamonds, but Ed takes the blind with a bid of eight hearts. He must have picked up some good cards in the blind because he's drawn his shoulders up, cocked his head to one side, and done this thing where he wiggles his chin.

"Then came Bun," he says. "I know when I bought her. Nineteen fifty-five. It was so damn hot. I couldn't get her bred, so I took her over to Harvey Smith's. He had a nice palomino. He tried everything to breed her, but he couldn't. Then I got Blaze."

"No," Sharon interrupts, "then we got Dilly. Now that was a horse with a hard mouth! She bit all of us and had this trick of moving to one side when you tried to mount her. What was the name of the spotted stallion that bred Dilly?"

"I know it. I just can't remember it."

"Lucky Strike," says Fran.

"That's it," Sharon continues. "Anyway, out of Dilly and Lucky Strike came Donamingo. And Donamingo was the stallion we bred with Blaze."

"She had some quarter horse in her," says Ed. "She was a hackamore horse, but we used a bridle on her."

"No. I used a hackamore on Blaze. We bred her with Donamingo to get Daiquiri."

"There's another horse that was so damn pretty but useless."

"I tried to break her," says Sharon, "but she was just green broke. Really skittish. You couldn't trust her."

"Mrs. Coltier tried to break her and Daiquiri broke her leg. She had a riding stable and thought she could handle any horse. She fell off and got her foot caught in the stirrup and Daiquiri dragged her around the corral several times."

Ed lays the queen of hearts, hoping in vain to flush the left bower. "Come on," he says, "where is it? Frances, are you holding out on me?"

"I haven't got it."

Sharon goes back to horses. "Blaze had another colt. Dobie. I remember watching him being born in the orchard. He was my horse. I raised him and I broke him. He was the last."

Even I remember Dobie. He had run with the cattle so long he probably forgot that he was a horse. Some mornings you'd find him stretched out on the lawn like a dog. He seemed ancient by then, the sole survivor of some vanished race, and now even he's gone.

Ed lays the ten of hearts. Sharon trumps it with the left bower and then sets her parents by taking the next two tricks.

"Christ O'Friday! You were supposed to have that bower, Frances."

"Why should *I* have it? I wasn't the one who bid eight hearts!"

Sharon sweeps up the cards and shuffles for another hand.

"So when did Blue die?" Ed asks himself. "By God, I figure Blue was thirty-two when I got rid of him. He had rheumatism and his hooves had turned up, and when he tried to eat grass it just ran down the side of his muzzle. I didn't want to shoot him, so I sold him to Vince Lily, who probably sold him for fox meat."

Blue had been Ed's pony when he was growing up. One of the places he would ride was to a tar-paper shack south of the farm to visit a friend. The boy owned a spotted roan with one milky eye, "moon-blind" they called it, and all summer the two rode their horses together, swam in the Root River and smoked cornsilk cigarettes. A few weeks ago Ed attended the man's funeral and stopped to offer condolences to his friend's aged mother.

"Do you remember me?" he asked the old woman.

"I should, but I don't."

"I'm Ed. Eddie O'Neill."

"My God, that little boy? I never expected you'd live the way you rode that horse."

ELEVEN

On a June morning in his ninth summer, Ed O'Neill crossed the yard from the farmhouse to the new barn in a buff-colored cowboy hat and boots that scuffed against the worn surface of limestone. Already the day was heating up, and the barn felt cool inside and smelled of fresh timbers. He could hear the horses chuffing in their stalls. Taking a bridle down from the hook, he slipped it over Blue's head and led the horse to the first stall, the narrowest because it shared the staircase leading to the haymow. He tied the reins to the gate and dragged his saddle a step at a time up the staircase until he was high enough to drop it on the horse's back. Then he walked into the stall and reached under the horse's belly to fasten the cinch. Not much bigger than a pony, Blue stood fourteen hands high and weighed 950 pounds. His mother was a bucking horse bought from a rodeo, mean and ornery as they come, her history written in overlapping brands that covered her flanks. She produced a good colt each year for three years before she died, and Blue was the last. In summer he was a strawberry roan, but every spring, after shedding his winter coat, he turned a storm-cloud blue.

The boy led the saddled horse into the sunlight where his older brother and sister were already mounted, reining their horses to hold them still. His father inspected the boy's outfit and checked the cinch. He himself wore a tall white sombrero crimped in the center, a new shirt, and a red silk kerchief knotted at his throat, all special-ordered from Stockman's Supply of Denver, Colorado. He was not a tall man but he carried himself erect, and when he mounted Prince, an enormous bay done up with a martingale, he looked like a figure on a statue. Ed reached for the saddle horn, turned the stirrup to place his left foot in it, then swung onto the horse. His mother had said good-bye earlier but now rushed out to the front porch, followed by his grandmother, stooped and ancient-looking in her black dress and apron, to wave as the riders trotted down the driveway, passed under the shade of the box elder, and turned north on the county road.

At the property line, they turned west and climbed the sandy road that bordered Sheehan's pasture, still steaming from the heavy rains the night before. John O'Neill rode first on Prince, a coiled lariat hanging from his saddle on a pommel strap. Next came pretty, dark-haired Theresa wearing her father's goatskin chaps and riding a bay gelding named Brownie. Then Ed, a foot shorter than the others even when he was mounted. Jim brought up the rear on Arizona Al, a chestnut stallion that had sired both Blue and Brownie, so the group riding to town that morning was family in more ways than one.

Their saddles creaked as the country rose and fell beneath them. Skirting the old Dubuque Trail, they crested a hill and descended into a wooded swale, splashing across a muddy stream swollen over the road from last night's rains. They turned north again to cross Willow Creek Bridge and trotted past white farmhouses and fields of blue-green corn. When the pavement began, the horses' hooves made a hollow sound against it as the highway zigzagged past the Poor Farm and Pinewood School. An automobile whooshed by, and Ed tightened the reins. More cars passed them, all going in the same direction. The fields fell away as they reached the outskirts of Rochester and turned west on Twelfth Street toward the fairgrounds. The traffic grew heavier still as cars streamed into the city for its diamond jubilee.

On Second Street between Third and Fourth Avenues, the riders took their place in line with the floats and people waiting for the parade to begin. Cecil Remington, who ran a riding academy and looked resplendent in a spotless white jersey and pants, joined the O'Neills. Everyone else looked as if they'd stepped out of a post-office mural. Ahead of them, Ed could see a knight on a white horse, soldiers in blue and gray uniforms, trappers and hunters in buckskins, Indians with long black hair braided down their backs, faces painted for war. Behind was a cyclist on a high-wheeled velocipede, a float depicting victims of the cyclone of 1888, another bearing veterans of the Spanish-American War. Some of the participants waited on horseback, like themselves; others stood around smoking cigarettes and talking. The boy, who did not consider himself in costume, was enthralled by the scene, which was how he might have imagined the Last Judgment, the dead of all time milling around the Pearly Gates, waiting to explain themselves.

The midday heat filtered down through the elms shading the street and onto the brick pavement. Ed felt his head cooking under his cowboy hat. Sweat dripped down his face. He'd had nothing to drink since before they left the farm, when he had leaned over the horse tank to sip cool water from the spigot. A boy his age walked past licking an ice-cream cone, and on the next block Ed could see the concession stand. Nudging his horse forward, he asked his father for a nickel to buy a cone.

"Forget it!" his father said from his great height. "You're supposed to be a cowboy today. And cowboys don't eat ice cream cones!"

His father took horsemanship very seriously. When Ed was first learning to ride, he would climb onto a horse's back just to enjoy the rocking motion of the saddle and the elevated view of the world it afforded—so much land spread out before him! One day he trailed a team of workhorses his father was using to grade the road in front of their house, when the boy's horse threw back its ears and flew off at a gallop. The reins hung too low to reach and the horse wouldn't stop. Finally his father stepped in front of the runaway, and Ed went sailing over the horse's head. He landed in the soft dirt, unhurt but wailing. His father promptly lifted him back into the saddle and said, "Now ride."

Drums rolled and at last the parade started to move. A parade marshal spaced the floats and riders so they wouldn't collide as they marched up Second Street. At First Avenue they turned south past the Chicago Northwest Railway depot and then east on Fourth Street, winding through the downtown. Turning north on Broadway, the procession marched toward the reviewing stand between Knowlton's and First National Bank, their brick facades hung with flags and bunting and banners reading Diamond Jubilee ~ 1854–1929. A drum major led the combined band and drum corps as it played the newly composed Rochester jubilee hymn.

> We sing our praise to pi-o-neers
> Who brav'd the red man's roving bands,
> And with a patr'-ot's zeal and love
> Built t—hey their homes with loy-al hands.

Behind the band came two boys dressed as medieval pages in tights and floppy hats, bearing a huge book inscribed "Historical Rochester." The knight in armor appeared next, followed by the hunters and trappers and a surveying party with compass and Gunter's chain, laying out the plat for these streets now jammed with parked automobiles and spectators. The O'Neills rode alongside a stagecoach that once traveled the Dubuque Trail, protecting the stage and its passengers from "the red man's roving bands"—members of the Improved

Order of Red Men, done up in black wigs and chicken-feather war bonnets, and riding spotted ponies. But Ed, who had no reason to believe otherwise, thought they were Indians, so he was alarmed when Blue snorted suddenly and bolted toward them. He pulled on the reins as the horse reared up on his hind legs, lunging toward an Indian pony that was obviously in heat. Ed pulled harder. As they closed in on the mare and its rider, a look of horror passed over the Red Man's face. Then Jim brought his horse alongside and swatted Blue on the head until the horse pulled back and Ed got him under control.

The remainder of the parade was a blur. Ed searched the crowds for a familiar face and saw instead only strangers, upturned and gawking at him beneath hats and straw boaters. He kept his eyes glued on his father's back as they rode through the slot of redbrick buildings beneath overhanging banners and a light-shot sky. The parade turned west at First Street and then proceeded to the county fairgrounds, where it dispersed. The floats and stagecoach were parked along the racetrack in front of the grandstand the rest of the day, but the O'Neills were finished playing pioneers. They left their horses at the riding academy, and while Jim and Theresa went off to enjoy the rides, Ed and his father walked across the road to watch the dedication of Rochester's new airport.

The ground was still wet and spongy from last night's downpour. They arrived too late to hear Dr. Charles Mayo's dedication speech, but were more interested in the aerial exhibition anyway. As a fleet of army and navy pursuit planes from Selfridge Field in Michigan and Chanute Field in Illinois staged a mock air battle in the sky overhead, the boy shaded his eyes. Black specks, very high, buzzed above them, chasing and overtaking one another. But he couldn't keep track of any single biplane, let alone the progress of the battle. It was like counting flies. Then Speed Holman, the famous Minneapolis aviator, performed a series of flying stunts—aerilons, wingovers, and barrel rolls—directly over the runway. That was more like it. A loudspeaker announced the imminent arrival of the Independence, a Ford trimotor owned by the Reid-Murdoch Company, which operated the largest canning plant in town. At first there was nothing but the vast expanse of blue. Then a far-off drone of engines could be heard, very faint but growing louder, more insistent, as the crowd scanned the sky. This was the moment Ed would remember, the enormous monoplane circling the field before it swooped down and bounced over the muddy runway, rolling to a stop in front of the yellow-roofed hangar. He and his father joined the crowd that surged across the rough field to the concrete apron where the trimotor was parked. They walked beneath its immense, slate-blue wings and examined the three rotary engines and the corrugated metal sides of the long, low fuselage. Inside, the plane was outfitted like a grocery store with products made by the Reid-Murdoch Company and signs proclaiming: The Monarch of the Clouds—The Pioneer Food Display of the Air!

In the afternoon, when they had seen enough of the diamond jubilee, the O'Neills retrieved their horses and rode east through town, crossing Badger Creek on Tenth Street, until they were out in the country and climbing the gradual rise toward the farm. Ed, who rode behind his father, kept turning around to search the skies for more airplanes. The ride home seemed intolerably slow.

ON SCHOOL DAYS, Ed rode bareback down the hill to Burr Oak School, pulling off Blue's bridle and sliding off at the last moment. The one-room school had changed little in the half century since his father had attended it. Twenty-odd scholars in eight grades were crammed beneath the sphinxlike gaze of George Washington's unfinished portrait. Their teacher, Miss Fleming, was smaller than many of the hulking farm boys she taught, and occasionally had to reach to deliver a blow. The students learned to read the two dresses she wore alternately—one wine-red and the other a somber green jersey—as barometers of Miss Fleming's mood, and slunk down in their desks on the days she wore the green dress. A regulator clock hammered out the hours, while Blue drifted in and out of view, a movable feature of the landscape—a windblown tail glimpsed through the south window, a roan-colored rump blending into the bald hills. If Blue had not wandered home by the end of class, Ed would try to slip the bridle over his ears, but the horse always managed to trot a little ways ahead of him, just out of reach, the two of them shadow dancing all the way home.

When Ed turned fourteen, his father kept him back in school a year to see if he wouldn't grow. Short even for an O'Neill, the boy barely stood five feet tall and weighed ninety pounds. But on horseback he was as agile as a monkey. If he could get a hand on Blue's mane, he was aboard without the horse's breaking stride. He liked to show off with trick-riding stunts he'd seen at the movies—hanging upside down from the horse's neck like an Indian, riding backward while standing up, holding on to the saddle horn and vaulting to either side of the horse at a full gallop. Too small to manage a plow or drive a binder like his brothers, he helped with the horses. In hot weather he would ride out to see if Bill, driving a four-horse grain binder through an oat field, needed a fresh team. Then he'd race back to the barn, bridle two pairs of work-horses, and ride them circus-style out to the field, standing on their wide rumps, four abreast. The first time some open-mouthed hired man saw this, he said, "By God, that kid's gonna get himself killed!"

But it was his father, not Ed, that a horse put in the hospital. After the threshing accident, John O'Neill requisitioned the boy's pony for the grocery run into town. Blue hated the old man's spurs and quirt, and the Boss hated any horse that wouldn't bend to his will. He had broken the horse as a colt, putting him in a corral for a week before trying to ride him. The first time he got in the saddle, Blue caught him with a willow branch that nearly took off the old man's head. Now they struck a deal based on their mutual helplessness. Blue would get John to town in thirty-six minutes flat; and in return he gave the horse the run of the farm. Other horses wintered in a straw shed over in the hollow, while Blue wandered the yard like a prize goose.

As a consolation prize for Ed's extra year at Burr Oak School, his father put him on a train, with Theresa along as chaperone, for the Chicago World's Fair. They rode the bumper cars and got stuck on the Ferris Wheel when their car stalled high above the Century of Progress. Theresa pointed out landmarks for twenty minutes while the car swung back and forth in the breeze off the lake. Ed's face turned pale green as he contemplated the earth far below. He was threatening to climb down when, at last, the wheel began to revolve again. He returned home no taller but wearing a black cowboy hat with white trim from Marshall Field cocked on his head.

That fall, Ed enrolled in Agriculture 1 at Rochester High School. The course was taught in a basement classroom by Ben F. Dunn, a beefy ex-sergeant who could blow an entire hour talking about the Great War if anyone got him started. When he wasn't reliving Flanders Fields, Dunn handed out bulletins on hybrid seed and animal husbandry from the University of Minnesota Extension Office for the class to cross-index in their three-ringed binders. "Book farming" was a comparatively recent phenomenon, and most farmers of John O'Neill's generation had done without high school or extension bulletins, but his son recognized that agriculture was about to become a different game altogether. He'd already seen increased yields from Minnesota No. 13, the first hybrid corn developed in the state. When Dunn handed out a new variety of hybrid seed, Ed raised some on a test plot, thinking he'd get rich, but the corn it produced wasn't very different from the hybrid they were already using. Dunn also organized field trips to nearby orchards and the state hospital to see its dairy herd of purebred Holsteins. No school bus was available for these trips, so the class crammed into whatever clunkers the farm boys drove to school, and a carload sometimes lost their way and got no farther than the nearest coffee shop.

When snow drifts made the roads impassable, John O'Neill paid a family in town $2 a week for Ed to board with them. The Binghams lived across from the high school and had eight kids, including a couple of girls who were close to Ed's age, so he didn't mind the change. So many hired men had marched through his own home that spending weekdays in the bosom of somebody else's family didn't seem unusual. On weekends, Ed hitched a ride home or skied back on a pair of pine skis. Once he braided a lariat to Blue's tail and had the horse tow him around the farm on a pair of wooden skis until Mame put a stop to it. "That's just mean," she scolded. "Him pulling you with his tail!"

In 1937 a crew strung utility poles across the lower pasture and up the driveway to a splintery pole in the center of the yard from which lines dangled to the house and barn. The farmhouse had electric lights run off Delco batteries for twenty years, but the Rural Electrification Act brought a world of changes. The cookstove and icebox were replaced by a refrigerator and an electric range; instead of pumping water into the sink from a sandpoint in the cellar, there was indoor plumbing and an end to the three-seater behind the house. The new barn had never been wired for electricity, and for the past ten years Ed and his brothers had hand-milked thirty-three cows twice a day by the smoky glow of kerosene lamps. Now they used a Rite-way electric milking machine from Montgomery Ward that could do the work in an hour and a half. The Century of Progress had come to the farm.

To be the youngest child in a large family is to witness

its slow undoing as older brothers and sisters embark upon their own lives. Catherine married and moved away even before Ed was school age. The younger sisters soon followed. Mary went to New York, and Theresa took a job as a manicurist on an ocean liner and sent postcards home from Rio and Buenos Aires. Bill and Jim stayed closer to home, settling down with their families at either end of the farm. By the time Ed graduated from high school, he had inherited an all but empty house.

While his brothers managed the farm, Ed became a hired man—shocking other farmers' corn, plowing their fields, driving a bundle wagon—hard, dull work that he'd done half his life, but it would do until something better came along. The Rochester Chick Hatchery wasn't any better, just easier. Located in an old barn off Third Avenue, it sounded like sunrise in birdland every hour of the day as chicks were hatched by the thousands. Ed's job was loading chicks from the incubators into cardboard boxes, twenty-five chicks to a section, four sections to a box. Holding the cheeping yellow balls of fluff between outstretched fingers, he'd drop them into cubicles, lay a piece of cardboard over their heads, then start another section, sometimes throwing in an extra chick or two in case one didn't survive the trip. Afterward he drove the boxes to the train depot to be shipped to rural post offices all over Minnesota, the Dakotas, and Montana—baby chicks seeing more of the world than he was.

THEN CAME the war.

Two weeks after Pearl Harbor, Ed and a friend drove out to California to look for work in a defense plant. After a stint at riveting school, they ended up at Consolidated Aircraft in San Diego. The factory was an enormous hangarlike building, two city blocks long, in which hundreds of men and women in gray overalls assembled B-24 Liberator bombers a piece at a time. He and Ben Hartley worked the swing shift, building wooden mock-ups for experimental aircraft like the B-32 or PBY. After work they stepped from the noise and glare of the factory into a dark, sultry night. San Diego was unlike any city they had ever seen. Stucco houses descended the hills like pastel staircases ending at the Pacific, and the streets and bars were packed, night and day, with zoot-suiters and defense plant workers, not to mention thousands of sailors and marines, all of whom were driven a little crazy by the knowledge that they would soon be crossing that ocean.

The Consolidated factory was next to an airfield, and during lunch breaks Ed and Ben sunned themselves and watched P-39s practice takeoffs and landings. Reasoning that the war would look better from a plane than on the ground, Ben talked Ed into enlisting in the Air Corps. They took the physical and both failed the eye exam. Instead of giving up, they wore sunglasses and drank carrot juice for a week. When they took the exam the next time, Ed passed every test except the height requirement. "You're a quarter inch too short," the recruiting officer told him, "but we haven't made our quota today, so you're in." Poor Ben, however, had flunked a second time. That night they drove down to Tijuana and got drunk for very different reasons.

Ground school, new cadets discover, has nothing to do with the ground except that they never leave it. For twelve weeks they studied navigation, meteorology and wind currents, everything about the kingdom of the air except how to actually fly. For that they were sent to Sequoia Field, a civilian airfield in the San Joaquin Valley. Their flight instructor, a reticent civilian named George Lavelle, usually took cadets on their first flight in a sturdy Stearman biplane nicknamed "the Yellow Peril." When Ed's turn came, however, Lavelle motioned him into the open cockpit of a PT-22 Orion monoplane. Propped up on extra cushions in the rear seat, Ed could barely see around the back of Lavelle's head as they sped down the runway. When its tail rose up, the plane no longer bumped down the runway but lifted up smoothly as if an invisible hand had taken hold of it, and they were in the air. The tin-roofed hangars and barracks fell away, and beyond them he saw green vineyards, truck farms, straight-running roads, and sunlight glinting off a river. This was not only Ed's inaugural flight as a cadet; it was the first time he'd ever been in an airplane.

Lavelle climbed fifteen hundred feet, then flipped the plane upside down. "How do you like this?" he asked—a rhetorical question, since the voice tube connecting the cockpits allowed only the instructor to talk. All the blood in Ed's body flooded into his skull; the pulsing in his ears replaced the engine's roar. Once he had adjusted to the sensation of standing on his head, he found they were still flying at the same altitude, but with the order of heaven and earth reversed. Above, instead of sky there was the floor of the valley, curving at the ends into yellow foothills and pine forests and the hazy blue beginnings of the Sierras.

Then the engine stalled and the plane spiraled downward like a leaf. This, too, was part of Lavelle's first flight routine. He'd stall the plane to demonstrate how to pull out of a spin and, in the process, test the cadet's nerve. After a few twirls, Lavelle got the Orion's nose down and once the propeller started windmilling, he kicked the right rudder and the plane leveled off. "Take hold of the stick," he said. "Just hold it steady."

Ed clutched it and watched the needle ball on the instrument panel waver slightly. When Lavelle told him to climb, he reined back on the stick and the Orion's nose abruptly tipped upward. Flying was not so different from riding a fast horse in the qualities it required—perfect balance and a sense of where you are at any moment. Trying to level out, Ed overcompensated and the plane leapfrogged until Lavelle took the controls again. It was a short flight, maybe half an hour, just a dip in the great ocean of air. But when they touched down, Ed understood the central lesson of flight: As long as a pilot keeps track of the horizon it doesn't matter whether he's flying sideways or upside down, since it isn't the blue sky he has to fear but the sudden return to earth.

At Sequoia Field the men lived in comparative luxury, six to a room, their meals served by Mexican girls. Since their names were arranged on the roll alphabetically, Ed became friends with a quiet, balding cadet named Roy Pelster, whom everyone called Pop because, at thirty-two, he was the oldest in the class. He was from St. Louis and liked to brag about swimming across the Mississippi River to Illinois on a dare. He was the only cadet with previous flying experience, although Lavelle had hinted that he'd picked up some bad habits as well. But while younger men washed out, Pop managed to survive. For their graduation picture, the class lined up in front of the barracks in leather flight jackets, which they had never worn in the desert heat, and a smiling Pop flung his arm around Ed, the shortest in the group and the only one whose officer's cap is cocked at an angle.

After they had moved to Gardner Field, north of Bakersfield, Pop asked Ed if he'd be best man at his wedding. Couples couldn't live on base, and they'd soon be overseas anyway, so what was the point? But Ed agreed. Pop's girl, a skinny blonde, arrived by train from St. Louis, and Ed held the ring while the couple exchanged vows in the base chapel. When the class graduated to another airfield, the newlyweds moved to an apartment off base and often invited Ed to stay overnight, yet marriage made Pop seem even older, a vision of the life to come.

Shortly before his twenty-fourth birthday, Ed boarded a C-54 transport at Hamilton Field and took off in darkness across the Pacific. Once they'd left the lights of San Francisco Bay behind, there was nothing to see outside the porthole windows but the all-encompassing night, so he dozed off. When he awoke, the sun was rising behind them as the transport descended to Hawaii. The men ate breakfast while the plane was refueled and then flew over more empty ocean to Johnson Island, nothing but a runway and a few buildings on a treeless speck in the vast expanse of water. They refueled again for the final leg, arriving in Port Moresby, New Guinea, at dusk.

After the dry heat of California, the humidity of the tropics was a difficult adjustment; it was like breathing through wet cotton gauze. While the men waited around for their new assignments, the army kept them busy with baseball games on the beach and tourist excursions in outrigger canoes. One afternoon the men climbed into army trucks for a sightseeing tour of the inland jungle. The trucks labored up a muddy road through green hills until the road ended and the men got out to walk single file along a path. The jungle was filled with hanging orchids and strange birdsong. Unable to see any distance, the pilots raced toward what they could hear, which was the sound of a river. As they neared a clearing, the sound became a booming roar. Three waterfalls descended through the jungle, one below the other, each with a pool of churning water at its base rimmed by wet, slippery rocks.

Ed had lagged behind the rest, and at the topmost pool he found them either frantically pacing its banks or staring dumbly into the water. Someone had fallen into the river. He had bobbed to the surface once and a fellow tried grabbing him by the hair, but there was little to hold on to and the man seemed to push away as if resigned to drowning or reluctant to pull anyone in with him. It was Roy Pelster. The current sucked him under and he was gone.

Four days later a soldier drove Ed to Port Moresby to identify a body that had washed up on the beach where the river emptied into the sea. There was nothing recognizable about the swollen corpse, nothing to recall the person he had been, except the balding dome of head and a gold wedding band on the distended left hand. It hardly seemed fair. Pop had traveled so far, halfway across the world, to fly in the war, only to be killed by a river.

EARLY IN September, Ed joined the 475th Fighter Group, which had already seen considerable action over Rebaul, Hollandia, and Wewak. Their nickname was Satan's Angels, and their insignia was the face of a leering red devil against the yellow stars of the Southern Cross. Ed's new squadron, the 431st, had the radio call name Hades. They were encamped at the far end of a landing strip carved out of white coral on Biak Island, off the north coast of Dutch New Guinea. Across a lagoon, the palm-thatched huts of a native village rose on stilts above the water. At dusk, with a purple sunset backlighting the palms, the village looked like the set of a Dorothy Lamour picture but not at midday, when the tide went out and the exposed coral in the lagoon reeked in the blinding sunlight. A few months earlier Biak had been the scene of fierce fighting. Its Japanese defenders had retreated into caves dug into the coral ridge, which, after weeks of steady bombardment, became their tombs. Remnants of their forces still hid in the surrounding jungle, sometimes raiding the base's food supply, but the fighting had moved beyond Biak, bypassing the living and the dead.

Upon arrival, replacement pilots were issued a booklet entitled "Combat Tactics in the Southwest Pacific Area." A foreword by the group's commanding officer addressed the new pilots in a detached third person, as if the CO had been caught thinking out loud: "When one considers just what he should say to a new sport who is reporting to an operational fighter group, the mind becomes confused in the complex maze of information it is necessary for the new sport to know." What the new sport learned was the myriad ways in which he could fall to earth. He could tumble from the sky in a dogfight or explode in a black puff of ack-ack, collide with a palm tree on a low-level pass or vanish forever in a tropical storm. He could be given the wrong coordinates and fly over empty ocean until he was running on vapors and the last thing he heard was the sound of rushing wind. Or he could parachute safely onto an island paradise, only to lose his head to a small man wielding a two-handed ceremonial sword. He could survive all these dire possibilities and finish off a victory roll for his ground crew by augering into the landing strip.

For the first month, the new sports practiced formations and tactics by flying long patrols over empty sectors or providing fighter cover for troop ships steaming toward the Philippines. Ed had had only thirty-one hours in the Lockheed Lightning when he joined the squadron, but the plane was far more stable than the single-engine fighters in which he'd trained. With its forktail and twin Allison engines, the P-38 looked like two planes joined at the hip. Once trimmed out, it practically flew itself. The problem was staying alert. Sunlight streamed through the Plexiglas canopy, and the superchargers muffled the engines to a dull rumble. Over his earphones he sometimes picked up the hometown voice of Tokyo Rose informing another squadron of its destination, leaving them to mull over her clairvoyance while she played Glenn Miller's "Chattanooga Choo-Choo." On convoy cover, he could look down on destroyers and troopships zigzagging north, a toy fleet pokered around an admiral's tabletop and carrying with it all the fortunes of war.

By spring, Hades Squadron had moved to Clark Field on Luzon and Ed inherited his own P-38. He had *Bonnie* painted on its nose for a girl he'd dated in high school, leaving room for any victory flags he might acquire. But the war in the air was winding down, most Zeros having been destroyed on the ground or withdrawn for a final defense of the home islands. Increasingly, the squadron flew ground-support missions, escorting bombing runs in the north and strafing the enemy on the way back. These low-level passes were dangerous but yielded glimpses of an increasingly strange, Lilliputian world: a tiny figure in khaki puttees and forage cap pulling the rope on an antiaircraft gun by the enemy airfield at Negros; the jungle canopy parting on the island of Panay to reveal women standing naked in a river as they washed brightly colored clothes; a string of packhorses at Balete Pass in the mountains of northern Luzon. A little taller than Shetlands but not so full in the body, these ponies carried Japanese supplies along the steep mountain trails and, more recently, fed the enemy. There were standing orders to strafe them.

In May, Hades Squadron took off from Clark Field with drop tanks under their wings filled with a mixture of gasoline and napalm gel. They flew north across Luzon's central plain, the land rising in green hills terraced with rice paddies until they neared Ipo Dam, where the foliage gave way to scorched earth. Japanese retreating from Manila had dug into jumbled hills around the dam, which controlled the city's water supply and the main highway north, and after ground troops failed to dislodge them, a massive air strike was mounted. The flight leader marked the perimeters of the strike zone with white phosphorus bombs, then circled above to direct waves of attacking fighters. Flying wingtip to wingtip, eight abreast, the formation dived through the smoke and leveled off at fifty feet to release the drop tanks. The shiny canisters tumbled end over end, bursting on impact in a great wave of flame and towering columns of black smoke that flattened off at the top like thunderheads. After dropping his tanks, Ed pulled back on the yoke to climb above the inferno. A wave of P-51 Mustangs followed up the strike to strafe any Japanese flushed by the flames, but Ed didn't see any return fire and the fighters seemed to be attacking the ground itself. What he saw was a vision of how the war would end.

ED RETURNED home to find that little had changed except himself. The farm seemed no different than when he had left, though there were fewer horses about the place. Buck and Brownie were long gone. And footloose Blue could have been anywhere.

"What's around to ride?"

"Well," Bill said, "there's this new horse up at the barn."

The white gelding had the stupid, chunky look of a plow-horse, but Ed threw on a saddle anyway, cinching it by putting his knee into the horse's belly until the air rushed out. He rode over east in the late afternoon sunlight to bring the cows in from the hollow. But when he tried reining the horse around to chase a stray, it plodded straight ahead as if plowing a furrow. Ed reached down and yanked on the bridle until the horse's head was in his lap, but its legs continued to trot forward. Finally, he smacked the horse on the side of the head and it seemed to waken from a dream. He managed to ride the gelding back to the barn, find Blue, and round up the cows. For the duration of his leave, he rode his own horse.

Ed reenlisted for another year's hitch because he loved flying. But his new assignment at Buckley Field outside Denver was basic training, which left little opportunity to get back to the blue yonder. Instead, he marched new recruits up and down the parade grounds, took them on camping trips, and taught them how to soldier. During this extended ground duty, Ed went on a double date arranged by a fellow lieutenant who had been nicknamed Killer for reasons unrelated to the war. They picked up the girls at their apartment and, after stopping for a few drinks, headed south to Colorado Springs in a merry mood. Driving through the countryside, Killer casually mentioned that Ed was a big dairy farmer from the

Midwest. Ed's blind date, a petite blonde with shy blue eyes, seemed particularly impressed.

"Really?" she asked. "Is that a dairy cow over there?"

At Ed's insistence, the car slammed to a halt beside a field dotted with brown cattle. Vaulting the fence, he approached a guernsey grazing in the middle of the pasture. Only then did he look around to see if there might be a bull nearby, but he understood that once you embark on a gesture like this it's fatal not to follow through. Stroking the cow's side, he squatted down and grabbed a teat. The guernsey looked back once, then resumed feeding. Ed gave the teat a pull and shot a thin stream of milk in the car's direction. A smattering of applause met him as he leaped back over the fence, and the broadest smile belonged to the curly-haired blonde in the backseat.

Frances Bruski knew perfectly well how to milk a cow. She had grown up on a ranch in the bleak, treeless plains of eastern Montana. Her father, the son of Polish emigrants, had homesteaded in the Badlands in 1907. When that land proved too rough for dryland farming, he crossed the Little Missouri River and homesteaded twelve miles south of Wibaux, where he raised wheat, oats, cattle, and a big family. The Bruski children honed their milking skills on rangy Herefords. When Frances was ten years old, her mother died, leaving the older girls to help raise their younger brothers and sisters in a hard-scrabble childhood that was over soon enough. The war had pulled a lot of high-school friends off isolated ranches and into the larger world, and Frances quickly followed. After graduation she lit out for the bright lights of Denver and met Ed shortly before he left the service. It was too late to paint her name on the nose of a P-38, so he proposed instead.

They married on a sweltering July afternoon when the temperature felt like a hundred in the shade. The bride wore a pale aqua dress, while the groom sweated in a double-breasted, pinstriped suit, his hair slicked back except for the waterfall lock that hung suspended over his forehead. Rushing down the steps of St. Bridget's, they found that their bull-nosed 1939 Chevy, parked under the pines for a quick get-away, had been graffitied with white shoe polish. Every inch of the car held some scribbled greeting—*"Sucker!"*. . . . *"You'll be Sorry!"* Ed peeled off his suit coat and swiped at the words with a wet rag, but the ghostly outline of *"She got him this morning, but he'll get her . . ."* had been baked onto the Chevy's blue finish. A crowd of well-wishers, their white shirts blazing in the sun, parted around the car as they drove away. On the road at last, they smelled something terrible. Stopping by the side of the road, Ed threw up the hood to discover that some bastard had smeared Limburger on the engine manifold.

After a week's honeymoon in Duluth, the newlyweds moved into the southwest bedroom of the farmhouse, right down the hall from the groom's parents.

THE PARTNERSHIP between John O'Neill and his three sons continued a pattern set almost at birth, and it was in-cidental that Ed ended up with the home place, since his older brothers had already established their own families at either end of the farm. But for Frances, the apprenticeship was just beginning. There had always been a daughter or daughter-in-law to be trained in the ways of the house. Having outlived her own mother-in-law's lengthy stay, Mame ran the household her way. "A job worth doing," she'd say, undoing the mistake, "is worth doing well." When her youngest son brought his bride home, Mame understood that here was the last in a succession of women to come under her roof and take direction, endure judgment, and finally inherit all that she and her husband had expended their lives upon.

While most farm work changed with the seasons, house-hold chores were ongoing, with each day of the week allotted its given task. Monday was wash day. Frances began by strip-ping beds, emptying hampers and hooks, and sorting clothes by color and use, the barn clothes in their own heap on the linoleum floor. She rolled the wringer washer and rinse tubs onto the porch if the weather allowed or into the kitchen if the day was cold. Depending on the amount of laundry, the cycle—sort, soak, wash, wring, rinse, wring again, hang to dry—extended into the afternoon. Some clothes moved through her hands so many times in the course of the day that they seemed to defy cleaning. Between folding dry clothes and putting others in a bag for ironing, she'd do the breakfast dishes and tidy the house. At 11:30 she put on a ham-and-bean soup for dinner. Coming in from chores, Ed would sneak up behind her at the stove, putting a cold hand to her cheek to show the difference in their jobs. After the meal, she cleared and washed dishes, then sat briefly and had a cigarette with Ed before going back to washing.

Tuesday, ironing day, must have seemed a relief. There was no end to the work.

Other obligations reached beyond the farm. Frances had married into a close-knit community, and though she had grown up on a ranch, Montana seemed distant enough in some neighbors' eyes to qualify her as a war bride. Now she assumed the parish duties that had circumscribed her mother-in-law's social life for decades. She joined the altar society, cooked for the annual Fall Dinner, delivered meals to the sick, and comforted the bereaved at wakes. In return, Mame inducted her into the customs of a small, clannish society of farm families whose intertwined roots reached back to Ireland.

Frances bore her first child a year after the wedding. When he became colicky, Mame insisted on rubbing the baby's gums with whiskey. By the end of summer, she was pregnant again. The piles of laundry on the kitchen floor grew logarithmically, as babies arrived as predictably as spring blizzards. The house resembled a nursery school. "How many are yours?" visitors would ask and tote up all the girls. Enough for a softball team. Why so many children when there was no longer any need for numbers alone to do the farm work? To raise a large family is to surrender one's privacy and freedom for something else. A hedge against disaster.

Two nights a week, Ed attended Ag courses on the GI Bill at his former high school. The instructors spoke of the bright future of agriculture to an audience of young farmers, most of them veterans who were particularly anxious to believe the best lay ahead of them. There was little reason to suspect it didn't. The U.S. Department of Agriculture, the University of Minnesota's experimental stations, and the county extension service—not to mention the companies that sold tractors, seed, or chemicals—all promised to free them from much of farming's drudgery. This technological revolution would be accomplished by substituting machinery and chemicals for human and animal labor. New hybrid seeds and heavy applications of commercial fertilizer would increase yields, while pesticides and herbicides developed during the war would reduce the need for cultivation. Here was a future that any farmer would want to buy into.

Between the epoch of horses and full mechanization lay a few awkward years of experimentation. A crew pitching oat shocks onto a bundle wagon may have appeared from the roadside like some graceful peasant drama, an Oberammergau of the harvest, but not to the sweating men on the wagon or the farmer nervously eyeing the weather. The war finished all that. With so many men overseas, nobody was left to gather the shocks or drive the horses, so the threshing rings came to an unheralded end along with the great noontide meals and long autumn days traveling between farms. The O'Neills replaced the circus of bundle wagons and bindle stiffs with a single buckrake. It was simply a scoop made by bolting six-foot oak tines to the front of a John Deere, and nothing about its operation was graceful. Throttling down a row of oat shocks, Ed would ram into each one with sufficient speed to impale it between the tines, showering himself in the process with a golden burst of chaff. When the tines were full, he'd race back to the separator so Bill could pitch the shocks into the feeder, then he took off on another strafing run. After buying a Ford self-propelled combine in 1951, he hauled both buckrake and separator to the elephants' graveyard at the end of the field road.

With fewer horses to feed, Ed converted oat fields into new cash crops like soybeans. He switched hayfields from timothy and red clover to alfalfa because its longer growing season meant a third cutting. Pulling a four-row planter behind his tractor, he could plant twice as much corn as his father ever had in rows as dense as teeth on a comb. He still monkeyed with sheep and hogs, but dairying paid the bills, so he culled the dual-purpose cattle into two distinct herds—Herefords for beef and purebred Holsteins for milking. He didn't use large doses of commercial fertilizer because his dairy cows provided nitrogen-rich manure to spread on the fields. When he sprayed 2,4-D, an herbicide developed as a chemical weapon during the war, he noticed less broadleaf but more new weeds like foxtail, and the soil seemed drier and more compacted from the heavy machinery.

Yields skyrocketed, but so did the costs. While prices for tractors, seed, fuel, and fertilizer went up, agricultural prices steadily declined during the early 1950s. Unable to control production or set their own prices for crops and livestock, farmers were caught in a worsening squeeze. The government's farm policy had ossified since the New Deal into a system of price supports for certain commodities, which guaranteed farmers the difference between the market price and the parity price. But farmers had become so productive that they exhausted the government's capacity to store the surplus it bought in warehouses and mothballed warships.

When the Republicans regained the White House, Eisenhower appointed an Idaho potato farmer named Ezra Taft Benson as his secretary of agriculture and charged him with dismantling the department's bureaucracy and eliminating the surplus. Benson, one of the guiding Twelve Apostles of the Mormon church, saw the issue in moral terms and, in the language of the times, stated that "no real American wants to be subsidized." Suggesting that the root of the farm crisis was a surplus of farmers, he moved to lower price supports to a level that would discourage production of unneeded commodities and eliminate marginal operators as well. These "free market" policies, however, removed the controls the government had on crop supply, and farmers planted more just to keep abreast of falling prices. When Elder Benson told a gathering of farmers in St. Paul that he would not extend government price supports to shore up sagging cattle prices, which had declined by 30 percent in a year, a Minnesota legislator likened him to "a man standing on the bank of a river telling a drowning man that all he needs to do is take a deep breath of air."

While the rest of the nation enjoyed abounding prosperity, many farm families slid into a private depression. Unlike the thirties, when everyone was in the same boat, they were virtually alone in seeing their incomes shrink. There were half as many farmers now as there had been during the Great Depression, and they couldn't agree on the best way to save themselves. The Republican-dominated Farm Bureau supported Benson's policies, while the more liberal Farmers Union lobbied for 100 percent of parity and a ceiling on government payments so the bulk of the money didn't end up in the pockets of a few large farmers. No firebrand such as Milo Reno arose to create a third party on their behalf. Instead of strikes and rallies, farmers settled into a slow war of attrition, and a whole generation of farm boys quietly took jobs in town, part-time at first, until they saw how much easier life could be. When they left the farm for good, it was sometimes in despair, sometimes with great relief.

One summer after haying season, a fast-talking organizer from the Farmers Union state headquarters asked Ed to accompany him on a membership drive. Ed would introduce him to a neighbor and, after a few comments on the weather, the organizer would launch into his pitch. The villain of the piece, aside from Benson, was the elusive "middleman," a Uriah Heep figure who produced nothing but ended up with the greatest share of the food dollar. The organizer talked until the farmer agreed to take out a membership. Then he and Ed went down the road to the next farm. They signed up the Sheehans, Fogartys, and Loshers. Their last stop was east of St. Bridget's to visit a farmer who was renting the place from his uncle. The nephew seemed genuinely interested until his uncle suddenly appeared around the corner of the barn. The old man, a Republican and a Farm Bureau member, hated unions of any stripe. The organizer might as well have waved a red flag in front of a bull. "What are you doing bothering the workingman?" the old man demanded. "Get the hell out of here!"

FOR YEARS John O'Neill stretched his credit to buy land every chance he got, adding a quarter section to the south during the war, until Woodlawn Farm occupied more than five hundred acres. It was a big farm, though he had to divide it among three sons. He was trying to buy his way out to a blacktop road over east, the old Martin St. George place, but the owner wouldn't sell. So he bought land along the Root River instead.

The new property was fifteen minutes by tractor east of the farm along a township road. Just past Johnny Baker's place, the road curled down to the river, crossed it on an iron bridge, then gradually climbed a hogback ridge that got higher and narrower until it plummeted away to the north, offering the first view of the land far below. John O'Neill had cobbled together 227 acres along both sides of Partridge Creek, where it emptied into a bend in the Root River. It was a steep-walled valley with a nearly vertical bluff to the north and a lid of blue sky overhead. The land was breathtaking but not much for farming. There was a ten-acre hayfield on a bluff top, and two fields in the bottomland that flooded every spring. John hired a bulldozer to carve a switchback road up the steep bluff to the hayfield on top. When the hired man accidentally drove over the side, the Boss leaped aboard the careening bulldozer and rode it down the hillside like one more runaway horse.

Mostly, John O'Neill had bought hardwood trees—yellow elms, basswoods, red oaks, and hard maples growing on the steep north slope. Driving that flume of a road in the morning, his sons would cross the valley in deep shadow, then watch the sunlight climb up the sides as they cut timber. They snaked the logs out behind a yellow Minneapolis-Moline tractor and rolled them onto a flatbed wagon with cant hooks to saw into lumber. The old sawmill in the yard south of the barn had once belonged to Berne St. George. It was powered, like a threshing machine, by a long canvas belt looped around a tractor's flywheel. Ed was chief sawyer. Standing behind the log carriage, he would pull a big iron handle that drove the log into the circular blade while Bill caught the board, flopping it to the ground so the blade didn't catch the end. When the lumber cured, they built a new house for Bill and his wife on the rise behind Stillwell's, framing it out with hard maple, which proved to be a mistake since maple breaks before it will bend, yellow elm for the sash work, and red oak for flooring and trim. Jim, who had quit farming to run a sheet-metal business, laid the floor out from the center in a concentric pattern as tight as a Chinese puzzle.

The Boss relinquished day-to-day management of the farm to his sons but still liked to ride the fence lines, checking the cattle and seeing his land spread out before him. Usually he took a square-fendered Jeep—he was almost eighty—but sometimes he'd saddle up and ride. In his cowboy hat and flapping clothes, he looked like a coat-tree on horseback. Suppertime was his favorite time for these jaunts. He'd just disappear without a word, and Fran would keep his plate warm in the oven while the rest of the family sat down to eat, the empty chair conspicuous at the head of the table. One night he appeared at the kitchen door as pale as a ghost. His clothes were muddy and torn. Mame dabbed at a cut on his face, while he sat down and explained what had happened. He'd saddled up Blue to check on the cattle over in the hollow. Coming down a steep cow path through the trees across from the spring, the horse had lost its footing and spilled them both.

"Well, I guess Blue is done for," the old man said with finality. "We both went down, and I got up first."

In July of 1954, Ed and Bill baled a second cutting of hay in a field near Bill's house. It was terribly hot and they took turns driving the tractor while the other rode the old Case hand-tie baler and twisted the wire around the bales. Ed had the scraggly beginnings of a beard that itched in the heat. He'd stopped shaving because the Alibi Inn was sponsoring a beard-growing contest for Rochester's centennial celebration, a Century of Progress. He'd considered riding Blue in the parade so he could say he'd ridden the same horse in parades twenty-five years apart. But Blue's riding days were over. His hooves had begun to curl up and he spent most days over in the hollow keeping company with the cows. They would both sit this one out.

As he stacked bales, Ed heard the drone of a small engine grow louder and more insistent until he looked up to see a blue-and-cream wing flash overhead before it disappeared beyond the treetops. The noise faded, then revived. The plane was coming back, lower this time, and when Ed heard its engine throttling down, he understood that it was going to land in the field.

The plane bounced twice and rolled to a stop on a level strip of grass beside the hayfield. The pilot emerged grinning from the cockpit and walked over. He was their sister Catherine's oldest son, Bob Sullivan. They shook hands, propped one leg on a bale, and regarded the airplane. The high-winged Taylor-Craft was a model the army had used during the war to instruct glider pilots because of its light weight. Would they like to go up, their nephew inquired, and see the farm from the air? Bill declined. But Ed, who hadn't been in an airplane since leaving the service, climbed into the cockpit. Sullivan turned the plane around and taxied back to the end of the grass strip to face into the wind. Since the Taylor-Craft had a tail wheel, its cockpit angled upward and Sullivan had to peer out the side window until he got up enough speed for the tail to rise. By then they were racing down the strip toward its edge of trees, the ground melting beneath them as the plane lifted into the sky.

They climbed to a thousand feet, and Sullivan banked west, flying over Sheehan's place. Down below, Ed could see Holsteins grazing on the green slope of pasture and, farther on, a car inching along the road to Marion. The sun flashed off Home Creek, curving among willows. Sullivan circled the farm. They flew over blue-green cornfields and swaths of cut hay. As they flew up the hollow, Ed saw the makeshift corral at the widest end, white-faced cattle, and farther up, all alone, a roan-colored pony.

"Go ahead," said Sullivan. "Take the controls."

The Taylor-Craft was so much lighter than the twin-engine fighters Ed had flown during the war that it seemed to float in the air. But after a few seconds the reflexes came back to him. Like riding a horse—once you learn, you never forget. If he had stayed in the service, Ed might have piloted jets in Korea instead of an old hand-baler through his father's hayfields. Then again, he might have crashed and burned.

Swooping low, Ed buzzed the arched roof of the barn and roared over the white farmhouse beneath its canopy of oaks. A dog ran in circles around the yard. Flying over one's rooftop is a recurring dream of childhood that dramatizes the central dilemma of growing up: whether to flee or stay put. From the distance of space, the attractions of home cannot help but shrink in perspective, although on this flight the opposite was true. As they circled around for another pass, the farm seemed more expansive, boundless, as if it went on forever.

"Why don't you land it?" Sullivan offered.

Flying over the hayfield where Bill stood waving, Ed tested the wind. But every time he made an approach to land, thermals buoyed the wings up and the plane hung suspended in the sky like a balloon—almost as if Ed couldn't bring himself to land it. Finally he gave over the controls to his nephew, who circled again and brought them gently back to earth.

TWELVE

In October the bull discovered the circles of worm-riddled apples beneath the orchard trees and soon bloated from eating too many windfalls. One night he emerged from the orchard, sides bulging like a cider barrel, black nostrils flecked with foam. He coughed and white froth shot out both ends. The apples had fermented in one of the bull's four stomachs, swelling the animal to nearly twice his size. If his stomach ruptured, the bull would die a horrible death, a death of excess.

Ed chased the rented bull around the pasture on the four-wheeler, trying to corral him until he could call Doc Predmore, but the bull eluded him with the foolish cunning of a drunk. Cornered against the barn, he whooshed past and disappeared into the night. The next morning, Ed walked down to the orchard expecting to find a bloated carcass. But the bull was alive, having somehow purged himself, and stood beneath an apple tree waiting for another windfall to drop.

The bull had misunderstood the central lesson of autumn, which is not that ripeness is all but that everything comes due. It's a poignant season. The spangled leaves, the torchy light, the wine scent of fallen apples—all send the wrong signals, as if fall was out of sequence, as if this was the resurrection before the death. The change of seasons in the Midwest can seem as abrupt as a border crossing, autumn a small republic you cross too quickly on the way to winter, leaving behind favorite customs and a familiar language. You put up storm windows and quarts of vegetables, drive to see fall colors before rainstorms beat them from the trees, and try urgently to gather everything before it's gone.

The garden is the first to go. All summer you follow its progressions, through the salad days to the rigors of tomato-canning time when the kitchen is as steamy as a Turkish bath and the sink overflows with Burpee Big Boys and beefsteaks put up against the coming bleakness. Then one morning you awake to a chill in the air. And while the maple blazing in the front yard is in its finest hour, the tomato vines have become terminal cases. After the first hard frost has leveled the garden, you pick through the wreckage, salvaging, among the acorn squash and pumpkins, a few hard, green tomatoes to set on the windowsill in the faint hope they'll ripen.

THE SUN is going down across the road, and, for the few moments it balances atop Sheehan's silo, the light divides itself around me, burnishing fields ahead while casting the barn and road cut behind in backlit shadows. A skein of geese fly across the empty sky, wings beating in unison like oars.

The far-off thrumming is not geese but the sound of a combine in a soybean field to the south. From a distance, the Massey-Ferguson appears to hover over the ground on a golden corona of dust and chaff. When it reaches my end of the field, the combine stops, the cab door slides open, and Dennis O'Neill edges along a plank mounted on the side to check the hopper.

"You don't get many days this nice," he says.

Dennis has two more days before he has to return to the fire station and will spend them combining Ed's soybeans and then his own. I mention that the good weather is supposed to hold.

He shrugs. "But I might break down and lose half a day."

There's just enough room in the cab for me to scrunch between Dennis and the sliding door. He starts the header reel revolving, lowers it to spin just above the ground, and then we push off, moving clockwise, carving away at the tangle of brittle stems and yellow pods as the field dips and rises. Normally a combine's header floats on flexible skids over uneven ground; but the hydraulic lift on the fourteen-year-old Massey-Ferguson is broken, so Dennis has to set the height manually. Leaning over the cab's inclined windshield, he keeps one hand on the lift and his eyes focused, through the revolving reel, on the ground directly ahead in the intent, neck-crinking posture of a computer programmer.

"I run it about an inch or so above the ground because that's where most of the beans grow. You can see the ones I've passed over."

I try to see the soybeans, but it's all a blur—snowflakes in a snowstorm. Every so often, Dennis swivels his head around to glance through a porthole to the hopper, where the cream-colored beans make a muffled pinging sound like rain on a tin roof.

We are riding across the field in a self-propelled factory. The combine revolutionized farming because it *combined* the multiple tasks of harvesting and threshing into a single operation. What had once occupied a traveling circus of men and horses could now be accomplished by one man who depended far less on his neighbors than on his banker. The black-paddled reel bends the soybean stalks forward, so they can be sliced off by a saw-toothed cutter bar and carried by auger into the separator, where the beans are shelled and channeled into the hopper while chaff and dust are shot out the back. The Massey-Ferguson does everything but haul beans to the elevator, which is what the grain truck parked at the edge of the field is for.

As the air cools down, the pods become tougher and the machine groans under the added strain. Dennis switches on four angled headlights that bore only a few feet ahead into the darkness. He's bent over the wheel, looking for chunks of limestone that may have floated to the surface with last spring's plowing. "You can see rocks a lot better at night than you can in the daytime. The headlights really set them off." The beams also catch any weeds the sprayer missed: lamb's-quarter, giant pigweed, devil's pitchfork. Occasionally a pale stalk of volunteer corn flies past like a ghostly pennant.

Combining is monotonous work, but it seems pretty serene if you're just along for the ride. Sailing through the night, the glassed-in cab takes on the self-contained atmosphere of a pilot house, perched as it is above the diesel's steady hum. The ground rises and falls like waves, and there is the pleasant sensation of being lost to the world. From the road, nothing shows but our running lights as the Massey-Ferguson trolls for soybeans in the dark.

Suddenly the combine changes rhythm, its steady chuffing underscored by a high-pitched trilling as if the night has filled with steel crickets. Dennis raises the head, sets the brake and jumps down from the cab, leaving the engine running. He starts pulling clumps of dirt and soybean stems from the teeth of the cutter bar. "I'm looking for a piece of wire or something," he says from under the reel.

I stand frozen in the headlights like a deer. I'm thinking about an item in yesterday's *Post-Bulletin* about a local man who was unplugging a corn picker when the husking rollers snagged his sleeve and slowly pulled him in. Some time later, a friend hunting in the area heard his cries and discovered the man caught up to the elbows. The hunter, who happened to have a cellular phone in his pickup, called 911. It took rescuers a half hour to arrive, and another hour and a half to extricate the farmer. None of this seems worth mentioning to Dennis at the moment.

"Here's the problem!" he says, emerging with a softball-size rock that had lodged between the header and the end of the cutter bar. He shot-puts it into a hedgerow.

Back in the combine, its pitch restored, we make a final sweep of the field, picking it clean except for a patch of lamb's-quarter in a low spot that the sprayer must have missed. Parking beside the grain truck, Dennis climbs out on the catwalk to swing the horizontal auger arm over the truck bed. He throws a switch and a yellow stream of soybeans pour out the chute. Dennis sticks his hand under the flow and retrieves a palmful of beans that look as if they've been dusted with pepper.

"See how dirty this is? That's not dirt. That's lamb's-quarter seeds."

The elevator will count the seeds and dock him for any foreign matter that shows up in a sample. He pops a few beans into his mouth to see if they're dry enough to crack, then spits them out. It's eight o'clock at night and so cold that we can see our breath.

Dennis grew up on the northeast corner of the farm. But like his cousins living at the other end, he naturally gravitated toward the middle, where there were horses and machinery to ride. Anyway, the home place was the center of operations for three families and it didn't much matter that Ed lived there. Now Dennis alone has returned to help his uncle bring in this year's crops. When I ask if he'll be on shift when the fire department burns down the old farmhouse, he smiles. "I think I'm going to skip that."

Obliqueness is the secret language farmers employ for talking about what matters most to them. One rainy afternoon when I was tearing down the old sheep pen, Dennis drove up to find me standing ankle-deep in the manure of ages. "How do you like farming now?" he asked. I don't remember what I said—something like, "I can use the exercise" or "This is pretty interesting"—only that he seemed disappointed by my response. Irony is one way farmers excuse themselves for caring about a job that gives so little return on labor. It's the wink when someone breaks down in a field or the price of hogs plummets or the rain won't stop or never got started. *How do you like it now?*

I steer the grain truck between cornfields in the dark, following the combine's running lights. Fully loaded, the two-ton GMC has the turning radius of a city bus, and after an anxious moment threading through the gateposts, I'm backing into the pole shed so the beans stay dry. We stand outside, the yard light shining overhead like a harvest moon. "Well," Dennis says, "I gotta do chores."

After his pickup disappears down the driveway, I walk across the yard toward the house. Everyone is inside watching the fourth game of the World Series, the adults gazing over the heads of the children at the TV screen, their faces framed in the warm light of the picture window. It's like looking at a photograph of the present, everyone exactly as I'd want to remember them on this October night in the very midst of their lives. A few steps and I'll be with them. I'll get a can of beer from the refrigerator and sit down on the couch and ask someone the score. So why am I standing out here? There's the brief illusion of holding time at a standstill simply by remaining apart from things, but it doesn't last long. The door swings open. I step inside and ask somebody the score.

WE ARE STAYING at Rita's for the weekend. In the morning we sit around her kitchen counter and drink coffee and take turns replenishing the kids' bowls with sugar-frosted gunk. Rita is a year younger than Sharon and as fair-haired as her sister is dark, but they share the same pale-blue eyes and leveling gaze, as if some question had gone unanswered. Growing up, they had been as inseparable as twins, but there is no direction to go from that kind of closeness except apart, and by high school they were running with different crowds and each felt jilted by the other. Marriage is the great equalizer, however, and when they bicker now it's over memories of childhood, which is a little like arguing about whether you dream in color.

While I wait for a ride to the elevator in Stewartville with their father, Rita recalls the last grain elevator to stand in downtown Rochester. "It was on North Broadway by the river and next to the railroad tracks."

"Roddis Elevator," says Sharon. "But what was the name of the bar down the street?"

"The Alibi."

"Dad always took us there afterwards and bought us a Hershey bar and an orange pop. Remember?"

For the girls, a trip to the elevator had been a treat in itself, an unexpected excursion into the greater world downtown. It was a dark wooden building where grain disappeared into a grate in the floor to be mysteriously lifted up to a lofty tower. They swung their legs on a bench in the office while their father finished his business. If he was waiting for feed to be ground, he'd march them down the block to the Alibi Inn. They always came in through the alley, past kegs and cases of sour-smelling empties, through the back door and down the long, dim cavern of a barroom at the end of which a plate-glass window looked out on the dazzling white street. On the bar side was a row of chrome-legged stools with red seats; on the other, half-round booths of the same slippery vinyl. The only illumination at midday, other than the blinding front window, came from a rainbow-colored jukebox against the wall or the electric tableaux for Hamms and Grain Belt suspended from the back bar. Spilling his change out on the bar, Ed would order a beer for himself and a bottle of pop and a candy bar for each of the girls. After being loudly admired—"Well, look at little Miss Salt and Miss Pepper!"— they were ignored while their father discussed prices or the weather with whomever, the conversation floating above the girls' ears, its cadence so different from the voices adults use with children. If they got squirrelly, the girls could spin every vacant stool top or chase each other around the booths or arm-wrestle or lose themselves staring at the framed picture of dogs playing poker that hung over the window. In too short a while, their father would announce that it was time to go.

ON THE DRIVE to Stewartville, we pass field after field of standing corn. The crop has survived a late spring drought, a killing frost on the first day of summer, and a cool, damp fall. Now it's too wet to pick. In some fields you could wring the ears like a sponge. One eager beaver took a load into the elevator only to have the drying fee cancel out the price of his corn. Ed had contracted to sell his corn in November and is playing a waiting game with the weather, hoping it will dry on the stalk before the snow flies. He has already invested $125 an acre in seed, fertilizer, and spraying, and that doesn't include crop insurance, taxes, or his own labor. Despite the poor harvest, corn prices are low.

"Cargill's sitting on all the corn they need," he says, "and the damn farmers are still planting to beat the band."

Not counting the water tower and church spire, the tallest structure in Stewartville is the All-American Co-op Elevator. Approached from Highway 20, its corrugated metal buildings and interconnected storage bins loom above the elm trees like a small oil refinery. Cornfields run right up to the edge of town on one side of the road, while a golf course and new subdivision push in the opposite direction. A sign in a muddy field: Future Site of Grace Evangelical Free Church.

Ed turns off before the business section, maneuvering the slippery grain truck through quiet, leaf-strewn streets, trying to beat the rush to the elevator. Already a small line is waiting at the grating shed—grain trucks, semis, tractors towing gravity boxes—all of them hauling soybeans. Ed skirts the line and pulls up between the Co-op office and a row of storage silos, stopping on the truck scale. While his load is being weighed, a tubular probe attached to a mechanical arm extracts a core sample of soybeans from the truck bed.

A voice over the intercom directs us to "Red driveway of C," and we circle around the Co-op to get in line for the grating shed. Since nobody is picking corn yet, the line moves at a good clip. (Dennis once pulled into the line with a load of corn at two in the afternoon and didn't get home until three o'clock the next morning.) When the truck ahead of us dumps its load of soybeans, a man in overalls and face mask waves us forward. The grating shed is a truck-sized passage in the base of the elevator. Ed drives ahead until a slap on the side of the truck signals that we're over the grate. Reaching under the seat, Ed pulls a red knob to engage the GMC's power lift and the truck bed begins to tilt upward. When it's fully extended, there's a bang as the grain door in the back is louvered open and then the hiss of flowing grain. With grain shovels and push brooms, the masked elevator men hurry the stream of soybeans through the heavy steel grate in the shed floor.

"Not much dust," Ed says, watching through the side mirror. "If they're dry, you can't see there's so much dust."

The beans pour into an unseen auger below the floor that carries them to the "leg" or cupped elevator that gives the building its name, and then to a horizontal auger that pulls them to whatever gray building they're destined for, drying or storage. From field to elevator is merely the first leg of the journey. Some of the beans will be trucked east to Winona and loaded onto barges to be pushed down the Mississippi River to the Gulf of Mexico. The rest will travel in the opposite direction, to a processing plant in Mankato to be pressed into vegetable oil for salad dressing or margarine or processed into meal so the farmer can buy them back as hog or poultry feed.

The food industry in this country is a pyramid with two

million producers at its base and a handful of processors at its apex. The giant corporations at the top exercise a virtual monopoly on food from farm to table. They sell seed and chemicals to farmers retail and then buy grains and livestock back from them wholesale. ConAgra, the nation's number-one flour miller, is the leading distributor of agricultural chemicals as well. It controls not only the buying and selling of grain but also its storage and shipment through more than one hundred grain elevators and thousands of railroad cars and barges. ConAgra and Cargill taken together account for half of all American grain exports. Because they control both ends of the business, these same companies were able to report record earnings and sales even during the eighties, when so many farmers lost their shirts.

We drive to the scale a second time so the empty truck can be weighed. The difference between the two weights is the load, in this case thirteen hundred pounds of soybeans. We wheel around the Co-op and park in front.

"Now I'll get the bad news. How wet they are. How much foreign crap. Just so long as they don't have to be dried. That drying will kill you. They'll ask if I want to store or sell them. I'm going to wait to see if the price goes up. They know they're going to get beans now because some guys need to make their payments."

A man behind the counter sifts through a cup of soybeans from the probe for any foreign objects—dirt, lamb's-quarter seeds, stray kernels of corn—before emptying the cup into a small plastic box that determines moisture content by measuring electric ions. Ed's soybeans test out at 15.7 percent moisture, which means that 4 percent of his load was water. He's docked twenty-five bushels. Since the price on the wall today is $5.08 a bushel, he's already lost $125 plus the mandatory cost of three months' storage.

"What's the good word, Glenn?"

Glenn scratches his neck a minute. "Well, it's getting pretty close to deer season."

When Ed drops me off, the kids are outside playing in a tree fort. Rita looks up from a sonata she's practicing on the piano. "Did he buy you a Hershey bar and an orange pop? Too bad. You missed the best part."

BY THE FIRST WEEK of November, a gray overcast has descended over the farm. A cold wind out of the northwest is spitting snow. Walking up the field road at dusk, hands in my pockets, I can hear the wind rustle the dried husks of standing corn. Just over the rise, the combine with a five-pronged corn picker mounted in front has run aground between two cornfields. Dennis is kneeling on the other side of the machine, wrenches fanned out next to him. He's wearing a ripped blue jacket with "Randy" stitched over the pocket and no gloves.

"Look at this sprocket," he says. "The bearing is supposed to fit in this, but it's completely stripped."

He'd picked a few acres of corn when he heard a click and the Massey-Ferguson almost imperceptibly changed tunes. An hour of troubleshooting and he found the problem—a quarter-size bearing that's part of the assembly for a vertical auger carrying grain to the hopper. The combine would cost $100,000 to replace, so downtime has to be figured into its operation. Since Dennis has to work on Monday, the corn harvest is postponed indefinitely until he can install a new bearing.

"Corn's still too moist. Some people will leave it in the field all winter if they can get by without feed. I'm going to run out in a few weeks."

All the light has drained out of the sky and into the snow-covered fields. The wind is bitterly cold. Dennis sweeps his wrench collection into a toolbox, then stares east as if he's forgotten something. In the fading light, it takes me awhile to see what he's looking at. Then I do: two yearling deer between the woods and the outermost field. Their semaphore ears stick out, alert, and I realize they're staring back at us.

"There's a big doe I saw a few days ago out standing in corn. I thought the corn was stunted, but it was full-sized. She's big all right."

This pair may be the doe's offspring, or maybe not. Plenty of deer cross the fields from the west to bed down in the hollow. It's a regular deer highway. But the two yearlings look at home here. They enter the far field and begin feeding, heads down, oblivious in this unexpected plenitude of standing corn that hunting season opens next week.

THE NIGHTS grow longer. The darkness neatly halves the days between work and sleep, although there is less of anything to do. On weekends we sit in recliners and watch the Packers lose, then the Vikings—always to a Sunbelt team whose quarterback looks like the star of surfing movies. Even the animals gear down as the world tilts toward winter. The early darkness acts as a soporific for everyone but Ed, who is the first to rise in the morning and the last to go to bed. When he can't sleep, he watches TV until he dozes off in the screen's blue light. "I get all the good shows at two o'clock," he jokes. "Lucy and Archie Bunker." Some nights when I can't sleep either, I listen to the progression of television shows through the thin walls of the spare bedroom: brief spates of music, a talk-show monologue, applause, a long stretch of movie dialogue, the hyena cries of an automobile commercial. He can't be interested in all this stuff. One night I recognized the Earl Scruggs bluegrass from *Bonnie and Clyde*, a movie I'd first seen at a theater in what now seems another life. I couldn't stop listening, scene after scene, even though the dialogue was an inaudible mumble, because I knew how the movie ended and understood there would be no release until I heard the whoosh of doves springing up from the roadside ambush and the long silence before the shooting starts. But I never did, so I must've fallen asleep.

SUNDAY MORNING I'm up before the others and watch from the living-room window as darkness ebbs and the yard light blinks off. The gray Olds Cutlass parked outside belongs to my brother-in-law Pete, the carpenter, who's waiting for me at this very moment above the hollow, hoping I will drive a deer past his stand so he can ambush it. I pour another cup of coffee. Finally, I put on my blaze-orange jacket and hike over east to find him.

The sky is pewtery, all shifting light and no heat. The windblown snow makes the open fields look grainy and larger than ever. I walk along the hedgerow to the edge of the woods and cut south toward Pete's stand, a wooded swale extending like a peninsula into the level field. Deer use its cover for crossing open ground, and, sure enough, as I approach the swale, a forkhorn buck breaks from the trees. Crashing through the undergrowth, white flag flying, the young buck reaches the top of the next rise and then pauses for a second to look back, outlined against the gray sky. No gunshot rings out. I aim my gloved finger at the buck and say "bang" just as it vanishes into the hollow.

It's a strange end to the fall. Sandwiched between Halloween and Thanksgiving, hunting season manages to combine elements of both. There are the blaze-orange get-ups, weird personifications on the radio ("When the buck's away, shop Prange's Lonely Doe sale"), flashlights flickering in the dark, and the posturing of men with guns. On the other hand, there is the companionship of friends, the anticipation of a feast, and the whiff of mortality that comes from knowing the true price of things. What most people find objectionable about hunting is not the death of animals, which is what farming is about on a larger scale, but the stag-party atmosphere that so often accompanies it. The awkwardness is a measure of how removed we've become from the animals we eat. Like many people, I used to be appalled by the annual procession of deer carcasses borne on car tops down the interstate. Where are they going? I wondered. Where have they been? Not the sort of questions one contemplates while passing a slow-moving stock truck on the way to the next burger joint. Gradually you suspect an absence of narrative in this Happy Meal existence.

I descend the hillside in a tree-grabbing slide to the hollow and wonder where Pete has hidden himself. It's windless and absolutely still. The trees near the spring are covered with hoarfrost and colorless except for a strand of bittersweet draped over the branches of a black locust. A dark shape passes overhead like some dread shadow, scaring the bejesus out of me, but it's only a wild turkey flying from its roost high in a white oak. I'm still watching it glide dreamlike to a landing in some brush at the far end of the hollow when someone calls my name.

"Here! I'm o-ver heeeeree!"

Since I'm partially deaf with no directional hearing, I have to slowly rotate until I finally locate my brother-in-law, a tall orange figure standing on the hillside above the spring, earflaps slightly askew, a neon-orange cushion dangling from his belt. He waves, then turns and walks away.

When I reach his stand in a clump of oaks, Pete is bent over a deer, working his knife through its white belly hair, as if he were cutting through Sheetrock to get at some wiring. Reaching up into the chest cavity, he severs the windpipe and turns the deer over to tip the steaming paunch onto the ground. He separates the heart and liver from the coils of bluish intestines and puts them into a plastic shopping bag. Then he wipes his knife and bloody hands clean with snow. This is the same forkhorn I had spooked from the wooded swale. The buck must have headed straight east before doubling back along this side of the hollow, following a well-worn trail through the woods as it fled, pausing just past this clump of oaks to sniff a few drops of doe scent Pete had put down.

"I aimed for the back of the head and hit him in the rear end. He went down like a rock."

Neither I nor the deer heard the shot. The slug must have hit the spine because the deer was dead when it hit the ground.

"I was freezing," Pete says, his arms stained to the elbows with blood. "I thought you weren't coming."

He slips a drag rope around the deer's neck and we skid the carcass down the hillside, leaving behind a pink trail in the snow. Once we get to level ground, I volunteer to hike back to the house and get the pickup. Everybody is up by now and getting ready for mass. Gunning the Jeep, I race back over the uneven road at full speed, scattering blackbirds across empty fields. But the cattle feeding at the wide end of the hollow pay no attention. They pretend not to notice as Pete and I swing the deer by its legs into the truck bed, as if this is some private feud in which they have no part.

THIRTEEN

The Rochester Fire Department set the old farmhouse on fire three days in a row, then put out the flames and drove away at the end of the exercise. By the time we arrive for the final conflagration, the house has taken on the bereft, deserted look of any abandoned homestead moldering in the woods behind a double-wide—a hole in the roof, plywood nailed over some windows, and smoke stains on the white sashes. Today all three shifts will gather to administer the coup de grâce. A basement for the new house has been excavated beside the old one, where the west wing once stood, so close, in fact, that the farmhouse appears poised to topple into it.

The driveway fills as friends and relatives arrive as if to watch fireworks at dusk. Everyone's in a picnic mood, and why not? Finally it's just an old house, whose destruction will mark a beginning as well as an end. The place has stood empty for weeks, but we all take a last-minute tour to jog memories or make certain nothing of value has been left behind. As with most prairie farmhouses, the illusion of size is left at the door; inside it's one small room after another, boxes within boxes, arranged around a central chimney. The electricity has been shut off, the rooms smoky and dim, and since I alone have no memories to jog, I try to picture a dozen people gathered in the dining room, three generations around the same table, night after night. There's nothing left now except for a broken console TV and a flame-orange armchair not worth rescuing. Deb and Steve have salvaged the wainscoting and banister to graft onto the modular home, to give it something of the old place. When I walk through the kitchen, Sharon is on her knees hammering at a hinge pin to remove a badly scratched door, although I can't imagine why.

The firemen arrive half an hour late in four lime-green engines and begin unraveling hoses and filling a plastic-lined reservoir in the driveway. They go about their tasks cheerfully because this will be a fire of their own devising, a blaze in which nobody is at risk but themselves. As the men finish their assigned tasks they are reduced to milling around like the rest of us, waiting for the fire to begin. One of the younger guys occupies himself by pitching stones from the driveway at an unbroken bedroom window until his chief waves him over for a talk.

When all is ready, the units gather by the trampoline pit to review the final exercise. Weighed down by bulky suits and oxygen tanks strapped to their backs, the men kneel down and bend their heads together as if reciting a pregame prayer. They start the blaze by igniting broken pallets and shredded paper piled in the small downstairs bedroom, the room in which Ed and all but one of his brothers and sisters were born. Columns of yellow smoke pour out the porch door as the fire spreads through the downstairs.

Out of uniform, Dennis has come to watch the fire after all, sitting on the lawn beside Ed and me. When a large fan is brought up to blow smoke from the house so the fireman inside can see, he calls it "positive ventilation" and wonders aloud if today's fire will include a training exercise called "Find the Dummy." Evidently it doesn't, since the firemen soon abandon the house without rescuing anything and stand back to let it burn.

"Wood burns two inches an hour," Dennis says. "So you

figure a house of this dimension will take about an hour to burn. When she starts to lose oxygen, she'll really start puffing."

The smoke turns black as the flames hit the asphalt shingles and creep along the roof line, blowing off the gables like sea spray. There's a slight breeze anyway, but as the heat's intensity builds, the fire generates its own whirlwind of dust and burning ash that forces us to retreat to the driveway. By now the firemen have turned off the pressure hoses and have nothing more to do with the blaze except contain it.

Flames break through the outer walls and the remaining windowpanes fall with a tinkling sound to the grass. Shingles on the siding begin to explode from the heat. When wind-whipped flames lick at the oak tree in the center of the lawn, Dennis tells some firemen to hose down the branches. The house is being consumed by flames, but nobody says much of anything. We're all too busy snapping pictures or video-taping or taking notes or otherwise documenting the event to think about whose house is burning. The fire seems nothing more than a special effect in a movie of our own making, as if it will go out once we finish the shot. A long-distance trucker who spotted the smoke two miles away in Simpson races up the driveway and seems genuinely surprised to find firemen hosing down trees while the house burns and the rest of us grinning like idiots. "Is this fire real?" he asks.

Sharon is taking pictures from the lower pasture as the flames eat through the northeast corner of the house. The wall has burned away to reveal a bedroom, its ceiling on fire. I tap her on the shoulder to tell her to move back from the heat but she keeps snapping away, and when she turns around, her eyes are red and brimming. "That was my bedroom," she says.

THIRTY YEARS EARLIER, a red-faced neighbor banged on the kitchen door and blurted, "Your pasture's on fire!"

The words, not entirely unexpected at this time of year, signaled a rush of activity as children bolted from the table, ignoring their mother's cries, and spilled out of the farmhouse. The air was hazy and smelled of burning grass. Uncles and older cousins appeared on the run from every direction. Their father pitched shovels, picks, and buckets into the back of the truck and roared down the driveway to the pasture gate. Behind the children came their grandmother, shading her eyes with one hand as she searched the lower pasture for the source of smoke. When she spotted the lean, familiar figure silhouetted against the flames, she sang out, "Johnnie, you fool! Get away from that fire!" in the same shrill voice she used at the piano, only louder, her shouts outdistancing the children as they ran toward the smoke.

Heart racing, legs pumping, Sharon chased the truck through the gate and down the incline to the lower pasture. Now she could hear the fire crackling through tall dry grass and weeds, a menacing thing with a will of its own. White smoke blanketed the figures stabbing at the flames with shovels and picks. And in the thick of it all was her grandfather, ignoring the younger men's calls to get the hell out of there, angry with them for thinking he couldn't handle his own fire.

Every spring her grandfather set fire to his pastures. And the grass always came up greener where it had been burned, or maybe it only looked more verdant against black ashes than dead-looking winter grass. On more than one occasion neighbors called the fire department, and as he got older the family monitored these seasonal fires more closely so the old man wouldn't hurt himself or burn down the house. For Sharon, though, spring meant rotting snow banks beside the barn and building dams in the ruts along the field road to catch the yellow-brown runoff and the pungent smell of manure spread on the fields. This was the season when her grandfather would resume his walks. Looking up from play, she often saw him in the distance, bent over a pile of brush along the creek or striding headlong across the dun-colored fields, a lone figure in a broad-brimmed hat, boots, and leather cuffs, covering ground with his weightless horseman's stride. Once he was pitching rocks into a bucket on the tractor and she asked what he was doing. "God's angry at me," he whispered. "So he dropped all these stones in my field for me to pick up."

Sharon never saw the fire that caught him, only the aftermath when her father helped carry him into the kitchen. Her grandfather's clothes were peppered with cinder holes and his boots scorched from trying to stomp out the flames. The wind had shifted and the fire caught his pants legs. Now he sat in his chair at the table, saying nothing as his son unlaced the blackened boots and removed the pants to reveal skinny white legs burnt raw along the shins. Her grandmother filled a basin with water and Epsom salts, all the while scolding him for being so reckless, so foolish, so terribly old.

After the fire her grandfather's movements were largely confined to a slow-motion shuffle between his bedroom and an oak rocker in the bay window of the living room, where he sat by the hour reading western novels and smoking cigars. He grew increasingly forgetful and contentious with those who cared for him, angry that he could no longer do for himself. But he'd let Sharon drink the sweetened dregs from his teacup after supper as a reward for lingering with him. And if she fetched the newspaper from the mailbox he would reach into his vest pocket, pull out a leather change purse, and hand her a dime. He called her Rosie, short for Rose of Sharon.

By October the yard light came on earlier and earlier until the barn loomed darker than the dusk falling outside. Cows entered through the south door, always the same cow in the lead, and proceeded down the center aisle, each falling off at its own stanchion with the slow deliberateness of people taking a church pew. Sharon and Rita were the youngest children allowed in the barn at milking time. Walking along the cement ramp above the stanchions, they emptied a coffee can of ground corn into each manger, feeling the cows' steamy breath on their hands, while their father worked at the other end, washing udders with a wet rag. The barn itself seemed alive and breathing in the still night air. There was the creaking of the water pump, the bellowing of hungry cows, the steaming arc of piss into the gutter, the hissing of the hot-water heater, the *thumpa-thumpa-thumpa* of the air compressor that ran the vacuum line overhead, and underscoring it all a thin wail of Western music from the Bakelite radio on the shelf. By the time the girls finished, their father had washed, belted, and attached milkers to cows in the first two stanchions. In the separating room, they set up milk cans and argued over who would put the paper filter in the bottom of the strainer. Chores done for the moment, they raced back across the barn and up the narrow staircase to the haymow.

Hay was stacked two to three stories high at both ends of the mow, its cavernous space dimly lit by three lightbulbs. An old hay-fork rail ran the length of the vaulted roof, and dangling from either end were two thick hay ropes. Each girl pulled the looped end of a rope around her waist and then climbed to the rafters. One scaled the ladder while the other scrambled up bales piled on the other side. At the count of three, the girls launched themselves into the darkness. It was like flying. When the ropes caught midway, they began to braid, spinning the girls in even faster revolutions until the ropes twisted to the knot above their heads and they collided. Kicking off with their feet, they'd whirl away in the opposite direction. If their brother Eddie or older sisters took a turn, their greater momentum caused the smaller girls to spin even more breathlessly out of control until two shrill whistles from below signaled a full pail of milk waiting to be emptied into the strainer, and they all galloped down from the mow.

The milking done, the girls unhitched cows from stanchions and watched them wander out the south door for the Night Pasture. While the older children scraped shitty straw into the gutter, their father swished each milker and pail with scalding water, dipped them into the water tank, and hung them to dry. He coaxed the last bit of milk through the strainer in the separating room, saving a pint for the collection of barn cats waiting for this moment. Once the strainer was scoured and hung, he capped the full milk cans, weighing one hundred pounds each, and rolled them to the side door for the morning's milk truck. Collecting the pail of house milk taken from a cow mysteriously selected for this honor, he walked back through the barn, turning off the water faucet and radio and light switches to plunge the south end into darkness. The girls waited for him to slide the north door open, surprised at the night's sudden chill and the overwhelming silence when their father shut off the water pump and they crossed the yard to supper.

Sharon and Rita shared an iron bedstead in the small room at the top of the stairs. Above the bed hung a gold-framed print of two children strolling along a darkly wooded path while behind them a white-robed angel (unseen by the kids) fanned its enormous wings. The angel's arms were extended, palms forward, as if herding the children away from some unforeseen danger. The picture illustrated a bedtime prayer —"Angel of God, my guardian dear / By whom God's love commits me here"—and was intended as an antidote to night terrors, but the angel was too spooky, too much a night creature itself, to be of much comfort.

A cascade of footsteps on the stairs woke Sharon early one morning. It was followed by murmured voices and someone sniffling into a handkerchief. Neither her sister nor their brother, sprawled in a cot at the foot of the bed, had stirred, so she went back to sleep. Later their father came to the door to wake them, a rarity since he was usually at chores by then. If he was in a particularly good mood, he sometimes called from the landing, "First up, best dressed!" But this morning he looked very tired and his voice was tight as he told the children their grandfather had passed away. That explains the noises, Sharon thought, wondering about the mechanics of moving a dead body down a staircase. "He died in his sleep," her father said. "It was painless. He didn't suffer." This was a detail she hadn't thought to ask about.

The wake was at Macken's Funeral Home, which looked from the outside like an elegant restaurant but smelled of church inside. After the unexpected holiday from school, the children sat mute in the second row of chairs and tried not to fidget as a parade of relatives and friends paid their respects. When someone tapped her on the shoulder, Sharon walked up to the open coffin and let her knees sink to the padded kneeler. Flanked by flower arrangements, her grandfather looked softer in death than he had in life, as if all the hurt had been drained out of him. She said a quick prayer. Then, glancing around to see if anyone was watching, she reached forward to touch the slender, translucent hands folded lightly across his good gray suit.

A priest began the rosary. "The First Sorrowful Mystery: The Agony in the Garden." A chorus of Hail Marys swept through the chapel like a dry wind.

The next morning, the procession moved from St. Bridget's into waiting cars to drive the absurdly short distance around the border of pines to the cemetery gate. The last cars had not yet left the church when the hearse pulled up to the graveside. The tombstones closest to the church were weathered slabs of limestone with curved tops and blotches of orange lichen in the lettering, while the newer stones were polished gray marble that held one's reflection and looked as if they'd last forever. Her grandfather's plot was in the middle of the cemetery on a rise overlooking the church and yellow stubble fields beyond. There was no headstone yet, only a gaping hole in the grass, and just to the right of it a flat stone with an

angel etched on one corner and her own last name carved
into it:

Ronald M. O'Neill
June 25, 1948
June 30, 1950
The Angels Will Watch Over Him

The gravestone belonged to an older brother who had died
before Sharon was born, leaving behind few traces of his short
life except this stone and a pair of bronzed baby shoes. The
shoes, size two Dr. Scholl's walkers, sat atop the highboy in
her parents' bedroom along with pocket combs, handkerchiefs,
and her father's balled-up socks. As a child, she'd heard the
bronzed shoes before she saw them. Coming back from errands
in town, her father would empty his pocket change into the
tray where the bronze shoes rested. The coins made the same
sound when she spread them on her parents' chenille bed
cover, then scooped them up to pour back into the tray. When
her parents came in, she'd ask, "Whose shoes are these?" Finally her mother sat her down and explained that they had
belonged to her oldest brother, Ronnie, who had drowned five
days after his second birthday when he fell into a water trough,
apparently trying to drink from the spigot. It was not the sort
of story a child expects to be connected to a pair of baby shoes;
and though it answered one mystery, it posed an even greater
one. Growing up on a farm, a child cannot help but be aware
of death, but the idea that a landscape as familiar as one's own
home could kill anyone, let alone a child, opened a world of
unforeseen possibilities.

A month later, the family sat in the living room and
watched another funeral. Drums rolled as a riderless horse
followed the slain president's flag-draped caisson down Pennsylvania Avenue. Her grandmother, who watched the television from a small upholstered rocker, grieved hardest of
all. With each funeral there was a similar feeling of loss and

foreboding, a fear of what would happen next. "Remember this," her father said in the same somber voice he had used on the morning of her grandfather's death. "This is history."

JOHN O'NEILL had died without a will, so the farm went into probate, and while the family sorted out his estate a succession of outside forces descended upon it. The phrase "eminent domain" was invoked with increasing frequency around the house, and always with an undertone of bitterness. To a ten-year-old it sounded more like "*imminent* domain," which made perfect sense given the urgency of the voices. Your *domain* was your property, your home, and *imminent* referred to matters that were pending. So when the term came up in her parents' conversations, Sharon understood that they were speaking of dark events gathering on the horizon, things about to happen to all of them.

What happened first was that Dairyland Power strung a 168,000-volt transmission line across the farm. The wires ran between seventy-foot H-frame poles erected along the highest part of the cropland. The power company offered landowners $25 for each hole it drilled. When a farmer on Irish Ridge climbed into one of the holes on his property, the pole crew from the power company retreated. The O'Neills and one hundred other landowners hired an attorney to sue Dairyland for greater compensation, but the case never reached court. "The lawyers went into the back room," Sharon's father would say, "and when they came out, it was settled."

At the same time, the family was fighting a losing battle with the highway department. A few years before John O'Neill's death, a surveyor had stopped at the farmhouse and spent most of the evening explaining the proposed route of a superhighway that would cut across the southeastern corner of the farm on its way to linking the coasts. On a map, he showed where Interstate 90 would cut kitty-corner through

Stillwell's eighty and connect with a widened Highway 52 by cloverleaf, slicing off the marshy land on the farm's northern border. The combined highways would consume eighty acres, mostly pasture, for right-of-way and landlock another seventy, for a total loss of 150 acres—one-fourth of the farm. The family's greatest concern, however, was that the interstate would cut off their access to the Root River land. But construction was years away, the surveyor assured them, and the highway department would almost certainly build an overpass for farm traffic.

For a long time, nothing did happen. After a survey crew came through, the children pulled up their orange stakes and used them for sword fights or to anchor gopher traps. Construction was down the road at Stewartville, always another summer away. Then, in 1967, a highway crew logged a four-hundred-foot-wide swath through the oak woods at Stillwell's and burned the slash in great berm piles that smoldered for weeks. The next year, bulldozers and earthmoving equipment scoured the swath into a wide corridor of brown dirt, leveling hills, diverting creeks into culverts, and filling the summer's stillness with noise.

One afternoon when the blasting and heavy machinery had quieted, Sharon, Diane, and Rita decided to ride the arc that had been cut through the farm. They were shy a horse, so Sharon doubled up on Blaze with Rita and rode south through the fields until they reached their uncle's pasture, where she slid off and caught a big Morgan that belonged to her cousin in Vietnam. They followed the county road as it curved past their uncle's farm toward Simpson. This was the route they took every summer to the Root River land, riding in a wagon behind the tractor, descending through a green canopy of trees to the sun-drenched bottom and then up the switchback to the hayfield. Now the road dead-ended at the interstate. (There was no overpass for farm traffic, nor would there ever be.) Scrambling down the soft dirt bank onto the roadbed, the riders turned their horses north. The sunken highway was sandy-bottomed and as broad as a dry riverbed. They rode past idled earthmovers and road cuts of stratified limestone with the drill holes still fresh. Sharon had trouble reining the horse back, and when he dropped to his knees to cool off in a sand bank, she leaped clear before he rolled. The Morgan wriggled on his back, stood up again, and she grabbed a handful of mane to swing back on. They rode up to the cloverleaf, two byzantine whorls of dirt at the base of Potter's Field, then turned west onto Highway 52, which was being widened to a four-lane. The bridge that would carry the county road over the highway hadn't been completed yet, so they spurred their horses up the slope to the old ruts of the Dubuque Trail and followed that back home.

Eventually the family sold the Root River land to settle the estate, since the interstate had turned a fifteen-minute tractor ride into an hour's commute. Nevertheless, the grandchildren were surprised when they didn't make the usual summer's trip to the river and the hayfield on the bluff. They had taken these things for granted, and now they were gone. They couldn't understand the decision to sell, because it contradicted everything they knew about farming. Their grandfather had sold crops and milk and livestock, but he had never sold land. The doctor who purchased the Root River land wasn't interested in farming, though. He'd bought it for the view.

That summer, the summer before high school, Sharon moved into Rochester to baby-sit for a cousin and his wife. It had seemed a good idea—helping out relatives, living in town. After they'd gone to work, she washed the breakfast dishes and cleaned the house, but that still left the afternoon to kill. She watched soap operas or took the baby to the fenced backyard and sat in a lawn chair reading. Sometimes she watched the boy next door playing catch with his brother, but when her cousin introduced them, thinking she wanted someone her own age to talk with, she wasn't interested. Days blurred together. Closed in by houses on all sides, she rarely ventured outside. It was a self-imposed loneliness, an interval of mourning to mark the passing of one's own childhood. When she returned home on weekends, her life seemed out of sequence; the hay already stacked in the barn, the calves rounded up, the first green apples discovered and eaten with salt. She had come home a stranger to all that.

On an August weekend in 1968, she watched the Democratic convention with her parents. On television, police and antiwar protesters collided in the streets of Chicago, one more disturbing event in a year of assassinations, riots, and state funerals. Her father sat on the sofa clenching his fists as demonstrators rained down shit from hotel windows onto the police below. On the street, a phalanx of cops charged through the protesters, flailing at them with nightsticks, dragging the fallen away. Despite the long hair, many of them looked no different, Sharon thought, from her older sister. For the first time, she realized that she and her father were on different sides of an issue that went beyond her choice of clothes or friends. Where he saw cowards defiling the flag, she saw kids being brutalized. "They're not doing anything wrong!" she yelled. He jumped to his feet, shouting, "They're bastards and they're going to ruin this country!" She stomped off to the kitchen.

For someone who'd spent most of her education within the confines of a three-room schoolhouse stuffed with cousins and neighbors, Mayo High School offered plenty of room for experimentation. Sharon alternated between two social circles. The first group lived on the southeast side of town in the kinds of houses she had babysat in the previous summer. The boys drove beaters they'd fixed up themselves and laid rubber when they left the parking lot, which was as soon as possible. Few went out for sports or the school play or did anything after class except cruise in their cars and go to work. In the summer, they threw keg parties in the countryside—a ring of cars at the end of a field road, radios blaring into the night. A couple of the girls dated older boys who were studying mechanical engineering or hydraulics in tech school at Granite Falls, but graduation held no immediate prospects beyond marriage or the draft or the job they held at the moment. But Sharon also dated boys from Pill Hill whose parents worked for the clinic or IBM. They drove to school in new cars and stayed to play sports. They partied at home when their parents went away to a conference and wouldn't notice what was missing from the liquor cabinet. They came back from Christmas vacation with tans that set off perfect teeth, and when they spoke of the future, it was with the assurance of people who'd been there.

Sharon's best friend was a girl named Liz, whose mother worked as a cocktail waitress. One night Liz's mother came home from her job to find a party in full swing, and tossed everyone out. Sharon, who had just gotten her license, borrowed Liz's car to drive another girl home. The streets were empty. A few miles later, she noticed a police car in the rearview mirror. Turning off the radio, she studied the dashboard. The lights were on; she wasn't over the speed limit. "Oh, shit!" the other girl cried. "He turned on the flashers!" Sharon kept driving, hoping the cop might be after someone else even though she'd seen no other cars. When she turned into a subdivision, the cruiser did the same. She told the girlfriend to jettison the beer under the seat. Out the window flew three bottles of beer, followed by a pint of vodka from the glove compartment. She was going through the ashtray looking for roaches when the cruiser pulled in front and cut them off. Two patrolmen got out and walked back to the car. One played his flashlight through the driver's window while the other walked past them and disappeared down the road.

"Why didn't you stop at the lights?" asked the first cop.

"What lights? Oh, you mean back at the Holiday station? I did stop."

"No," he said, drawing out the word. "You didn't."

He was checking her license when the second cop came back, cradling the bottles the girls had pitched out the window. He put them in the cruiser.

At the police station the girls sat on a bench and stared at the brown linoleum while they waited for their parents to arrive. The brightly lit room was quiet except for the dispatcher's radio and a balding, pink-skinned policeman in short sleeves behind the counter who spoke into the microphone to answer questions or give directions. Occasionally a policeman walked through to shelve papers or stop at the counter before stepping back into the night. Nobody said anything to them. Shortly afterward the door opened and Sharon looked up to see her father walk into the room, chin down, head held slightly to one side. Turning toward the bench, he looked right through her, then walked to the counter and slowly rested his forearms on top as if they carried the weight of the world.

"Ed?" the dispatcher asked.

He nodded without looking up.

"Ed O'Neill?"

His features softened as he looked into the man's face. "Baldy? Baldy Mertz? Well geez. . . ."

They laughed, gesturing toward the bench, and Sharon brightened a little, hoping that maybe things wouldn't go too badly now that the tone had changed. Baldy motioned her over and explained how he and her father had gone to school together, blah, blah, blah. . . . She didn't dare look at her father during this reminiscence, but tried to adopt a posture that conveyed both interest and profound regret. The ride home was absolutely quiet.

The next morning the house seemed empty. It was eerie. Maybe everyone had left before the storm could break. Sharon was standing before the bathroom mirror applying mascara when her father walked in behind her and leaned on the edge of the tub. She waited for him to explode so she could offer some kind of protest, engage in the arguments that had become rote by then. But he didn't. He just sat there, looking at her, and she felt ashamed. Finally he said, "I guess you're just one of those people who has to learn by experience." Then he stood up and walked out.

As she got older, Sharon no longer helped in the barn; the work had stopped being play, and her father didn't push it, since she'd gotten a job after school. He injured his back and was laid up for two months in constant pain. A doctor suggested surgery, while the chiropractor he'd been seeing warned that surgery could leave him worse off and scheduled him for three adjustments a week. The only thing they both agreed on was that he needed rest. The milk check was the family's only steady income, so even though he talked about selling the dairy cows, he couldn't. Instead he brought in a hired man, a drifter who slept in the small room at the top of the stairs and was an awkward presence at the dinner table. When the hired man suddenly quit, Eddie took over the milking and Uncle Jim came in the evenings to help with chores.

None of the children had been groomed to take over the farm. By accident or omission, they had been reprieved from a life they hadn't asked to be reprieved from. Their options were wide open—which is to say, they were free to make their own mistakes. Near the end of senior year, Sharon decided she wanted to go to college. Her best friends were planning weddings after graduation, but she thought she might have a future beyond Rochester if she could only figure out what it was. Farming was out of the question unless she married a farmer, and the only ones she knew were relatives. She had been considered a good artist ever since a fifth-grade teacher praised her for being the only one in class to correctly draw a horse whose legs bent in opposing directions. Making things with paint or clay was a logical extension of a tactile childhood, but studying art also seemed presumptuous, so she settled on art education as a more practical field. There were always jobs for teachers.

Mankato State University was two hours away, distant enough to seem like an escape, yet not so far as to require an airplane ticket to get home. Her parents were as curious about the destination as Sharon was the day they drove her to college. They took Highway 14 at a leisurely pace, her parents in the front seat remarking on the scenery, noting the crops and whether a town had grown larger (Byron) or smaller (Clare-mont) in the years since they last came through.

The campus was split between a sloping valley formed by the Minnesota and Blue Earth rivers and the wide prairie above it. They stopped at the registration building first, then at accounts payable, and finally at a cream-colored dormitory on the lower campus, where her parents helped carry up the same olive-drab footlocker her mother had taken from Montana on her own flight from home.

After Sharon was settled into her room, they drove to the athletic fields on the upper campus, where the Minnesota Vikings held their summer training camp. They watched linemen the size of silos collide with one another. Sharon and her father talked stats and the team's prospects and just enjoyed watching a conflict in which they found themselves in agreement. Then they drove back to the dorm. There were no tears at saying good-bye. Each generation on the farm had raised its children only to help them move away, to watch them leap free of all that had once truly mattered.

Before getting back in the car for the long ride home, her father gave her a hug and one last piece of advice. He said, "Stay out of trouble."

FOURTEEN

By Thanksgiving, cows are feeding in the yellow stubble fields over east. A two-man combine crew picked the corn in a single day. Twenty dollars an acre. Despite the poor harvest, prices are down because the sun managed to shine in Illinois and Iowa, where farmers enjoyed a bumper crop. After the corn was picked, Ed opened the gates because each day the cattle glean in the stubble is another bale of hay he won't have to feed this winter. The cows look enormous against the flattened horizon, rummaging through the wreckage of fields they eyed anxiously over the fence all summer.

Steve and Deb's family are still living with the folks. The basement walls for their new house have already been poured, but the factory in Waseca is running behind schedule for delivery. There's nothing between the driveway and lower pasture but an unfinished basement and a slump in the ground where the limestone foundation of the old farmhouse was bulldozed into the cellar and covered with fill. Dirt is a good insulator and even now, weeks later, the heated limestone breathes a thin geyser of steam into the chill air.

Fran has roasted a turkey with stuffing, while the rest of us arrive bearing mashed potatoes, candied yams, homemade pickles, creamed corn, butternut squash, a broccoli-and-cheese hot dish, and two kinds of pies. It's a small entry fee to attach ourselves, for the weekend, to a family larger than our own. Of course, it's easier coming into a family through the backdoor of marriage, thus avoiding the guerrilla warfare of adolescence, and one's subsequent failings or achievements don't necessarily reflect on the family at large; in-laws enjoy a kind of diplomatic immunity. Nevertheless, the fact that so many of my wife's siblings return home on a regular basis, and not just for ceremonial gatherings, speaks well for their collective memories of childhood and, by extension, their parents' success as parents, as the kind of married couple we'd like to imagine becoming.

When the newest son-in-law, Cindy's husband, arrives from his job at Marigold Dairy, he thumps a five-gallon tub of vanilla ice cream on the kitchen counter. "I made this myself," says Marty.

A card table is set up for the kids in the family room, and the adults take their seats at the kitchen table. As we hover over steaming platters of food, Ed wonders aloud if we should say grace. The invitation hangs in the air. Several wiseacres say the word "grace." But the newest son-in-law, thinking perhaps that he has the most to be grateful for, proposes a simple doxology.

"When I was growing up," says Marty, "we always said what we were thankful for."

It's probably a wonderful custom, but this is a family in which one's luck, good or bad, is always underplayed.

People groan.

"Sounds Protestant to me."

"You know the difference between Baptists and Presbyterians? Presbyterians are Baptists that drink."

"You know what they say about Lutherans? They won't have sex standing up because they're afraid people will think they're dancing."

We say a short, uninspired grace.

Marty Kiley had the good fortune to marry the last eligible

O'Neill daughter. To avoid all the hoopla of a church wedding—bridesmaids in matching taffeta and lectures from a priest—the couple eloped to Lake Tahoe, returning from their honeymoon the same afternoon we demolished the west wing of the old farmhouse. They drove up in a Japanese pickup just as Ed was carrying a blue roof section on the Bobcat's tines to the Night Pasture to burn. If they were surprised to find part of the bride's home in smithereens, they looked too tanned and happy to show it. We drifted inside to watch a video Cindy had brought back of the wedding ceremony. The couple stood on the wind-buffeted hotel grounds facing the lake, the bride holding a bouquet of baby roses against her wine-red dress. The justice of the peace, ministerial in a gray suit and rimless glasses, read a few lines from *The Prophet* and invoked the wedding ceremony of the "early inhabitants of this beautiful region we call Tahoe." Fast-forwarding, we watched the bride's and groom's faces go somber at the exchange of vows, as if they'd been transported to a cliff face and asked to gaze upon their own mortality. So much of modern life is a matter of keeping options open that marriage can seem a frightening proposition; even if it doesn't turn out to be a life sentence, you always assume that it will be. Afterward, the wedding party popped open bottles of champagne.

As a gift to the newlyweds, the bride's parents have hired the Legion hall and a band for a wedding dance on Saturday night. Marty is grateful but seems a little apprehensive about Ed's taste in music.

Whenever a song comes on the radio, he asks, "Does the band play this?"

THE STREETS of downtown Rochester are strung with Christmas lights the night we drive to William T. McCoy Legion Post 92 for the wedding dance. I've been up since 4:00 a.m. to hunt deer on the Wisconsin side of the Mississippi

River, so the day seems a long tunnel that began in darkness and blood at one end and, sixteen hours later, is concluding at the other end in darkness and the promise of a hangover.

While I was hunting, Sharon and her sisters spent the afternoon decorating the Legion hall with green, white, and red balloons and crepe-paper streamers. The colors, which suggest both the upcoming holidays and, unintentionally, the Italian flag, are a cheery antidote to the grim photographs of former post commanders that ring the dance floor. Even the vanilla sheet cake has green and red sprinkles. For the last wedding dance for which he'll foot the bill, Ed has booked the Village Tavern Masters, a three-piece band from Dodge Center, whose flyer promises "real genuine original beer drink'n foot stomp'n heel kick'n Music." In addition to the drummer, what appears to be a father-son combination switches instruments every other song, so the band seems larger than it really is. After puffing their way through "Beer Barrel Polka" on tuba and concertina, they pick up a bass and lead guitar for a weepy "Blue Eyes Crying in the Rain." The father sings lead vocal, though the lyrics are all but lost when somebody's kid gets his head stuck in a folding chair. It's a good introduction to the rigors of married life—a few notes of music underscored by chaos.

The crowd is evenly split between O'Neills and Kileys and their respective satellites. The groom stands at the bar, bolstered by members of his softball team, one of whom shakes his head and keeps repeating, "You're the last of the last, Marty!" Waiting in line at the bar, I try to decipher the tattoo on the bartender's right forearm. It's either a heart with wings or a flying hamburger.

"Get your deer yet?"

This time of year it's a question that passes for hello. The answer is a qualified yes. A friend filled my tag by shooting a big doe and we paddled to shore with it slumped between the thwarts, slush ice rubbing against the canoe. But nobody at the table wants to hear the tiresome details; they're more interested in Sharon's new job, which involves tragedy of a different sort. She's working as a part-time teacher on an adolescent behavioral health and chemical-dependency ward at the local hospital, admittedly an odd career move for someone with a master's in art education. Her students are a mixed bag of aberrant behaviors: cross-dressers, sexual perpetrators, interrupted suicides, "huffers" who get high on gasoline fumes, schizophrenics wired into a switchboard of voices. Most are the products of some form of abuse—physical, sexual, emotional—just use your imagination. All of them are children and what they have in common, besides the drugs or loony behavior that got them institutionalized in the first place, is that so many come from fucked-up homes. It's a sobering thought at a wedding dance to consider all the ways families destroy their own.

The band honks out a polka version of "That's Amore" as we line up for the privilege of paying a dollar to dance with the bride or groom. Hopping from one foot to the other, Marty presents a moving target, holding the women at arm's length, all except for Dennis and Bridget's daughter Kelly, whom he sweeps up like a doll and waltzes in great circles around the floor. His lovely bride, on the other hand, endures a succession of flat-footed bear-huggers, myself among them. A few twirls, and my turn is over quicker than a fair ride. Gradually the floor fills with other couples, softball players and parents who've sent their children home with baby-sitters. Wired to the same current, Ed and Fran two-step past in practiced, concise movements, smiling as they orbit around the bride and groom.

Those who remain seated are subjected to a roving in-law armed with a video camera. From table to table, he asks the guests if they have any advice for the newlyweds. Not surprisingly, they do. There must be a thousand years of matrimonial experience in the room waiting to be tapped. The older generation, gazing back on forty-odd years, is more generous in their comments than the younger couples, still mired in child-rearing, whose outlook is bruised and sardonic. It's like the left side of the brain talking to the right.

> "Take the good with the bad."
> "Separate bedrooms."
> "Life is fifty-fifty. You've got to give as well as take."
> "Be careful."
> "Love and kindness helps."
> "Don't have a kid who sticks his head in a chair."
> "Be careful."
> "Never go to bed angry."
> "Remember, marriage is more like seventy-thirty."
> "If they'll turn to the Lord, they'll last a long time."
> "My advice to the bride? Keep your legs shaved!"
> "Be happy. Love each other."
> "If you can't be good, be careful!"
> "Vote Republican."
> "I haven't finished my beer yet!"
> "Forgive and forget."
> "Keep your head down on those ground balls, Marty."
> "Be careful!"
> "I've already given my advice. It's on a tape somewhere."

Imagine an anthropologist in the distant future unearthing this video with its jerky camera work and background roar, looking as if it were shot at sea during a typhoon. What does it say about marriage that so many women spoke of forgiveness and the sacrificial quality of love? What can it mean that only the men warned the couple to "be careful"? What did I mean when I said it?

A friend of the bride's, winner of several karaoke contests, takes the microphone and wows the guests by singing "Crazy" in the torchy style of Patsy Cline. She follows it up with "I Fall to Pieces."

I'm tired and ready to go home but not, Sharon insists, until we dance one last time. We walk onto the shadowy floor and wait for the beat to sweep us along. When she starts squeezing my palm to time our steps, I tell her to knock it off. Married life is so crowded that at times it's claustrophobic, a mild dose of multiple personalities—though the idea is that two heads are better than one, and sometimes, when you're sailing together smoothly across a dance floor, they are. Meanwhile, nephews and nieces are dodging around the floor in a game of tag. As if that doesn't present enough of a challenge, someone has sprinkled dance wax on the brown-and-cream linoleum until its surface is as slippery as ice. It's all I can do to hold on to my wife as we polka in half turns across the room, weaving past children and in-laws, picking up speed until their faces and the photographs of deceased post commanders blur together and I think: This must be love.

ON A CLEAR MORNING in January, hoarfrost against a gray-blue sky, Steve and I chase cows from the corral so we can put their calves into a holding pen for a trip to the auction barn in Lanesboro. This is the final event in an agricultural year that began last spring when these same calves came into the world as shiny, wet bundles waiting to be licked dry.

The corral is bright with sunlight on snow and pocked with frozen clods of manure. Flocks of sparrows feast eagerly on the fresh droppings. The black calves, now weighing six hundred pounds each, cluster at the far end of the corral breathing clouds of frost. Keeping an eye on the one horned cow that hangs back with her calf, we get the youngsters moving along the fence toward a makeshift alley we made by parking a manure spreader perpendicular to the gate. Once they're boxed in, Ed starts up the Bobcat. The calves are used to its deep-throated roar, since this is the machine that fed them bales of hay all winter. Now, with the bucket down, Ed uses it to intimidate them into the pen. After the gate slams shut behind the last one, he calls the stock truck.

The temperature is climbing into the thirties, meltwater dripping off the barn roof. The night before, it fell to twenty below. This has been a winter of extremes, thaws followed by freezes, a roller-coaster of weather that's hard on livestock. Already this year one farmer has lost thirty calves to pneumonia.

A pickup hauling a gooseneck trailer the length of a yacht pulls into the driveway an hour later and backs through plowed snow to the holding pen. The young driver has peach fuzz on his chin and yellow curls falling from under his hat. He carries a fiberglass wand with a few inches of rope at the end that he flexes like a trout rod to load the calves—a tricky job because there's no ramp and the cattle have to step up to get into the trailer. But the driver doesn't rush them and must be new to the job because he seems to enjoy it. When Ed asks what the hauling charge will be, he grins and shakes his curly head.

"I was wondering that myself."

Fran manages to keep one eye on *The Price Is Right* in the living room while peeling potatoes at the kitchen sink. When a contestant gives a spectacularly wrong answer, Bob Barker knits his eyebrows together in faux exasperation and the studio audience explodes with laughter. Ed changes into a fresh shirt, slacks, and walking boots. He sits at the kitchen table and grabs a handful of pistachio nuts.

"How much money should I bring home, dear?"

This is an exchange they've practiced for decades, an inside joke, because farmers have no control over prices for what they raise. It's always a buyer's market.

Nevertheless, Fran stops peeling to consider the question as if she has entered an isolation booth. "Twenty-one thousand?"

"Christ, I'm only selling nineteen head! I bet I won't get eight thousand."

"You'd better!"

THE HIGHWAY DESCENDS in a steep S curve to Lanesboro, which sits in the bowl of a limestone valley cut by the Root River. We drive out of the shadow of the bluff and cross a bridge into a small town given over to its past: storefronts and white frame houses converted to antique emporiums and Indian jewelry shops, bed-and-breakfasts. An abandoned railroad grade that runs along the riverbank has been turned into a recreation trail. Every summer legions of bicyclists sweep into Lanesboro like an army of occupation, swaggering down the sidewalks in helmets and funny shorts. The town's other economy is hidden except on winter mornings, when the only traffic consists of stock trucks heading for the cattle yards along the river.

Five hundred feeder calves have been trucked in for today's sale, quite a few of them from Iowa to judge from the blue license plates in the parking lot. Ed wedges his Buick Regal between two pickups and we stroll down the drive alley to check out the competition. Two acres of wooden pens and catwalks stretch along this side of the river. After the wet harvest, farmers who can afford to are buying calves to fatten on corn that isn't worth anything on the grain market. Instead of paying elevator storage and drying fees, they'll feed their crop to a granary-on-hooves that four months later they'll turn around and sell as fat cattle. We pass the narrow, confessional-size compartments where the bulls are penned. Bull pens. When I peer through the slatted windows, the stalls are empty. Another couple of gates and we find Ed's black calves at the far end of the yard. They appear not to recognize us but swarm together, heads up, as if swimming a current while trying to see where it's taking them. They look better than the small, manure-splattered Herefords next door who've been penned overnight. Some of them, Ed says, he can hear wheezing.

The auction barn is unheated, so we wear everything we brought. It's an overwhelmingly male crowd, lots of sideburns and Brylcreem, their occupation made conspicuous as much by what's missing—the pinned-up sleeve or prosthesis, limbs lost to augers and power takeoffs—as by the nylon jackets and muddy bootpacs. One man has brought his dog. The mood is social but no less serious than you'd expect from a group of small-time gamblers who've convened to bet the farm. Where else can you watch a man risk an entire year's worth of hard work on a few seconds of luck?

The delicious smell of frying hamburgers from the concession stand just inside the door competes with wafts of manure from the auction ring. Balancing steaming cups of coffee, we have to climb nearly to the roof to find a seat in the bleachers. Luther Olsen, the auctioneer, sits on a wooden platform above the gate through which cattle will enter the ring. He's a long-eared man in a black cowboy hat, a pair of dark-framed glasses riding on the edge of his nose. Looking for selling points, he asks Ed if his cattle have had their shots.

"Just black leg. In October. And they've been penned overnight."

Luther jots all this down. His wife went to nursing school with one of Ed's older daughters.

On their way to the ring, the cattle pass over a floor scale that flashes their combined weight on a large electric scoreboard above the auctioneer's platform. Luther divides this sum by the number of cattle to arrive at an average weight per head. As the gate swings open, the first lot bursts into the ring. Four fawn-eyed Limousin steers hit the brakes and skid on the sawdust. Average weight: seven hundred pounds. The steers put their heads together and begin to pinwheel, tails out, trying to melt into the center.

"Feast your eyes on these steers! They've had their shots!

They've been cut with a knife. They're wormed and weaned and ready to go! Let's start at eighty."

The PA system flattens out Luther's already wire-thin voice, so when he speeds through numbers it sounds like someone strumming his lips and trying to yodel at the same time.

"Now a quarter . . . now eighty and a half!"

Two men, one in a striped western shirt and the other in plaid, stand at either end of the sawdust ring with buggy whips to keep the cattle moving. The yard men are so busy searching the bleachers for prospective bidders that they hardly notice the steers racing between their poles. They grimace and gesture, a vaudeville routine in themselves. Pointing the butt end of their buggy whips at the bidders, one shouts "Yep!" and the other shouts "Yo!" as enthusiastically as if the cattle were their own. The bidding is all but invisible, a flick of the wrist or a nod of the head. The steers sell at $85.50 per hundredweight and disappear through a side gate.

"Who bid?" I ask Ed.

"Guy in the green cap."

That eliminates half the crowd, leaving only those wearing John Deere or Pioneer caps. There must be a state ordinance that Minnesotans cannot remove their feed caps once they're inside an auction barn. Ed and I are the only ones in the bleachers who aren't wearing an advertisement for an implement or seed company on our heads, except for three Amish men across the ring in broad-rimmed black hats and galoshes. They sit in ascending order of age, their beards ranging from short and brindled to Mosaic.

"Different man's cattle," Luther says as another half-dozen steers rumble through the gate below him. "They're a Charolais-Angus cross. A fancy kind of cattle. Who'll give me eighty-three?"

Then Luther's voice is off to the races.

Lot after lot of cattle emerge from the gate until it seems that every calf in Minnesota is lined up head to tail behind the door waiting to get into the ring. The audience, for their part, never seem to lose interest, as if this is the most fascinating exhibition of meat on the hoof they've ever witnessed, as if each calf is a fable of profit or loss waiting to be deciphered.

The smaller the calf, the higher the price per pound, and steers bring more than heifers. But as the afternoon wears on, there's a noticeable decline in the bidding. At one o'clock, nine black heifers, the first of Ed's three lots of calves, enter the ring.

"Here comes a set of cattle up by Rochester. O'Neill cattle. And a fancy kind they are. I believe you told me they've had the black leg and been penned. I've got seventy-seven . . . Now a quarter . . . Now seventy-seven and a half . . ."

Ed's hands are clenched around the edge of the bleacher. One bidder sits across the ring in a red-checked shirt, and another's somewhere behind us. The yard man in the ring points first at one side and then the other, his hands moving metronomically up and down.

"Now seventy-eight and a quarter . . . Now seventy-eight and a half. Sold at seventy-eight and a half!"

The next two lots of calves go in a kind of blur. The steers sell for a few more cents per hundred weight. Ed looks at his watch. All of five minutes have transpired.

"That's it," he says. "That's the last of them."

We watch a few more lots, then walk down to the office to pick up the check. The calves have nearly brought Ed's target price of $9,000, less $250 for commissions, insurance, transportation, and a dollar per head to the Meat Board ("Real Food for Real People"). The next farmer, who'll sell them as fat cattle, will pay the same fees all over again.

Across the street from the parking lot a bay horse is tied to a hitching post next to a black buggy tilted forward on its harness shafts.

We stop at the White Front Cafe for a late lunch. The

decor of wooden booths and counter with stools can't have changed much since V-E Day. A few spoonfuls of hamburger soup and the price of the calves starts looking better.

"I'm pretty well satisfied," Ed says. "But if I'd sold them before the snows in October, I'd of done better. They were selling in the eighties to a dollar a pound. And that shrink hurt, standing overnight with nothing to drink. They easily lost fifty pounds apiece."

On our way out of town, we pass an Amish buggy, perhaps the one from the auction, though it's hard to tell, since they're all pulled by bay-colored horses. This reminds Ed of a story he heard about an Amish farmer whose three sons got to taking a buggy ride in the evening to a bar in Lanesboro. They'd sit by themselves at a corner table and listen to the jukebox and drink beer with their hats on. Eventually the old man got wind of this and rode into town one night. When he found their buggy parked outside the bar, he unhitched the horse, put it on a lead, and took it back home.

"I'd like to have seen those boys pulling a buggy up that hill!" Ed laughs. He heard the story from a cattle dealer in Lanesboro, but it's really another version of the Prodigal Son's return.

We crest the hill and follow a high ridge above the river valley, a height from which the countryside falls away. We pass hills and wooded coulees. The snow looks bluish against a line of dark clouds and the pink-tinged sky to the west. We drive through Fountain and Chatfield as the land levels off into snow-covered fields. We pass Black Angus cattle feeding in windswept stubble, and Ed recalls with a kind of wonderment how, in what now seems a distant age, he had driven cattle by horseback with his father. This was during the Depression, when there was no market, so they drove the thirty head down the highway into Rochester, crossing a bridge at Third Avenue (where the K-Mart is now) to the stockyards to be weighed, and then out Forty-fourth Street to the state hospital to be made into soup. His father rode Brownie and he was on Blue.

"I was in on horses," he says, "and I was in on planes. Now how many people can say that?"

By the time we get home, the yard light is blinking on. Ed lays the check on the kitchen table like a trump card. "Well, Frances, we're not very damn rich. Read it and weep."

Fran studies the check for a long time. "They didn't even spell your name right."

FIFTEEN

On a chilly night in January we drive to Rochester for Catherine Sullivan's wake. We hang our coats in the hallway at Macken's Funeral Home and I see Theresa O'Neill in the anteroom talking with people I don't know. Then we walk into a vast green-carpeted room where most of my wife's extended family are assembled in small groups, talking quietly about the woman whose death has occasioned this gathering while managing to avoid looking at her flower-banked coffin.

I hadn't seen Catherine since our visit to the nursing home last spring, when I'd brought along that photograph of her family in which she posed on horseback long ago, looking as delicate and fair-haired as a Dresden doll. I'd kept her so busy answering questions about her grandmother that I asked almost nothing of her own life, which had begun with the century. She had taught in a one-room school, boarding with a family named Sullivan, and when their doughboy son returned from France, she married him. They raised a large family and, after their children dispersed as far away as Texas and Arizona, she went to work in a florist shop. Sharon recalls how the Sullivans would come to the farmhouse on Sunday afternoons and stay for supper. Catherine always brought a bundle of freshly cut flowers—roses, azaleas, and begonias—and now, in winter, the room smells of those same flowers.

BUD BAKER PULLS UP the driveway with a load of cows and a bred heifer, or "heiferette," that Ed bought at the auction barn in Zumbrota to build up his herd. The snow is deep enough that Baker spins his wheels trying to back the stock trailer up the slight incline to the holding pen. He keeps getting stuck and we keep digging him out. After twenty minutes of this, my feet start to go numb. Finally, Ed hooks a rotary snowplow to the back of the tractor and furiously clears a wide path by driving around the yard in reverse, piling the snow in enormous drifts.

When Baker opens the trailer gate, the cows are too spooked to come out at first. When they do emerge, it's in a great rush of hooves, their tails stiff with panic. They bolt through the holding pen and into a side corral, where they'll be sequestered from the herd for a few days until they calm down. The leader, a spotted cow, trots around the side corral twice, sizing up the old plank fence, then makes a heart-stopping leap over it, smashing through to the corral. With another leap, she clears a second fence into the cowyard. I ask Ed if he wants to try and catch her.

"No. I'd say we've had enough fun for one day."

The next morning I wait in the barn for Ed to finish feeding the cows from a dwindling supply of hay. The tanklike roar of the Bobcat builds and fades as he transports bales from the pole shed east of the barn to a rebar rack in the cow yard. My job is keeping an eye on a sick cow in the holding pen. She dropped a stillborn calf last week, then began to bloat early this morning. Bloating occurs when foam in the rumen, or first stomach, prevents a cow from belching; and since a cow normally belches two hundred gallons of gas a day, she soon inflates herself as surely as if hooked to an air compressor.

Doc Predmore is on vacation, so we're waiting for another vet to show up. In an emergency, there's a way to release the gas by jabbing a knife just under the short ribs, but I wouldn't want to try it. Through the window over the stanchions, I watch the cow stretch her neck to breathe, gasping for air.

I slide the south door open and the Bobcat rumbles into the barn in a blaze of snow-reflected light. Cold weather is the only time Ed wears a hat, a gray pile cap, ear flaps akimbo, that makes him look like the last cossack on the last yak roundup.

He parks the Bobcat halfway down the aisle, lowers the tines, and climbs down to look at the engine. "It's leaking transmission oil. I've got to get that fixed."

He fills a bucket with water for the sick cow and we step out the side door to the holding pen.

"Oh Christ, she's down!"

Ed swings the gate open, but it's too late. The cow is tipped over on her side, legs splayed, tongue hanging out, her teats turned purple. Her eyes, open and fathomless, hold a wide-eyed look of horror as if she'd seen what was coming. Ed pushes on her stomach with his boot and she exhales an evil stink, death's breath itself, and gives up the ghost.

"Shit. She's gone. Probably my fault for giving her too much corn last night. Shit."

Back at the house, Ed phones the vet. "We won't be needing a house call," he tells the secretary. "Wouldn't do any good now."

She asks if Ed wants the vet to come out and post the cow, but he decides that knowing for certain what killed her isn't worth the expense. The next call he makes is to a renderer.

WINTER DRAGS ON into March with no relief in sight. There aren't any memorable blizzards, no snow days to keep the children from school, only overcast skies and dismal weather.

Temperatures that might have felt mild two months ago now seem wretchedly, even malevolently, cold. It is the season of disappointment, when every break in the pattern of storms proves short-lived, another instance of false hopes. Cows run on their own calendar, though, and many are ready to calf. On Palm Sunday, Ed goes out into a cold rain to ferry bales from the pole shed to the haymow so the cows can shelter under a roof. By the time the pole shed is empty, he's soaked to the skin. That night he starts coughing and two days later we get a phone call that he's been admitted to St. Mary's Hospital with pneumonia.

We drive down on Easter under a leaden sky, arriving at the farm in the early afternoon. Ed's condition has stabilized, although he'll have to remain in the hospital on oxygen until the end of the week. His absence couldn't come at a worse time for the cows. Having followed their fortunes throughout the years, he alone knows each cow's time and the history of her past deliveries, can match newborn calves with sometimes lackadaisical mothers if they separate, and shove a cow's insides back in if she suffers a prolapse. What is required now is the practice of animal husbandry in its most literal sense. Already Ed has lost three calves since he went into the hospital.

It's spitting snow, a perfectly shitty day, as Steve and I walk out to check on a roan cow that hasn't been letting her calf suck. Steve, who has kept watch on the herd between ten-hour shifts at work, says the calf will die if it doesn't get some colostrum on the first day. Cows and their calves are scattered about the muddy yard, bedded down beside the old granary or in the lee of the pole shed to keep out of the wind and too miserable to care as we move among them. In the middle of the yard we find a dead calf lying in the rain like a sodden black rag.

"I could swear that calf was up a few minutes ago," Steve says. He thinks this calf and the others that died are the offspring of cows Ed bought this year, which might explain why they were so cheap. But we don't know the cows well enough to be certain. That's part of the problem.

Peeking around the corner of the pole shed, I find the roan cow in question lying on straw in the back with her calf. She's not letting her suck, but at least the calf has moved in with her, so there's hope. We stand in the center of the cow yard and slowly turn in a circle to take an inventory of calves. Four black ones, one in the corral, two brown ones, a spotted pair, and the hungry calf in the pole shed.

"I count ten. Is that what you've got?"

On the way out, I pick up the dead calf by a hind leg and drag it behind me through slick mud to the pickup and throw it in the bed. Then we drive over east to the edge of the hollow and stop beside a ravine stuffed with junked water heaters and tin cans and rolls of rusty barbed wire. I chuck the dead calf on top of three others and walk back to the truck.

MOST OF THE DISHES people bring to pass for supper are the same ones they brought for Thanksgiving—except for the ham, of course, and Kathy's chocolate pudding and Cool Whip concoction called Better than Robert Redford Pudding. But an undercurrent of anxiety runs through this gathering, not only about Ed's condition but also about the long-term fate of the farm, since the connection between the two is painfully obvious. After years of not thinking about the future, suddenly there's an urgency to act, to do something even if nobody knows exactly what should be done. On Saturday night all the grown children except the two who live out of state, Eddie and Sharon, met at Rita's house to map out a strategy. They had arrived at several decisions. First, the farm should be taken out of the folks' names as soon as possible. Second, the farm should be kept whole and intact, not sold off as real estate or divided among the eight heirs. Everyone clearly wants to preserve the farm—they don't want to be the ones to undo what three generations before them have accomplished—yet none of them, with the exception of Eddie, is capable of farming it. One reason people don't switch careers in midlife to become full-time farmers is that it takes so many years to learn the intricacies of crops and machinery and livestock. Some of the blame must rest on Ed's shoulders, since by carrying the torch alone all these years he absolved his daughters from having to learn the operation themselves; the resulting illusion was that the farm ran itself. Now, in a panic, we realize it doesn't. The solution the sisters have come up with is to try to manage the place as a kind of collective farm, with each couple contributing according to their means and talents. Some could donate time, others money, but there seems to be more of the former than the latter.

Sharon missed last night's meeting because our kids had the flu, and ever since we got down here she's been playing catch-up. While the rest of the family sits in the living room, she slices up pineapple for a fruit salad in the kitchen and tries to assure her mother, as well as herself, that the circle will remain unbroken.

"Why not? You did it. We're not the first family to go through this. You took care of Grandma and Grampa. And Grampa Bruski."

"No. Dad always had an income. We never had to take care of him."

"What income did he have?"

"He sold the farm."

A silence falls upon the living room as everyone stops talking to listen in on the conversation in the kitchen.

"Come out here and talk," Rita calls, "so we can all hear."

Sharon and Fran carry their drinks into the living room. At the moment we seem not so much an extended family as a collection of very different couples, each with distinct hopes and fears for the future and, I realize for the first time, a certain amount of suspicion. For once, the sons-in-law are quiet and let their wives do the talking. They sit and stare at the carpet, faces impassive as stones.

"We already talked about this," Linda explains. "You're going over the same ground we covered yesterday."

Linda, the youngest in the family and its traditional peacemaker, starts the meeting by reiterating the decisions they arrived at the night before and by reminding everyone that "the key is good communication." Because she couldn't attend Saturday's meeting, Sharon has prepared a two-part proposal of her own, which she hands out to her sisters. The first part is almost identical to the group's, that the land stay in one piece, but it's the second part that nobody likes—assuming the expense of taxes, insurance, and liability. Her tone, as usual, is blunt and matter-of-fact.

"I think we've got to be realistic. If we get a working business plan that produces income, great. But if it doesn't, part of the responsibility of ownership is assuming costs."

"Why not rent it out," Kathy says, "and the folks can have that income?"

"Fine. If that works out. But there's damned little income from land rental. It might work if we could contract, long-term, with a young farmer starting out who can't afford land. It would give him a chance to build up to it, acquire equipment and livestock . . ."

"Oh, no! Get rid of the cows! They're nothing but a headache!"

"But, Kathy, this is a beef farm. How many farmers are going to be interested in a few small fields? What I'm saying is that we have to separate the issue of ownership from income. Don't tie them together, because one may not support the other."

"Well, what's this going to *cost*?"

At this point the discussion begins to unravel. The sisters can't agree on what expenses to assume, and their husbands are still staring at the floor. So when the children grumble that they're hungry, we all escape into the kitchen to fill our plates.

After supper I'm helping to clear the table when Rita taps Sharon on the shoulder and says they need to talk before she goes home. Sharon mixes another drink and they go into the family room and sit down on the couch. Rita begins by saying how good it was for everyone to get together the day before and share what was on their minds. But that's not the reason they need to talk now. She tells Sharon that some people at the meeting had expressed their reluctance to work with her "the way you are." Who? Rita is not at liberty to say. She is merely an emissary, a go-between, trying to work things out between the parties involved. When Sharon asks what she's done to offend, Rita tells her that it's not so much a specific action as what she says, and it's not so much what she says as how she says it.

I don't hear about this until later, when we're lying in the fold-out bed in the family room after everyone else has left or gone to sleep. "I'm not going to apologize for my personality," Sharon says, louvered in moonlight through the window blinds. "I've stopped beating myself up for who I am." I'm angry for her and wonder how anyone could be so heartless, except that we've had these arguments ourselves. I've used those same words; what's new is hearing them as a bystander. I've known other women who grew up on farms, and who judged themselves by the physical standards of that particular world only to find that in the larger society such strengths became liabilities. Traits that served them well in the one— forthrightness, independence, a certain toughness—failed them in the other, so they learned to stifle the best part of themselves, and from their awkward, self-imposed shyness you could tell how hard that must have been.

———

IN THE MORNING Sharon and Linda accompany their mother into town to see the estate lawyer and then drop by the courthouse for probate records. When they return, I drive into Rochester to visit Ed at St. Mary's Hospital. He's sitting upright in bed eating breakfast at two in the afternoon.

"Haven't eaten since yesterday."

Ed had a lung scan this morning because of a spot that showed up on his X ray, so breakfast was delayed. He's off oxygen at the moment, but his face looks gray and his voice sounds far away. We seem to have been here before, if not in this very room then in another one just like it, having exactly this conversation. It's a double room, and the other bed is mussed but temporarily vacant.

A doctor drops in briefly to look at Ed's chart. He's tall and young and speaks with a German accent. "Haff you received the results from your lung scan yet? No? Vell, you will probably haff them later today."

Ed is recovering from the pneumonia and will be out of the hospital in a few days, but the root cause is a progressive disease, and its effects will never improve. Emphysema attacks the alveoli, the air sacs in the lungs, the great network of tributaries that carry oxygen from the air to the blood, reducing their elasticity so that while breathing in is still relatively easy, the expiration of air becomes a painful, conscious effort. When I try to comprehend what that's like, I picture the strongman in *La Strada* who every night performs the trick of breaking a steel-link chain around his chest by filling his lungs with air. Only imagine that with each performance another link is removed, pulling the chain tighter across the chest, so that each breath requires greater effort and brings less air. A man of less robust health to begin with would hardly stand a chance.

Clearly it's an effort for Ed to speak, so I babble on about the weather and fence-mending, trying to fill the gaps, but he cuts to the chase.

"How many calves?"

"Ten."

"Is that alive or dead?"

"Alive."

Then I mention the four calves piled in the gully. Sad news, of course, and all the more regrettable because they might have been saved if Ed wasn't stuck in a hospital bed. He knows this. Trying to be upbeat, I tell him that I carried a white calf that had wandered away from its mother back to the cow yard.

"Probably would have gotten back on its own."

We're still discussing cattle when a woman wheels her husband, Ed's roommate, into the room in a wheelchair. He's about Ed's age, emaciated and clearly a goner, a terminal-cancer patient with jaundiced, waxy skin and a grimace on his face like someone being eaten alive, which, of course, he is. An orderly helps him crawl onto the bed, then roughly draws the curtain around him and leaves. As the drugs wear off, the man begins to groan. We try to pick up the conversation as if we can't hear the man groaning in the next bed, and all the while I'm wondering about his wife, who has no one to talk to at this point, only the long vigil. She's not glum, however, and puts on an uncannily cheerful face, that being what a dying man would most want to see, not a reflection of his own pain.

"Excuse me," she says, coming over to our side of the room, "but did I hear you say you have dairy cows on your farm?"

"Beef cattle," Ed replies.

"Oh. But did you ever raise dairy cows?"

"Too long I did!"

"Maybe you know my husband then? We worked for Consolidated Breeders for twenty years and got all around."

She says her husband's name, but Ed shakes his head. He only tried artificial insemination once, back in the 1950s, and the experience wasn't fruitful; none of the cows got bred. He mentions that his neighbors, the Sheehans, operate a dairy farm, and perhaps her husband had serviced their cows. If that's the case, we've seen his handiwork grazing on the grassy hills across the road.

The woman goes back to her chair beside the curtained bed, and I find that I've run out of things to talk about. I don't want to tax Ed's breathing anymore, so I get up to leave. "Well, I'll tell everyone at home that you're looking good."

The woman sings across the room, "Does that mean he's good-looking?"

This, of course, is survival humor—a specialty of people who've survived a lot already, from depression and war to their own failing bodies—and it must be working. Ed not only smiles but manages a wan blush, because he's among the living and will be going home soon enough.

"Yeah!" I shout back. "I guess it does!"

On the elevator ride down to the first floor, I find myself smiling as well, and when the doors open I fairly skip down the street beneath the overcast skies. I feel strangely ebullient, better, in fact, than I have felt all this long, piss-poor day, because I'm alive too.

SIXTEEN

On the fourth Sunday after Easter, Sharon and Fran stand outside on the deck smoking cigarettes. Mother and daughter share the same posture—the small of their backs against the railing, one arm held against the waist to prop up the elbow of the other arm, which brings the cigarette to the lips then withdraws it. Beyond them, the new house looks as if it's always been there, though the grass in the bare ground around it is just starting to come in. The low roof affords a clear view to the lower pasture, where flocks of red-winged blackbirds have gathered in box elders along the creek. On the sunlit hillside across the road, Sheehan's cows loom big as billboards.

"The smoking lamp is lit," Ed says when he's ready to drive to mass. His recovery from pneumonia has been swift. The ruddiness is back in his cheeks and he's resumed all the farm work except for putting in this year's crops. Already this morning he's been out on the four-wheeler to check on the new calves and come back with a handful of pasqueflowers.

During the drive to St. Bridget's we pass acres of disced brown earth ready for planting and, every so often, a gravel driveway leading back to a white farmhouse beside a windbreak of pines and idled machinery. The geometry of corn and soybean fields won't be apparent for another month or two. Without crop cover, the land's natural topography is laid bare, whaleback hills and stream-cut ravines, so much earth and sky stitched together with barbed wire. From this height I can see the land drop away to the west to Rochester, the spire of the Plummer Building reaching high above the gray flood of buildings. To the east, the countryside spreads unbroken. Stillwell's, Clark's, the Baker twins, Schoenfelder's—the names of quarter sections tick off from memory as if they were a part of the landscape itself and not connected to anything so temporary as men's lives.

Turning south through Simpson, Ed says, "I see Ritchie O'Connell is cleaning up his junkyard."

The parking lot at St. Bridget's is fuller than usual today, so Ed noses the Buick under the branches of a Scotch pine bordering the cemetery. Four generations of O'Neills lie buried within these borders, each occupying a plot of ground no bigger than a flower bed—that bit of earth we all finally inherit. Two hundred years of a family whose lives were ushered in through the church doors with baptism and brought here at the end for burial. The latest grave, Catherine's, is still fresh.

We have come today to watch Deb and Steve's youngest, Allison, receive her first communion. She is a sweet-natured kid, quiet, with close-cropped brown hair and a last child's shyness. Dressed in a white satin dress, veil, and cotton gloves, she looks like a child bride. The two boys in her communion class stand around in bow ties and cowlicks and practice looking morose.

Bells are peeling through the rope hole in the belfry ceiling. Inside the church they sound muffled and far off as we take a pew and wait for the procession to begin. A pair of appliqué banners that read "He Is Risen" and "Sing Alleluia" in gold and pink hang on either side of the altar. Babies draped like shawls over their mothers' shoulders gape back at us. The church is stuffed with them—bug-eyed, wobbly-headed, wet-lipped—church babies. We swivel around to watch the communicants, their hands pressed together at chest level, march up the center aisle singing the entrance hymn, "Immaculate Mary," one of my favorites because of its upbeat, almost martial air. I haven't heard it much since Mary's general devaluation in the Church, pushed aside for a shadowy character like the Holy Ghost, and I flub the first line, which is not, as I recall, "Im-mac-u-late Mar-y, our hearts are on fire!" The new translation in the hymnal is more restrained, ending with "your praises we sing," an image too bloodless to impress itself on anyone's childhood. At that age, I was in a swoon of religion and didn't sing hymns so much as shout them, thinking Catholics had an ironclad lease on the next life.

Three of the children take turns reading the response, the Twenty-third Psalm, the one everybody knows, with its reference to "verdant pastures." The first boy is inaudible until Father Santos adjusts the microphone. Allison, the second reader, sounds throaty but as clear as if she were repeating the day's news.

The theme of today's gospel is the good shepherd: "Whoever does not enter the sheepfold through the gate but climbs in some other way is a thief and a marauder. The one who enters through the gate is shepherd of the sheep; the keeper opens the gate for him. The sheep hear his voice as he calls his own by name and leads them out."

Santos runs through the gospel in a weary, distracted voice, perhaps because he's soon to leave the parish, barely a year after arriving. His tenure here has met with a mixed reception, so he may feel a sense of relief. Since the diocese has yet to assign another full-time priest, St. Bridget's may end up a mission church with no resident pastor. But Santos mentions none of this; his homily, addressed to the half-dozen children who are about to receive communion for the first time, seems conciliatory when he reminds them that the word means "coming together."

I am not thinking about the church at the moment but the

farm, which has recently changed hands. After meeting with the estate attorney, Ed and Fran decided to gift the farm to their children while maintaining a life estate interest in it. This means they'll continue to operate the farm, assuming both profit and loss, as long as they live. But ownership has passed on to the next generation. The gift is as a whole: Each grain of soil belongs to all eight children and cannot be divided. This arrangement won't be permanent, of course, since eight people can't run such an intimate business as a farm; it's merely a postponement of hard decisions to come. But for the time being this decision will protect, in the lawyer's words, the "corpus of the farm." I like the physical metaphor, the notion of land as a body, something alive to which we are connected by blood and responsibility. The farm, after all, is what has brought us together.

Dennis has agreed to put in this year's crops. With his help and Ed's guidance, the farm could last another generation, maybe more. Who knows? Linda and her husband are driving down from Ely in a month to repair fences and tear down some old sheds. Rita has said she'll be there, and so will we. None of us can imagine what the land will be in the future, only what it has been and is now. All we can hope is that whoever lives there will know something of its past.

Watching my niece make her way up to the altar, I'm moved by the solemnity with which she takes the host from the priest's hands into her own and puts it in her mouth. Swallowing gingerly, she walks back down the center aisle without moving her lips, and I wonder if her heart is on fire. The pianist thumps out a closing hymn, and we step outside into the blazing sunlight to find the car and make our way home.

NOTES

11 The white wife of Captain Seth Eastman, commander of Fort Snelling, composed a poem of eight stanzas interpreting the Great Seal of Minnesota. The first stanza begins:

> Give way, give way, young warrior,
>   Thou and thy steed give way—
> Rest not, though lingers on the hills
>   The red sun's parting ray.
> The rocky bluff and prairie land
>   The white man claims them now,
> The symbols of his course are here,
>   The rifle, axe, and plough.

Quoted in the Reverend Edward Duffield Neil's *The History of Minnesota from the Earliest French Explorations to the Present Time* (Minneapolis: Minnesota Historical Company, 1882), p. 517.

16 J. B. Jackson calls the grid "the symbol of an agrarian utopia composed of a democratic society of small landowners" in his essay "Jefferson, Thoreau & After," from *Landscapes: Selected Writings of J. B. Jackson*, ed. Ervin H. Zube (University of Massachusetts Press, 1970), p. 5.

That Thomas Jefferson thought highly of farmers is evident in his remark: "Those who labour in the earth are the chosen people of God, if ever he had a chosen people, whose breasts he has made his peculiar deposit for substantial and genuine virtue." *Notes on the State of Virginia*, ed. William Peden (Chapel Hill: University of North Carolina Press, 1955), p. 164.

The quotation from Black Elk is from *Black Elk Speaks: Being the Life Story of a Holy Man of the Oglala Sioux* as told through John G. Neihardt (Lincoln: University of Nebraska Press, 1961), p. 198.

John Ball, the eighteen-year-old surveyor who conducted the initial survey of Marion Township, also laid out the city of Winona and later distinguished himself in the Civil War. Wounded three times in one battle, he mustered out with the rank of lieutenant colonel and died in 1875 at the age of forty. Winona named a GAR post after him.

17 Government land warrants are explained in Merrill Jarchow's *The Earth Brought Forth* (New York: Johnson Reprint Company, 1970), p. 52.

28 The "young and old are dying as fast as they can bury them . . ." is quoted in Kerby A. Miller's *Emigrants and Exiles: Ireland and the Irish Exodus to North America* (New York: Oxford University Press, 1985), p. 285.

29 The custom of the American wake is described in Arnold Schrier's *Ireland and the American Emigration 1850–1900* (New York: Russell and Russell, 1970), pp. 83–91.

The Ireland-Liverpool-America sailing route is described in John Francis MaGuire's *The Irish in America* (London: 1868), reprinted by Arno Press in 1969. MaGuire is particularly critical of English shipping lines and includes a letter from a passenger: "The serving out of water was twice capriciously stopped by the mates of the ship, who during the whole time, without any provocation, cursed and abused, and cuffed and kicked, the passengers and their tin cans, and, having served out water to about 30 persons, in two separate times, said they would give no more water out till the next morning, and kept their word."

30 The plight of "Bridget the ill-tempered Irish servant girl" and others like her is described in great detail by Hasia R. Diner in *Erin's Daughters in America: Irish Immigrant Women in the Nineteenth Century* (Baltimore: The Johns Hopkins University Press, 1983). Diner points out that, more than in any other emigrant group in the nineteenth century, those who left Ireland were largely "young, unmarried, [and] female."

31 An account of the one-month tour of duty by the Pennsylvania "emergency men" in the Civil War is taken from a letter by a veteran signed "S.F.J.," in Theodore Bean's *History of Montgomery County* (Philadelphia, 1884).

32 Two versions of "The Red Hand of O'Neill" legend can be found in Jeanne Cooper's *Ulster Folklore* (Belfast: H. R. Carter Publications Ltd., 1951), p. 50, and John Biggs-Davison's *The Hand Is Red* (London: Johnson Publications Ltd., 1973), p. 8.

36 The acreage planted on the O'Neill farm comes from the Agricultural Census of 1880.

38 The " 'west room' [was] reserved for family mementoes, for the old people and especially for the dead. Here the body is placed during wakes . . . and it is possible that there was an association between death and the direction of the setting sun." Quoted in E. Estyn Evans's *Irish Folk Ways* (London: Routledge & Kegan Paul, 1966), p. 44.

52 "Minnesota Fence, Boundary, and Animal Control Law," a pamphlet of the University of Minnesota's Agricultural Extension Service, defines "at large" as "permitting an animal to stroll, wander, rove, or ramble at will without restraint or confinement."

57 Thoreau may have been influenced by the health claims of guide books such as J. Wesley Bond's *Minnesota and Its Resources* (Chicago, 1856) in which the author states: "From a residence of over six years in Minnesota, I can safely say that the atmosphere is more pure, pleasant, and healthful, than of any other I have ever breathed on the continent of North or South America." Bond also advises potential settlers: "Don't waste time going east for a wife. *You* want a whole-souled, strong, wholesome Minnesota woman."

57–8 All quotations from Henry David Thoreau's travels in Minnesota are from Vol 2 of *The First and Last Journeys of Thoreau, Lately Discovered Among His Unpublished Journals and Manuscripts*, ed. Franklin B. Sanborn (Boston: Bibliophile Society, 1905).

58 The Sioux words for wildflowers are from *A Dictionary—Oie Wowapi Wan of Teton Sioux* compiled by the Reverend Eugene Buechel, S.J., ed. the Reverend Paul Manhart, S.J., in cooperation with the Institute of Indian Studies, University of South Dakota (Pine Ridge, S.D.: Red Cloud Indian School, Inc., 1983).

60 "To make a prairie . . ." is from *The Poems of Emily Dickinson*, edited by Thomas Johnson (Cambridge: Harvard University Press, 1958), p. 1178.

65 The Methodist circuit rider's account of a prairie wildfire is from Paul Angle's *Prairie State: Impressions of Illinois, 1673–1967 by Travelers and Other Observers* (Chicago: University of Chicago Press, 1968), p. 162. Nicholas A. Woods's advice to "ride madly before the wind" appears in his book *The Prince of Wales in Canada and the U.S.*, 1861, pp. 301–302.

70–1 Most of the information on alfalfa and soil in Olmsted County came from an interview with George Polk of the county's Agricultural Stabilization and Conservation Service.

73–4 The statement that white hunters planted corn in gopher mounds "upon the prairies that have thus been mellowed" is from Henry Schoolcraft's *Narrative Journal of Travels through the Northwest Region* (Ann Arbor: University Microfilms, 1966). The debate over whether Minnesota would become the Gopher State or the Beaver State is recounted in Judge Charles Eugene Flandrau's *The History of Minnesota and Tales of the Frontier* (St. Paul: E.W. Porter, 1900), pp. 242–44. The ballad lyrics "The Gopher girls are cunning. . . ." are found in Theodore C. Blegen's *Minnesota: A History of the State* (Minneapolis: University of Minnesota Press, 1963), p. 202. I saw the newspaper cartoon of the "Gopher Train" in a display at the Olmsted County History Center.

Notes

82 The natural history of the pocket gopher is from the chapter "Chisel-Teeth" in Victor H. Cahalane's *Mammals of North America* (New York: Macmillan Company, 1961), pp. 426–33.

86 "And nothing to look backward to with pride . . ." is from "The Death of the Hired Man," in *The Poems of Robert Frost* (New York: The Modern Library, 1946), pp. 37–44.

107–8 The four types of accidents most dreaded by threshers were entanglement in belts, boiler explosions, fire, and bridge breakthroughs—though not necessarily in that order—according to Thomas D. Isern in *Bull Threshers and Bindlestiffs: Harvesting and Threshing on the North American Plains* (Lawrence: University of Kansas Press, 1990). In addition to Isern's wonderful book, my information on threshing comes from interviews with former bindle stiffs and bundle-wagon drivers.

113 The year 1914 was the "parity base" the Agricultural Allotment Act used for establishing a fair price ratio between farm prices and nonfarm products. The concept of parity first appeared in an essay submitted to the Farm Bureau in 1921 entitled "Equality for Agriculture?" The unsigned pamphlet was written by George N. Peek and General Hugh S. Johnson of the John Deere Plow Company. The origin of *parity* is explained in Robert West Howard's *The Vanishing Land* (New York: Villard Books, 1985), pp. 165–68.

115–16 The description of the mass rally of "agriculturalists" in Mayo Park is in the September 5, 1932, edition of the *Rochester Post-Bulletin*.

116 "They sound like some far-off foreign country . . ." is from Bruce Bliven's "Home Thoughts from Afar" in *The New Republic* (August 31, 1932).

J. P. Morgan's question—"What is happening in Iowa?"—is quoted in William Carter's *Middle West Country* (Boston: Houghton Mifflin, 1975), p. 119.

Milo Reno's speech, "Our organization is the last hope of the American farmer . . ." is from a newsreel included in the documentary film *The Radio Priest*, produced and written by Irv Drasnin, Public Broadcasting Service, 1989.

118–19 Accounts of "penny auctions" and other activities of the Farm Holiday Movement not taken from contemporary newspaper accounts are from John L. Shover's *Cornbelt Rebellion: The Farmers' Holiday Association* (Urbana: University of Illinois Press, 1980) or David L. Nass's *Holiday: Minnesotans Remember the Farm Holiday Movement* (Marshall, Minn.: Plains Press, 1984).

124–5 An excellent source on Father Coughlin's relationship with Milo Reno is Alan Brinkley's *Voices of Protest: Huey Long, Father Coughlin and the Great Depression* (New York: Knopf, 1982).

125 "Are you not apprised of what is happening in Iowa . . . ?" is taken from Coughlin's radio address "The March of the Workers,"

in *Driving Out the Money Changers* (Detroit: Radio League of the
Little Flower, 1933), p. 30.

125 Coughlin referred to FDR as "Franklin Double-Crossing Roosevelt"
at a national convention of Dr. Francis E. Townsend's supporters.
Coughlin later apologized.

The money changers had been driven from the Temple, but "they
landed in the White House . . ." is from a speech Coughlin delivered
in St. Paul on September 20, 1936, and reported in the *Rochester
Post-Bulletin*.

127 "His face is completely lineless . . ." and other observations on the
National Union for Social Justice's convention are from Jonathan
Mitchell's "Father Coughlin's Children," which appeared in *The New
Republic* (August 26, 1936), pp. 17–21.

131 An article in the *Rochester Post-Bulletin* of August 3, 1992, estimated
the real-estate value of the Olmsted County Fairgrounds at $5 per
square foot.

136 The statistics on the declining number of hog producers are from
an essay "Pork Industry's Numbers Shrink as It Heads to Ma-
turity," by Steve Marberry, that appeared in *Feedstuffs* (April 13,
1992).

The ranking of agribusiness giants changes constantly. As of 1994,
the top-five hog producers were Murphy Family Farms (North
Carolina), Carroll's Foods (North Carolina), Premium Standard
Farms (Missouri), Tyson Foods (Arkansas), and Cargill (Minnesota).
Successful Farming (October 1994).

143 "Farm Projects Can Be Psychologically Damaging" was written by
Neal C. Barnard, M.D., on a George Washington University Medical Center letterhead. Barnard simply inverts Margaret Mead's 1964
study of violent criminals, then redefines violence to include raising
animals for slaughter and projects a sorry future for children involved in 4-H livestock projects.

170 "Combat Tactics in the Southwest Pacific Area" by Captain Thomas
B. McGuire, Jr., was originally published and distributed by the
Fifth Fighter Command and reprinted in William N. Hess's *Pacific
Sweep* (New York: Kensington Publishing Corp., 1978). McGuire,
the second-leading American fighter ace in the war, died in a crash
on Negros Island when he violated his own rules by attempting a
quick turn at low speed to come to the aid of his wingman.

179 The statement "no real American wants to be subsidized . . .",
made by Ezra Taft Benson, was quoted in *Time* (April 13, 1953),
p. 25. It was Minnesota's Representative Eugene McCarthy who
compared Benson to "a man standing on the bank of a river telling

a drowning man that all he needs to do is take a deep breath of air."
Time (February 23, 1953), p. 25.

194 Information on ConAgra is from Osha Gray Davidson's *Broken
Heartland* (New York: Doubleday, 1990), p. 30, and A. V. Kreb's
article "The Future of Farming," *Prairie Journal* (Summer 1992),
p. 6.

A Note About the Author

John Hildebrand is the author of *Reading the River: A Voyage Down the Yukon*. He lives in Eau Claire, Wisconsin, and teaches at the University of Wisconsin.

A Note on the Type

This book was set in a digitized version of Janson. The hot-metal version of Janson was a recutting made direct from type cast from matrices long thought to have been made by the Dutchman Anton Janson, who was a practicing type founder in Leipzig during the years 1668–1687. However, it has been conclusively demonstrated that these types are actually the work of Nicholas Kis (1650–1702), a Hungarian, who most probably learned his trade from the master Dutch type founder Dirk Voskens. The type is an excellent example of the influential and sturdy Dutch types that prevailed in England up to the time William Caslon (1692–1766) developed his own incomparable designs from them.

Composed by PennSet,
Bloomsburg, Pennsylvania

Printed and bound by Quebecor Printing Fairfield,
Fairfield, Pennsylvania

Designed by Cassandra J. Pappas